For Anne and Bill

Contents

v

List of tables, figures and boxes

Tables

Figures

Boxes

Glossary

Theoretical explanatory terms

Bonding social capital – exclusive, integrative and clannish, binds groups together and helps them to get by

Bridging social capital – essentially inclusive, bringing diverse people together and helping them to get on in society

Challengers – those occupying less privileged positions in the social field who may be disadvantaged by the status quo, relative to the incumbents, and thus may only wield slight influence over operations in the field.

Doxa – the conventional wisdom operating within a field

Field – a social terrain or structured social space where actors, with varying resources, engage in individual or collective strategic action to obtain some scarce resource or goal

Habitus – early socialisation of social conditions that over time have been internalised into a series of mental and bodily dispositions which then govern our actions

House advantage – a gambling term that denotes the predictable long-term advantage to the casino (house)

Incumbents – those who are already settled in the social field and enjoy positions of power; they seek to retain this advantage and to keep the favourable status quo

Independent operators – someone who is not affiliated to any specific gang but is criminally active and known to all gangs within the social field

Illusio – a shared principle or general acceptance (specific to the field itself) that the field goals are worth pursing in the first place

Network – a social grouping of connections and relationships

Proximate fields – fields that are linked but not geographically connected

Repertoire – the stock of specialised skills of a person or group

Sanction – a threatened or actual penalty for disobeying rules. While these are largely negative, they may on occasion be positive

Social field – *see* field

SNS – social networking sites

Strategic action field – a unit of collective action with a constructed social order whereby actors interact competitively but with a shared understanding of rules, goals, logic and legitimate action (*see also* field)

Strategic actor – someone operating within a social field or strategic action field

Gang terms

Baby mother – a young woman who has a child outside of marriage (may also mean single mother or previous girlfriend)

Badman – a notorious gang member who is generally considered dangerous

Beef – an argument/fight or ongoing conflict/vendetta

Blind moves – to engage in any action or business without being fully informed of all the current circumstances or current information on the issue

Boy(ed) – an insult referring to the individual as a boy (boi). This term also has connotations from the days of slavery as someone with no power who can be ordered about

Bredrin' – (brethren) a close companion, family or friend

Bruv – (brother) close friend but a commonly used term similar to pal or mate

Chicken cash – loose change which young people use to buy take-away food

Cook house – a place, often a domestic house, where drugs are boiled down and 'stretched' or cut in order to increase the quantity and dilute the quality. Such work involves dealing in kilos and considerable amounts of cash will be on the premises

Country – the provinces outside London (*see* going up country)

Deal – to sell illegal drugs

Dry snitching – to inadvertently or indirectly provide information about someone to a person in authority or to another person who is not privy to the information

Elders – a senior gang member

Endz – neighbourhood; also one's own local neighbourhood

Falling – *see* slidin'

Fam (family) – close friend or buddy

Feds (federal agent) – the police

Fishing for strays – a hunting mission conducted by a gang for individual rivals who are isolated and alone on rival or disputed turf

Floater – an 'independent operator' who can move or 'float' between gangs without being affiliated to any specific gang

Going up country – out of London to the provinces, i.e. taking a consignment of drugs to another town or location

Honey trap – where a young woman is used to set up a young man, usually a rival gang member

Hood pass – an informal validation or permission to enter an area

Line up – sexual activity with one person after another

Link(ing)- a casual sexual partner; offering regular sexual contact with another person

Macs – machine guns

ManDem – group of men/fellow gang members

Moist – soft, weak (indicating ripe for victimisation)

NFA – no further action (police term)

Olders – a gang member, probably in late teens, who had previously been a younger but not advanced

Playa' (player) – someone who is an active participant in gang life

Rep (representation) – to represent an area, gang or person

Rollin on a job – accompanying others on a job

Runners – those who help to sell drugs and run between the dealer and the buyer

Screwing – deliberately holding the stare of another individual without looking away; a dirty look

Set-up – to use guile or deceit to place someone is a dangerous or difficult situation

Shank(ed) – a knife/to be stabbed

Shotting – selling drugs illegally on the street

Sket – derogatory insult for a young women with a perceived sexual reputation; a slut

Slidin' – to suffer a decline in one's respect and status

Slippin' – (to slip down an alleyway) to enter an area or neighbourhood that is not one's own

Snitch(in') – an informer, or grass; considered a traitor

Squeeze, the – a provocative and pre-emptive street encounter in the form of a direct challenge or confrontation

Steaming – where a large group of boys or gang members will run through a train/bus/market/shopping centre robbing or assaulting people as they go. A fast and frightening event that is over in seconds.

Stripes – acquired peer respect for achivements

Tinnies – young gang members aged 8-12

Wannabees – young people who emulate gang members' behaviours and attitudes

Wasteman – dispensable, unconnected, useless

Wifey – a serious girlfriend who is considered marriage material

Youngers – a young or subordinate gang member

About the author

Simon Harding is a senior lecturer in criminology in the School of Law at Middlesex University, north London. He has lived and worked in London for over 30 years as a market researcher, housing consultant, youth researcher, crime consultant, diversity trainer, community safety manager, local authority director, and lecturer. He co-devised acceptable behaviour contracts in 1999 shortly before joining the Home Office as regional crime adviser for London. Since 1999 he has been an independent adviser on hate crime, equalities and diversity to the London Metropolitan Police Commissioner.

He obtained his doctorate in youth justice from University of Bedfordshire having previously earned an MA (Hons) from Edinburgh University, an MA from Middlesex University, a BTP (Bachelor Town Planning) from London South Bank University and a Diploma in Marketing from London Metropolitan University. His current research interests include gangs and group offending, street cultures, hate crime, policing and community safety.

He has recently published a second edition of *Unleashed: The phenomena of status dogs and weapon dogs* (Policy Press, 2014). This publication has led to numerous media appearances on TV, radio and in print.

Acknowledgements

I would like to acknowledge and thank the following for their assistance, support and encouragement over the past few years and their help in bringing this book to life, notably Professor John Pitts, Professor Jenny Pearce and Professor Tim Hope, for their invaluable advice, guidance and support. I would also like to offer my sincere thanks to the late Jock Young who offered me great encouragement for this work. I am equally indebted to Professor Anthony Goodman and Dr James Densley for kindly reviewing early drafts and offering advice and suggested amendments. My thanks also to Dr Tim Bateman, Professor Margaret Melrose, the officers of the Metropolitan Police Service, the staff of Lambeth council, and local residents of Lambeth and London Probation Service. Grateful thanks is also offered to the staff at Policy Press for their assistance and professionalism. My gratitude is also due to all the staff and individuals from the professional charities and agencies who gave up their time to be interviewed and also to my partner for showing both patience and understanding.

In particular I offer my admiration and thanks to the all the young people interviewed for this work, for their time, their knowledge, their experience and I offer my sincere admiration for their spirit of survival.

Preface:
living and working in the social field

My interest in the world of gangs dates back almost 30 years through a long history of living and working in Lambeth, London SW9.

I first worked in Brixton, SW9, in 1981, covering the April riots for my university newspaper. From 1982-85, I was a frequent visitor to many of the multiple squats in and around Brixton before finally moving to Brixton in 1985. I was then to live and/or work in Lambeth until 2012, including five years living on Loughborough Estate, SW9. The estate is home to over 3,000 families and consists of two separate parts: Old Loughborough, which is brick built 1940s former London County Council (LCC) properties, up to five storeys in height; and New Loughborough, comprising six 11-storey tower blocks dating from the 1950s and 1960s, interspersed with some flat-roofed, low-rise properties. The tower blocks were brick-built rather than concrete slab prefabricated system-built and reputed to resemble ocean liners when viewed from a certain angle. Although I lived in one I never did find that angle. In immediate proximity to this estate was Angell town – a low-rise, 1970s brick-built warren of interlocking streets and cul-de-sacs, which by 1985 had developed a notorious reputation. One hundred yards away were Coldharbour Lane and Southwyck House, an eight-storey, neo-brutalist, deck-access block built in the 1970s and often mistakenly thought to be Brixton prison. Built in a horseshoe-shaped crescent, it was called the barrier block, as it was planned to act as a sound barrier to an adjacent motorway. The crescent shape faced away from Brixton town centre such that the edifice presented a cliff-face rising out of the street, with tiny windows in place for soundproofing against motorway traffic. The motorway was never built. Rumour had it that the Danish architect killed herself shortly after the block was completed as it was 'facing the wrong way'. Within a few years of completion, Southwyck House, along with Angell town, became dumping grounds for poor black families. An invisible line between them constituted the infamous Brixton 'frontline', a line that could not be seen, but could often be smelt by virtue of the cannabis smoke which pervaded the air at every corner. Here young and middle-aged African Caribbeans often openly sold drugs to the young, middle-aged white professionals, artists and leftwing squatters who lived in Brixton town centre. Following the riots of 1981, this romantic image was increasingly replaced by the grimier reality of heroin and crack dealing, of muggings and gun crime.

During this time, I became keenly aware of the privations of the local community, especially those in receipt, as I was for a time, of unemployment benefits. I became knowledgeable about how the estate, and local underground economy, functioned; who committed the vandalism and petty crime; where to buy stolen goods; how to buy drugs from the basement of the local taxi office; when to buy drugs down at the 'frontline'; the 'wall of silence' following a crime; the imperative of not grassing. I became increasingly aware of the local gang, the 28s, later known as the PDC.

During proposals to regenerate the estate via a Housing Action Trust in the late 1980s, I observed the local matriarch using the youth from the estate to organise stiff resistance and noticed PDC members moving freely around the estate into areas that became increasingly 'off limits' to me. I observed them monitoring closely any tenants voting for estate regeneration during their watchful presence at council tenants meetings. Slowly I became aware of how it all worked; I was living in a crime hotspot; the young men slouched in stairwells and walkways were observing and reporting on police movements; my neighbour's 'boyfriend' was actually her pimp; my movements were monitored and I was burgled four times; there were gangs in the neighbourhood.

Throughout this period, two key events had a strong impact on me personally: first, being caught up in the 1985 Brixton riots (triggered by the police accidently shooting a black woman while raiding her house to arrest her gang-affiliated son) and second, having a verbal altercation with two young female neighbours and subsequently being violently attacked by their brother, leading to my taking several weeks off work. Slowly the fog began to lift and I began to view things differently. Although I moved away from the Loughborough Estate, I continued to live and work in Lambeth until 2012, travelling through SW9 daily. From 2005–08, I was Assistant Director for Community Safety in Lambeth. Gang issues had by then emerged as a serious community concern and I quickly became immersed in managing London's most extensive gun and gang project; convening and managing a multi-agency Gangs Commission for Lambeth; participating in the multi-agency Five-borough Gang Alliance in London and funding a series of multi-agency interventions for gang-affiliated young people.

It is this lived experience that fired my interest in better understanding the complex set of relationships I witnessed daily.

Simon Harding
January 2014

ONE

Introduction

'Poverty is the worst form of violence.'
Mahatma Gandhi

The social field of the gang in London SW9 is a dangerous arena of social conflict and competition for some young people.

While gang researchers struggle to articulate this domain, or to even acknowledge it, the young men and women within it live a daily reality that remains largely unexplored in the UK. This world is often distanced and remote, and, for many adults, estranged, inexplicable and impenetrable. It is a world where social norms are inverted; where rumour and gossip lead to death and injury; where personal slights become 'beefs', then feuds; where family members are fair game for reprisals; where boys are 'soljas' and dead at age 15.

For those young people caught up in violent street gangs, this world exists in the London SW9 postcode (see Appendix A).[1] While many residents in SW9 have no contact with gangs, none remains oblivious to them and all are affected. For young people in the social field of the gang, daily life is now governed by fear and an all-pervasive, unabating anxiety. This daily reality of fear and stress lead some to deal with the world as if it is unreal; a place unaccountable to adults and societal norms; a self-biographical world of hyperactivity, excitement and drama, replete with opportunities for distinction; a place to personally transcend and transform. For others, this reality (which generates a blank-staring fatalism) means harsh and rapid violence predicated on a belief that this is all ordained and it will all end soon.

For those of us living outside the social field of the gang, this appraisal is bleak and disturbing; our first response is to reject it as alarmist and inflated. It is, however, an accurate summation of many young people's views on gang life in London SW9.

Worryingly, however, the indications are that in recent years this social field has become even more violent. In the past few years, a range of gang-related incidents, including several murders, have occurred in Lambeth, with several occurring in SW9. Some of these are illustrated in Table 1.1.

Table 1.1: Recent events attributed to gang activity in Lambeth

Date	Event
2006	15-year-old stabbed to death in rival gang fight involving 30 people
	Gunman shoots two 17-year-olds in crowded McDonald's restaurant
2007	17-year-old shot dead at crowded Streatham Ice Rink
	15-year-old shot dead inside his Clapham home
2008	19-year-old member of OC gang shot dead in Myatt's Fields park
	18-year-old stabbed to death by six youths on bikes
2009	16-year-old chased and savaged by pitbulls, then stabbed to death by rival gang
	24 year-old man shot dead through a window with a MAC-10 pistol
	19-year-old DJ knifed to death following confrontation over a rumour
2010	22-year-old gunned down in Gypsy Hill. Six convicted of murder
	15-year-old stabbed to death by rival gang at school entrance in West Norwood
2011	25 year-old gunned down in motorcycle drive-by shooting in Stockwell
	Five-year-old girl paralysed as gunman sprays Stockwell shop with bullets to attack rival
	18-year-old shot dead near his home in Tulse Hill
	14-year-old schoolgirl lures armed gang to home of 'friend'
	Lambeth police declare 'high state of tension and conflict' between known gang-related groups, launching an unprecedented borough-wide Section 60 Search Order
	Six fatal stabbings or shootings in Lambeth between April and May, prompting Emergency Violent Crime Summit, Community Leaders Forum and bid to Greater London Authority for extra cash to tackle gun and knife crime
2012	17 year-old fatally stabbed in unprovoked attack
	15 year-old fatally stabbed on Loughborough Estate

Source: BBC News; LCPCG reports and minutes; *South London Press*

In addition, as shown in Appendix B, the borough has experienced an 18% rise in serious youth violence (1 April to 21 November 2010), the highest rise in the Metropolitan Police Service (MPS) grouping of boroughs with a similar profile.[2] Youth victims have increased by 65% and weapons are increasingly used in violent offences, including a 16% increase in knife offences (April to November 2010). The most serious violence (grievous bodily harm, attempted murder and murder, wounding) has also increased by 26% (21 November 2009 to 21 November 2010).[3] Local partnership reports identify gang-related activity as responsible for half of Lambeth's shootings, one in five stabbings and one in five incidents of violence against the person. Moreover, these figures only relate to reported incidents, further indicating that in some areas of the borough violence and gang-related activity is both constant and increasing significantly. These areas are increasingly dangerous for young people who are increasingly dangerous for young people, who are increasingly at risk of victimisation. So how do we explain both endemic and increasing gang-related violence in SW9? I attempt to provide some answers to this question by offering an ethnographic analysis of the area in which I lived and worked for over 25 years.

Searching for answers

I began this search for answers by exploring in depth the variety of both UK and US sociological and criminological theories and perspectives offered by academics on the topic of gang life. By reviewing the most topical and recognisable perspectives (see Chapter Two) I sought insight into the right questions to ask before searching for the right answers. I concluded that classic and contemporary research leaves several key questions regarding UK gangs, unanswered.

I should declare at this point that I intend to sidestep the tricky debates about definition and re-focus on other aspects. For this study I use Miller's revised definition (1992):

> ... a self-formed association of peers, united by mutual interests, with identifiable leadership and internal organisation, who act collectively or as individuals to achieve specific purposes, including the conduct of illegal activity and control of a particular territory, facility, or enterprise. (Miller, 1992)

Moreover, I quickly reached several initial conclusions: that classic ethnographic works such as *Street corner society* by William Foote Whyte (1943) still have much cogency; that a general theory of the social order of gangs remains elusive; that details of gang processes and behaviours are frequently overlooked; that research is frequently blindsided to gender; that interpersonal relationships within gangs are often taken for granted rather than explained; that research often fails to take account of the disparate phenomena that are so often observable; that many gaps still exist in our understanding of street gangs; and that despite many valuable and rewarding insights into gang life, much contemporary UK research is confirmational reportage of limited explanatory value offering few, if any, fresh insights. What is missing is often the glue that binds it all together. Lastly, explanatory perspectives on UK gangs lag some way behind US counterparts.

Adopting a fresh approach: field analysis

I increasingly felt that a new perspective on UK gangs was needed, one that illuminates the variety of interrelationships, networks and behavioural dynamics crucial to understanding the evident complexities of UK gangs – which until now have too frequently been either denied or simply labelled 'messy'.

I therefore set out to reveal these structures and networks, internal conflicts, struggles, behavioural dynamics and power relationships in the violent street gangs of south London using the approach of social field analysis. A social field is essentially a social terrain where actors, with varying resources, engage in individual or collective strategic action to obtain some scarce resource or goal (Bourdieu and Wacquant, 1992). Defining a social terrain as a social field is a useful device for identifying the social actors and their relationships. Therefore field analysis requires an investigation and understanding of the internal structures, dynamics and internal workings that come together to shape the field. Field theory permits us to consider these relationships and explore their interactions, demonstrating their ability either to transform or maintain a field. While quantitative research, so favoured by American positivists, permits observation of fields over time, qualitative research permits identification of key actors and their relative positions in the field, thus providing a denser account of field evolution.

Often these underlying structures and dynamics of a social field are not always observable and deeper structures might only be revealed through theory or by developing mechanisms of measurement to explore variations that later result in observable change. These deeper structures are linked to unique historical and cultural contexts. It is only by understanding these deeper structures, contexts and processes in a social field that we can move closer to providing empirical purchase on the phenomena. Fligstein and McAdam (2012, p 194) note that realist field analysts seek to incorporate these 'historically and culturally contingent meanings' (Bourdieu and Wacquant, 1992) and Bourdieu's theory of fields is perhaps the best-known example of this approach.

In applying field analysis (Bourdieu, 1991, p 33), I hoped to identify assumptions about the gang as a social field. The applicability of social field analysis to gangs is confirmed by Swartz's comment that 'field analysis of this type provides for an attractive structural mapping of arenas of struggle over different types of capital, power and privilege' (Swartz, 1997, p 293).

In line with Bourdieusian field analysis methods,[4] I set out to research the relationships of power in the social field and how this is determined by the outside world, before considering how capital is distributed and who are the actors/players in this social field.

Bourdieu's theory is that action in the field is generated by the encounter between opportunities/ constraints and its interface with the habitus, (an internalised cognitive framework by which actors interpret the actions of others in their social field). The habitus becomes a useful starting point for considering any relationship between agency and structure.

Of the many theoretical perspectives employed by gang scholars to interpret gangs, social field analysis remains glaringly absent. I propose that social field analysis provides an holistic interpretive frame to identify and analyse the characteristics of the violent street gang, as well as its social structure and key actors; the relationships of power and capital; capital acquisition and retention; and gender dynamics. I then determine how all these issues are guided by the habitus.

I have adopted this underused methodology to generate a broader theory of gangs and their regenerative social dynamics. In so doing, I acknowledge my indebtedness to Bourdieu, Waquant and Fligstein and McAdam for providing the interpretative lens for my theoretical perspective. Having established the utility of social field analysis (Bourdieu, 1969, 1984, 1991) to gang research, I shall offer here a brief introduction to the theories I establish in detail throughout the book.

Street capital and the street casino

The goal of actors within a social field is to overcome their unequal allocations of skills and resources to achieve advantage that will lead them ultimately to success. To do this, they become improvisers, employing strategic actions that will either maintain their privileged position in the field, or advance them slightly towards their goal. In this field of struggle, all actors are developing strategies to survive – sifting and surfing information, making and breaking relationships, as all young people do – only in the social field of the gang, this has endless repercussions. Like the social field of prison, this social field operates at a high level of emotional intensity, only with fewer adults. Here, information technology has fundamentally altered social spaces creating new dimensions for building reputations and new opportunities for disrespecting rivals, often to deadly effect. The intensity, lack of rational actors and constant dynamic make this social field unique in many ways.

Identifying one's position, and that of others, in the field is critical, as all actors must be able to measure their current position, their trajectory and their personal capital allowance. To address this key issue, I argue that this is achieved through my concept of street capital, which I theorise acts as a tradable asset within the social field, one that actors seek to exchange for economic returns.

Street capital acts as a way of measuring, accrediting and exchanging types of capital in the gang's social field. It can be viewed as an amalgam of street knowledge and street skills (cultural capital); internalised behaviours and ways of being and thinking (habitus); local history, family connections and networks (social capital); relationships, reputation, status and local levels of recognition, honour and prestige (symbolic capital). All these are high-value resources on the street. I argue that in street life, street capital is the premium capital. Instantly recognisable and universally understood, this commodity operates as the prime source of capital in this social field. This is a highly volatile, tradable commodity and the strategic actions of individuals, groups and rivals generates dramatic daily fluctuations. Insufficient street capital brings victimisation; thus all actors must strategise daily and hourly to manufacture, maintain and maximise their street capital.

I argue that the social field of the violent street gang is a field of struggle where young people must constantly manage risks. It is often a world of depressing limitations and alarming normative violence. In this social field, young men quickly understand that hegemonic masculinity in the form of paid work will pass them by, or merely offer the low-grade manual grind accepted by parents but now scorned by offspring. The gang offers a chance to 'do masculinity', to construct a new street persona, a new personal brand, a new hero. It offers a field of opportunities, a social arena of competition; a place where crude bodily capital and the street code are as important as wearing the right togs; a place where distinction will come to those who survive. Some actors become skilled at this 'game', while others fail.

My theory envisages the gang social field as a place where gang members, affiliates and associates are all 'players' ('playas') in 'the game' – the constant search for street capital that ultimately leads them to distinction. Here street capital equals casino chips, which can be won, lost or traded. This is the world of the street casino with daily winners and losers; where friends are in constant competition; where information is power; where game strategies determine who is knocked out and who keeps playing; where you must learn to play by the house rules; where you are hyper-vigilant of other players; where players can be excluded or exploited; where talk, vocabulary and actions only make sense to other players; where at all times you must survive by building street capital and maintaining your reputation. Only by doing all this, can the players access what they all strive for – economic capital – which facilitates what they seldom achieve but all want – a way out.

Conducting the study

Of London's numerous gang-affected areas, the London borough of Lambeth was an obvious choice because of my knowledge of the area. In selecting possible case study areas, SW9 was an early contender. It offered a designated postcode, mixed housing tenures and recognised gang-affected neighbourhoods.[5] SW9 has high levels of crime (see Appendix B). It contains London's highest number of problematic drug users, records above-average levels of crack cocaine use (Lambeth First, 2011a) and has been the subject of several Osman Warnings.[6] Indeed, four areas in SW9 are among the 10% most deprived in the UK and out of 21 Lambeth wards, SW9 displays some of the highest volumes of crime in terms of reported total notifiable offences (TNOs).[7]

Within the borough of Lambeth, the SW9 Royal Mail postcode area was thus selected for the purpose of this study (see Appendix A). It includes six local council wards: Coldharbour; Stockwell; Vassall; Larkhall; Ferndale; and Oval. A recent Community Engagement Survey by Lambeth Community Police Consultative Group (LCPCG) (2010) identified areas of SW9 as some of the least safe spaces in Lambeth. The local council also identified numerous gang interventions.

London SW9 is also the focus of structural factors that limit both life chances and opportunities for residents. Briefly, these include spatial and social exclusion; dwindling investment and resources; high levels of population change, including new arrivals; and high levels of poverty and disadvantage.[8] These areas of acute deprivation now experience increased concentrations of crime and youth victimisation (Hope, 1994, 2003) and increased concentrations of black and minority ethnic (BME) communities (Pitts, 2007a).

A concentration of poverty

A concentration of poverty[9] and disadvantage is a recognisable feature within the wards of SW9, the degree of which is illustrated in Table 1.2. These neighbourhoods are characterised by high unemployment, high levels of social and rented housing and high levels of population churn and immigration. This concentration of disadvantage, or neighbourhood effect (Pitts, 2008b) suggests that young people living in these wards in SW9 experience significant degrees of deprivation, indicating reduced life opportunities and, in some cases, increased availability for and proximity to, the social field of the gang.

Child poverty in Lambeth is another key indicator of levels of deprivation. In 2010-11, the proportion of dependent children living in either out-of-work or in-work, low-income families was 57.3% (11.7% higher than the UK average).[10]

Table 1.2: Profile of deprivation in Lambeth, SW9, by ward*

Coldharbour	*By far the most deprived part of the borough* 38% of residents receive Child Benefit (LA 28%) 44% of residents receive Housing Benefit (LA 22%) 29% of residents receive Income Support (LA 12%) 51% of residents are employed (LA 59%) 53% of residents are aged 18-34 (LA 45%)
Ferndale	28% of residents have lived in Lambeth less than two years (LA 21%) 47% of residents are social tenants (LA 38%) 20% of residents receive Council Tax Benefit (LA 14%)
Vassall	58% of residents live on housing estates (LA 40%) 52% of residents are in socioeconomic class DE (LA 28%) 31% of residents receive Housing Benefit (LA 21%) 18% of residents receive Income Support/Jobseeker's Allowance (LA 12%) 17% of residents are aged 18-24 (LA 12%)
Stockwell	78% of residents live on a housing estate (LA 40%) 52% of residents are social tenants** 19% of residents are owner-occupiers (LA 30%) 43% of residents receive Housing Benefit (22%) 48% of residents are in socioeconomic class DE (LA 28%)
Larkhall	17% of residents are aged 18-24 (LA 12%) 29% of residents have lived there for less than two years (LA 21%) 39% of residents are economically inactive** 47% of residents are socioeconomic class C2DE**
Oval	65% of residents live on housing estates (LA 40%) 36% of residents are in socioeconomic class DE (LA 28%) 53% of residents are aged 18-34 (LA 45%)

Note: * Lambeth average is shown in brackets (LA) ** LA figure not available

Source: Lambeth First (2011b; 2012)

Limited opportunities

Young people in SW9 experience both spatial and social exclusion. For many, this exclusion is most immediately noticeable through reduced access to legitimate opportunities for older adolescents, (Merton, 1938; Cloward and Ohlin, 1960; Durkheim, 1964). Limited opportunities or desire to pursue what many believe is beyond their reach (Evans, et al 2001) effectively seals young people into their lifeworld (Berger and Luckman, 1966) or the social field (Bourdieu, 1990) of the gang. These opportunities are further diminished by the processes of globalisation (Sibley, 1995; Jones, 2002) and these 'global processes of change impact upon place[,] significantly affecting youth opportunities' (Macdonald and Marsh, 2005, p 206).

Dwindling recreational alternatives

The repositioning of youth services (Jeffs and Smith, 2008) and reduced provision has largely affected young people in deprived communities, notably those at risk of joining gangs. Recent budget cuts have decimated local youth services and government projects. In 2011, Unison calculated that youth service cutbacks in England and Wales approximated £137 million pounds in April 2011/12, surpassing the 2010/11 cuts of £61.6 million (UNISON, 2011). The absence of youth provision, especially 'a lack of legitimate things to do and places to go', was identified by Morrell and colleagues (2011) as a trigger for the 2011 August riots. The majority of socially excluded young people believe there is 'a lack of things for them to do' in their communities (The Princes Trust, 2004, p 2).

Convulsive and dynamic communities

The borough of Lambeth, with its population of almost 300,000, is characterised by above-average population density, and rented and social housing. Rapid population increase is also evident, although this varies across wards (see Table 1.3).

Lambeth is further characterised by high levels of residential mobility or population churn. In 2010, 33,600 people moved into the borough and 35,900 moved out, indicating population churn of 24.5% (approximately 70,000) of the total borough population. The council claims this is not 'an inherently negative phenomenon', although churn nevertheless affects community sustainability, with 35% of Lambeth's population resident for less than five years (Lambeth First, 2011a, p 7).

Table 1.3: Population increases and ethnicity characteristics, by ward (2001-12)*

	Population increase 2001-12	Ethnicity characteristics
Coldharbour	6%	74% are from minority ethnic backgrounds (LA 51%), predominantly from black Caribbean (17%), black African (21%) and 10% mixed/other ethnic group Fewer residents speak English as their main language (69%) (LA 82%)
Ferndale	9%	Only 35% white British (LA 47%)
Vassall	7%	Black residents account for 41% (LA 23%)
Stockwell	10%	68% are from ethnic minority backgrounds (LA 51%) including 11% Portuguese; 7% Polish; 19% non-specified white other origins 38% of residents do not have English as their first language (LA 18%)
Larkhall	16%	19% of residents are black African (10%)
Oval	20%	8% of residents speak Portuguese (LA 4%)

Note: * Lambeth average is shown in brackets (LA)

Source: Lambeth First (2011b; 2012)

These figures echo the urban succession and social ecology theories posited by Park et al (1925) and Shaw and MacKay (1942) of the Chicago School regarding invasion, conflict, accommodation and assimilation of populations into the inner city. Some of this increase is from new immigrant communities settling in the borough in new emergent communities.

Lambeth's population is already very diverse, with over 37.3% of the borough's population from BME groups. Interestingly, the largest non-white ethnic group is now black African (11.8%), whereas it had previously been black Caribbean (10.1%). This represents a notable change in the borough's ethnic composition. BME communities are also disproportionally represented in some wards, as shown in Table 1.3.

The majority of the borough's child population is overwhelmingly BME (59%), compared with a London average of 37%. In Lambeth schools, this rises to 81%. Over 140 different languages are spoken in Lambeth, with English the second language of 45% of state school pupils.

BME communities also experience a higher concentration of poverty and deprivation. Unemployment is higher for black residents (57%) and those of mixed ethnicity (56%) than for white residents (20%) (Lambeth First, 2012).

Discredited neighbourhoods

These macro issues directly affect young people but also have a profound impact on the neighbourhoods in which young people reside. Table 1.2 illustrates the levels of deprivation experienced in the wards that make up London SW9. Where poverty and disadvantage is concentrated (Dean, 1997; Pitts, 2008b) communities become discredited (Baum, 1996). This stigma further extinguishes legitimate opportunity for young people. Increasingly, these excluded areas in the UK are racialised (Pitts, 2007a). Moreover, as areas of acute deprivation they will experience increased crime and youth victimisation (Hope, 1994, 2003).

It is from this world of 'distressed and disadvantaged neighbourhoods and communities characterised by structural neglect, poverty, poor housing and severely circumscribed labour market opportunities' (Goldson, 2011, p 11) that gangs emerge.[1] I suggest we owe the young people involved a moral and social responsibility to understand this world, to explore this social field and to seek answers to the many as yet unresolved or contested questions about gangs rather than to simply deny its reality.

Researching the social field

The data collection methods I employ included semi-structured, in-depth qualitative interviews; participant observation; media analysis of documentation collated over four years; web research on social networking sites; and a field diary.

As an experienced youth researcher, I made effective use of facilitative techniques to manage short attention spans and allow young people to articulate experiences in the third person. For the purposes of the current study I therefore devised a set of 'show cards', allowing respondents to 'unpack' comments and feelings without highlighting any knowledge deficit. These methods proved extremely valuable throughout the study. The show cards covered both interpersonal and community matters, legal and illegal issues, and expressive and instrumental crimes.

Crucially, I wanted to conceptualise the differentiated spaces where various gang activities and behaviours took place and to tease out the differentiated tactics used by gangs in certain spaces, at different times. To do this, I adapted the concepts from the Duluth Model.[12] This training model illustrates the connectivity between actions, patterns, control and domination over women in a domestic violence setting in relation to different spaces or environments, for example, public space. It thus illustrates the tactical choices available to abusers, from authoritative power to direct personal control or use of sanctions. Adapting this model provided me with a template for how gangs might control their social field. Tactics were then identified appropriate to the differentiated spaces used by gangs and possible activities grouped into categories, which I then used on show cards.

Show cards permitted respondents to rank priorities or group variables (for example, most dangerous activity), permitting easy visual recall of topics and allowing multiple perspectives or scenarios to be discussed simultaneously. Though primarily devised for use with young people, they were used with all respondents to great effect.

In line with a field-analysis approach, I undertook interviews with non-gang-affiliated people who lived/worked in SW9. Residents (n = 7) were accessed using snowballing techniques while police officers (n = 10) working with gangs were accessed via the Lambeth MPS Superintendent. Professionals working with gang-affiliated young people – Community Safety Officers, and London Probation Service and Youth Offending Service workers (n = 15) – were accessed through service directors. Gang-affiliated young people (n = 20) were accessed through three local SW9 charities working with young people aged 16-25, either gang-affiliated or at risk of affiliation. New arrivals (immigrant) young people, aged 16-20 (n = 4) were also accessed in this way but interviewed in a focus group. The research study began in October 2008, with fieldwork conducted from April 2010 to April 2011 and again from August to December 2013.

As part of the ethnographic approach, I undertook 60 site visits for participant observation, (Stephens et al, 1998), with each visit entered into a field log and used to monitor activities and changes in patterns observed or evidenced on the ground. Observing local tenants and residents meetings and local Safe Neighbourhood Panels soon became impracticable because they were often cancelled.

Ethnographic methods often generate rich research findings and this study was no exception; interviews lasted two to three hours, with all digital recordings then transcribed verbatim by me.

Content analysis of local media generated multiple examples for contextual discussion. Social networking sites were identified by random snowballing following leads from respondents. These were accessed live and reviewed over a three-year period. They allowed assessment of how incidents 'played out' online and identification of common themes, but most importantly gave insights into gang presentation, location, marketing, terminology, symbolism, age groups and so on.

Undertaking gang research always highlights ethical considerations for the 'dignity, rights, safety and well-being' of participants, (Stuart et al, 2002, p 3). To avoid possible stigma of interviews on gangs, I adopted the investigative field title of 'What is it like to live to live here?' and later 'Surviving the neighbourhood'. Both provided an easier point of entry into questions, identification of positive attributes and spontaneous raising of gang issues by respondents. A map of the case study area was presented to all respondents.

Anonymity and terminology

Ethical consideration was given to the appropriateness of revealing the location and names of gangs active in the area. It is argued, most notably by Aldridge and colleagues (2008) (but also by Klein, 1971; Hobbs et al, 2003; Ralphs et al, 2009) that introducing anonymity in published research reduces stigma to local communities. Referring to gang research undertaken in *Research city* (Aldridge and Medina, 2008), Aldridge and colleagues argue against 'strengthening' gangs through research publication, noting that local communities did not wish to further glorify gangs as 'brand names' and sought to limit 'identifying talk'.

Herein lies a key methodological point of difference, as I argue that this approach is situated in traditional labelling theory and is not conducive to a more realist perspective of social field analysis. Adopting a field-analysis approach ensures the centrality of local historical context to any understanding of local dynamics and the interactions of actors. Without such context, the history or habitus cannot be fully explored, assessed or elucidated. Without situating the research study, local residents' perspectives cannot be contextualised nor established gang history validated. For example, in SW9, it is impossible to ignore the long-standing history between the black community and the police, and the connection between the Jamaican community and drug dealing. Such aspects must be central dimensions of social field analysis and cannot therefore be ignored. Indeed, it is the habitus of such areas that affects and governs actions within the social field of SW9 (see Chapter Four).

The central relevance of local historical context and habitus is further heightened when researchers seek to map changes or evolutions over time. Without situating or contextualising gang research, evolutionary insights are dulled and claims of change cannot be tested by those with local knowledge. This is a crucial element in moving beyond field reportage to field analysis.

Moreover, anonymising the findings from SW9 or the gangs involved inhibits understandings, denying realities on the ground. This view was shared by local residents, who are highly cognisant of local gangs and their histories but are realistic and informed about the discourses widely available in the public domain. They know the reputation of SW9 for gangs and are realistic about their existence. They do, however, seek a better understanding of this phenomenon. Abstracting any findings, some argued, would deny their experiences.

While seeking to avoid stigma is a worthy objective, it fails to account for the social field which the gangs themselves inhabit. It may also potentially deny the the reality of enormous contemporary changes occurring for young people (and for gangs) e.g. the impact of social networking. The challenge therefore is not to worry that research will glorify 'gangs as brand names', but to enter the social field of the gang – where brand names already exist with a currency and street value. The challenge then is to explore why they exist, for whom they hold relevance, and how are they monitored, advertised, and so on. The issue of stigma is relevant to those outside the social field of the gang rather than those within it. I have therefore chosen not to anonymise the findings.

Similar arguments to those above are often expressed about the terminology 'gang'. For some researchers, (Aldridge et al, 2008; Hallsworth and Young, 2008; Ralphs et al, 2009; Hallsworth and Duffy, 2010), the term is often misattributed and widely misunderstood. For Hallsworth and Young (2008), who remain sceptical of the existence of gangs in the UK, the term 'gang' and the subsequent discourse of 'gang talk' is to be avoided. The term 'gang', however, drew wide consensus among my respondents. Although one or two respondents preferred to set their own slightly amended vocabulary, as interviews progressed, the term 'gang' was used easily by all. While for some, it is something that 'dares not speak its name lest it become manifest', it remains a term commonly utilised within SW9. Despite the lack of consensus as to a definition, the term was used in the research and throughout this book.

Chapter outlines

Chapter Two places my research within the context of contemporary UK gang research, identifying three pre-eminent perspectives on gangs by UK scholars. It then approaches the academic contributions to the gang agenda of both UK and US scholars, considering areas of consensus and debate within themes or topics. The aim here is to identify commonalities and also gaps in our understandings. These gaps are then identified in an emerging research agenda.

Chapter Three details my search for an explanatory model that might explain the rise in violence occurring in London SW9, the subject of this enquiry. I then propose my theoretical perspective, field theory, as derived from Bourdieu, Waquant and organisational theorists such as Fligstein and McAdam, as a useful interpretive lens to view the gang, its internal dynamics and its myriad of interpersonal relationships. Having utilised field theory, I turn to social field analysis to further explore the gang. This approach establishes the gang as an 'arena of structured conflict'; moreover, it accords to us the useful insight of actors within this arena (field) as being constantly in conflict and convulsively struggling towards mutually agreed goals. I establish a linear narrative metaphor of a casino where actors are variably placed in this social field determinant upon the quality and weight of their casino chips (capital). Each seeks advancement to distinction within the field. Having detailed the social field, its underlying logic and its links to the habitus (the internal blueprint that guides social actions), I then move on to develop my unifying concept of street capital, illustrating its centrality to the social field of the gang. I propose that street capital acts as the premium capital in the social field of the gang.

Chapter Four considers how the code of the street and the habitus of the neighbourhood act in unison to undergird the social field, acting as a set of 'house rules'. I reveal how actors in the social field employ various forms of strategic action in order to advance. This is done by employing the gang repertoire – a menu of tested actions, inspired by the habitus of the social field and employed strategically by gang members. I expand this concept to consider three separate repertoires: an expressive repertoire, an instrumental repertoire and a sanction repertoire.

Chapter Five sets out in detail how social order is maintained within the social field, offering a deep analysis of gang organisation, hierarchy and structure – which not only exists but is both clear and evident in this social field. It argues that structures have evolved over the past few years and gangs now present with three clear age banded tiers: elementary, mature and advanced. Movement between tiers is achieved by competence and increased street capital rather than by age. Opportunities for upward advancement are provided through auditioning, testing and upward transitioning. The chapter considers the characteristics of the social skills needed to be a competent actor, and finally addresses the constant and ubiquitous change in the social field arising from the ever-present struggle between incumbents and challengers, which can lead to gang fracturing and desistence.

Chapter Six expands on the metaphor of the casino game and considers how the inequitable distribution of capital in the social field leads young people to develop strategies to accumulate street capital. It then considers how street capital is manufactured through reputations for both individuals and gangs and how it must be maintained and maximised, and expands the concept of gang reputations and street names/brands with concepts of marketing and fast-tracking reputations.

Once in 'the game' young people in the social field of the gang must defend their reputation or street capital. Others seek to test them and steal their street capital. Chapter Seven develops this concept by revealing what players must do to stay in the game and what they must do to win the game.

Chapter Eight expands the theory of street capital with an in-depth example of 'the game' in action and how habitus, street capital and the gang repertoire relate to the so-called 'postcode beef' 'postcode beef'. It suggests that territorial disputes offer an opportunity for street capital to be instantly adjusted; territorial incursions are strategically employed as personal violations to discredit rivals and diminish street capital. It also refutes the notion favoured by the media that gang violence is driven primarily by 'postcode beefs' and drug dealing.

Chapter Nine establishes the social field as a landscape of risk for young people, illustrating how young people navigate this landscape by reducing and mitigating their chances of victimisation. To navigate and survive this violent landscape, young people must learn the rules of the game quickly, often from school. Here they recognise the influencing factors for gang affiliation and learn the various narratives of street families, protection and peer pressure.

Chapter Ten addresses the mechanisms for survival in this landscape. These include the imperative for young people to risk manage their lives, self-restrict movements to avoid victimisation, to challenge and confront. The chapter also considers the risks at the boundary of the social field before detailing the risks specifically evident in relation to ethnicity.

Chapter Eleven is titled 'Creating the house advantage', by which is meant the importance gained by having critical information on everyone in the social field. This is a process that favours incumbents and leaders. The chapter develops the concept of the centrality of information technology and social networking sites, arguing that this has fundamentally changed gang dynamics and operations. It details how information is used, traded and marketed, using social skills, through the 'network' – a social network of connections.

Chapter Twelve argues that the social field of the gang is highly gendered and that girls and young women begin the game with fewer allocated 'chips' than men. It further argues that young women are central to the social field and that they often develop strategies to build capital and survive in different ways from men, relying instead on social skills. They become key traders in information, which makes them key players. However, for those with little social skill, the social field becomes an even more dangerous place, exposing females to sexual abuse and exploitation.

In the social field of the gang, social order is maintained through the imposition of sanctions. The sanctions repertoire thus acts as the tested menu of affirmative or negative sanctions. Each can be employed to influence street capital and reputation. For many, this acts as a wheel of fortune (Chapter Thirteen), offering instant wins or losses.

Chapter Fourteen argues, by way of conclusion, that social field theory has enormous utility for gang studies. It permits a deeper analysis of the multiple interpersonal relationships and motivations explicit within gang dynamics and processes, allowing insight into what has too often been labelled 'messy' networks. It also offers an insight into the cumulative impacts and stresses of living in and surviving this social field. Finally, it summarises the original aspects of my theory before offering some policy insights arising from my general theory.

Notes

[1] It must be stated that SW9 is not the only postcode in Lambeth where violent street gangs exist or are evident in local communities. Nor is Lambeth the only local authority in London where gangs exist and serious gang-related youth violence persists.

[2] The UK Peace Index from the Institute for Economics and Peace (IEP, 2013) identified Lewisham as the least peaceful place in the UK, with Lambeth in second place, followed by Hackney, Newham and Tower Hamlets in east London. Violent crime in Lambeth was identified as being three times the national average. The authors defined peace as 'the absence of violence or the absence of the fear of violence'. Research was based on Home Office crime data, including public disorder offences and weapons crime, and police officer numbers.

[3] On the morning of 8 April 2014 some 700 police officers were jointly involved in raids on the homes of gang members across London and the UK, with the Brixton GAS gang specifically targeted. According to Justin

Davenport (2014), the crime correspondent of the London Evening Standard, 'Detectives say the Brixton-based Gas Gang has expanded its drug-dealing operations and is now linked to several towns and cities around the UK.' The piece continued by quoting Detective Chief Inspector Tim Champion, of the Trident Central Gangs Unit:

> We are targeting this gang because it is one of the most dangerous in London whose members are involved in knife and gun crime. We have disrupted their activity and the feedback we are getting is that this has suppressed violence... We have seen a 6.5 per cent reduction in knife crime among the under-25s but this is an ongoing process. ... The majority of our priority gangs now have tentacles in the county forces.

The article further claimed that 'At least six killings have been linked to the Gas Gang and eight suspected members are in jail for murder or attempted murder.'

[4] In his analysis of Bourdieu's sociological research method, Swartz (1997, p 142) considers three steps in this approach: research must relate the particular field of practices to the broader field of power; What are the forms of economic or cultural capital specific to the field under investigation? How are they distributed and what are the dominant and subordinate positions for all?; research must analyse the class habitus brought by agents to their respective positions and the social trajectory they pursue within these fields.

[5] Lambeth featured significantly on the Gangs in London website (2011). Lambeth has a strong reputation for gang activity, including one of south London's most recognised gangs, the PDC, (Pritchard, 2008). The location has been subject of numerous recent gang initiatives and incidents (Pitts, 2007b; Lambeth First, 2008). The borough strategic crime assessment 2011 states clearly 'a high proportion of youth violence can be attributed to gang tensions or is committed by individuals with gang links', noting 'widespread but sporadic gang and group violent activity in Lambeth, centred in areas of social housing, and producing the high risks of serious youth violence and associated offending' (Lambeth First, 2011a).

[6] Osman Warnings (warnings of death threat or high risk of murder issued by the police to the expected victim) in Lambeth are reportedly increasing, with approximately four high-rated and 20-40 medium-rated warnings issued weekly (private correspondence with Lambeth MPS).

[7] Lambeth First (2011b) identified the crime ranking for the six wards that are part of SW9 as follows: Coldharbour ranked first out of 21 wards for

reported TNOs; Ferndale ranked third; Oval ranked fifth; Vassal ranked eighth; Stockwell ranked 12th; and Larkhall ranked 11th.

[8] For a more detailed discussion of these issues, see Pitts (2008b).

[9] The data for this chapter are all sourced from Lambeth First, *Lambeth strategic assessment 2011* (Lambeth First, 2011a) and *State of the borough report 2012* (Lambeth First, 2012).

[10] Centre for economic and social inclusion, Child Poverty Toolkit, www. cesi.org.uk/statistics/tools

[11] Pitts (2008b) summarises these conditions as a 'concentration of disadvantage' (58); The Kenny Report (Imafidon, 2012) also outlines these conditions. Klein and Maxson (2006, 149) note that 'communities spawn gangs'. However they also found 'little evidence to support neighbourhood characteristics as predictors for individual-level gang joining'. They posit that neighbourhood characteristics may be more relevant to understanding the emergence or persistence of gangs in communities.

[12] The Domestic Violence Power and Control Wheel (the Duluth Model) as pioneered by the Domestic Abuse Intervention Project in Duluth, Minnesota (1984); www.duluth-model.org

TWO

Academic gangland

During the past ten or 15 years, the UK has witnessed an increase in street gang culture and the emergence of violent urban street gangs which are active in a small number of urban areas. This phenomenon includes recent changes in gang composition (increased organisation with ever-younger affiliates staying in the gang longer), (Pitts, 2008b; Densley, 2013), presentation (links to the drug economy and so-called 'postcode beefs') (Pitts, 2008b; Densley, 2013) and a concurrent upswing of serious and seemingly chaotic gang-related violence (Centre for Social Justice, 2009). This phenomenon has brought sensationalist media headlines and dissensus among academics as to gang organisation, membership, behaviours and even their existence.

In the US, a similar situation was reported where a 'major escalation' of youth gang problems was experienced from 1970 to 2000 (Miller, W., 2001). A striking feature of this growth was the emergence of gangs in smaller towns and cities, from 1970 when fewer than 300 cities reported youth gang problems to 1998 when more than 2,500 US towns and cities reported youth gang problems.

John Hagedorn gives life to Miller's dramatic quantification by narrating the gang renaissance in the US in the 1980s (Hagedorn, 1998) followed by its subsequent 'institutionalisation' and 'globalisation' (Hagedorn, 2007, 2008). Located in 'abstract spaces', and emanating from 'local histories of economic restructuring and community defeat', Hagedorn situates the modern global gang as 'organisations of the socially excluded simultaneously occupying the spaces of both prison and ghetto' (Hagedorn, 2007, p 25). Academics now report that membership of violent street gangs is on the rise globally (St Cyr and Decker, 2003; Decker and Weerman, 2005; Salageav et al, 2005; Weerman and Decker, 2005; Hagedorn, 2008).

The identification of this phenomenon has precipitated recent academic studies on both sides of the Atlantic, highlighting divergent perspectives between contemporary gang research in the UK and the US, while raising questions about the applicability of US research to the UK. Though informative, and largely contextual, this growing body of work illuminates the limitations of current research, raising many unanswered questions. While in the UK academics have queried the very existence of street gangs (Goldson, 2011), contemporary

US research has shifted focus to singular aspects of street gangs: definitions (Klein, 1971, 2006); Chicano gangs (Moore, 1978); gang formation and causality (Spergel, 1995); risk factors (Thornberry, 1998); levels of organisation (Decker et al, 2008); increasing levels of membership (Decker et al, 1998); the multiple marginality of immigrant communities (Vigil, 2002; 2010)[1]; and globalisation and institutionalisation (Hagedorn, 1998).

Though often a crowded discipline, I suggest that gang research has yet to fully embrace the explanatory value of sociological concepts such as habitus and social field analysis (Bourdieu, 1990). I intend to now rectify this omission and add to this academic landscape using these sociological approaches as the theoretical underpinning of my own research. Before detailing my contribution, I first wish to review the alternative perspectives that are most recognisable to the contemporary debate on gangs. It is possible to consider the UK discourse on gangs either historically, theoretically or thematically. I begin this excursion into academic gangland by grouping UK theoretical perspectives on gangs. I follow this with an analysis of several research themes indicating areas of consensus, while highlighting research debates and gaps.

UK gang research

Youth gangs are not new to the UK (Patrick, 1973; Pearson, 1983; Davies, 1998). Traditional studies of UK gang and youth groups have often undertaken an ethnographic case-study approach (Patrick, 1973), focusing on intergenerational territorially based traditions or sub-cultures (Downes, 1966; Parker, 1974). The rich and expressive sub-cultural tribal groupings emergent in the UK in the second half of the 20th century, (zoot suiters, rockers, greasers, beatniks, mods, hippies, skins, suedeheads, boot boys, soul boys, New Romantics, New Wavers, goths, ravers, EMOs, skater punks) seldom ever found expression as gangs, but emerged as rebellious adolescent breaks from parental conventionality via their focus on art, music and fashion. Any violence generated here (mostly through alcohol and tribal contest) was recreational. Such groupings emerged *from* the street (as forms of youth or street-style), but they were not *of* the street, nor oriented towards it, and thus differ considerably from the contemporary violent street gangs that are the subject of this book.

While youth sub-cultural expression dominated thinking on youth group offending for the Centre for Contemporary Cultural Studies at Birmingham University, Willmott (1966) argued that more serious offending was related to excitement and group identity. Such work pre-empted the current vogue of cultural criminology (Katz, 1988; Presdee, 2000; Hayward, 2004).

Whereas American sub-cultural theorists focused on gangs and delinquent behaviours, UK sub-cultural studies questioned their extent and sought to locate UK debates within UK class-based structures, a discourse complicated by lack of a universal definition of gangs and a paucity of UK research resulting in overreliance on US theoretical concepts. This was further complicated by the plethora of UK sub-cultural groups and a sensible reluctance to view such groups as gangs. This, however, was to change.

From the late 1990s, increased UK media discussion generated highly politicised debate as to the existence of street gangs in the UK and the applicability of US terminology to this emergent issue. Around the millennium, reports began to emerge in the UK, largely from local youth workers and practitioners, of an increased prevalence of a more violent form of street gang, often linked to drug markets and street robbery, utilising high levels of violence involving knives and firearms. Such issues first surfaced in Manchester (termed 'Gunchester' by the press). Authorities responded with Operation Crome and in 2001 the creation of the Manchester Multi-Agency Gang Strategy. Regionally, violent street gangs were becoming the subject of academic study (Mares, 2001; Bullock and Tilley, 2002; Shropshire and McFarquhar, 2002; Bennett and Holloway, 2004), leading to research by Aldridge and colleagues (2008) funded by the Economic and Social Research Council.

For some, these activities indicated an evolution of group offending and serious youth violence (Pitts, 2008b; Toy, 2008), with the groups involved and their targeted use of violence emerging, not from youth culture, music and fashion, but from blocked opportunities, multiple deprivation, poverty and links to ongoing criminal activities, such as drug dealing. Others viewed this as the 'dramatic rediscovery of the gang' (Hallsworth, 2013).

In London, however, the increasing emergence of violent street gangs and their propensity for weaponised violence was largely overlooked by academics, leaving the media to frame the debate. When academics did catch up with events, both nationally and in London, the debate was all but truncated by claims that violent street gangs were nothing more than a product of media moral panic (Hallsworth and Young, 2004). Such contributions, while claiming to be 'getting real about gangs', simply denied the realties on the ground, now increasingly presenting to partnership practitioners in London. Overwhelmingly,

London practitioners viewed these emergent violent street gangs as UK home-grown and not simply US imports. However, calls by some academics not to evoke US cultural references usually had the effect of doing just that, thus confusing the debate even further.

In the absence of any leading academic research, key gang-affected London boroughs established the Five Borough Alliance in London.[2] This was followed by flurry of activity from government agencies: the Home Office (2006), which offered a controversial and largely discredited definition; the Youth Justice Board (Young et al, 2007), which articulated a labelling theory position warning of the danger of 'talking up' gangs (preferring the term 'peer group offending'); the methodologically questionable Communities That Care (2005), which reported on their extensive quantitative schools survey that found low levels of gang affiliation and thus offered little clarity. This activity was followed by the government's flagship initiative, Tackling Knives and Serious Youth Violence Action Programme, which was unable to attribute falls in serious youth violence over four years to its extensive activities (Home Office, 2011). Since this somewhat faltering start to study and conceptualise the emergent phenomenon of violent street gangs involved in drug markets and often fatal weaponised violence, a contemporary UK gang discourse has begun to emerge, albeit one shaped by these early perspectives.

Contemporary UK developments

This brief excursion through the contemporary UK gang's discourse only tells part of the story and it is perhaps useful to view this discourse in a different way. It can be argued that the UK conceptualisation of gangs derives from either a 'risk factor paradigm' (Farrington 1995), which posits that gangs are the end result of 'defective attitudes, beliefs and behaviours', or from a 'youth governance thesis', which posits that youth crime has changed little from before and any concerns regarding rising violence are elevated by interested groups, for example, the police, media and government (Pitts, 2008b). While the former paradigm leads to a correctionalist and managerialist response, the second underplays the realities of socioeconomic and historical influences. In addition to this paradigmatic meta-narrative that influences research, the contemporary UK discourse on gangs falls broadly into three theoretical perspectives, as follows.

Governance through crime/Left idealists

Hallsworth and Young are major contributors to gang research in the UK, not least via their typology of urban collectives (Hallsworth and Young, 2006), which for a while gained traction in the UK. Despite compelling evidence of their existence, for Hallsworth and Young UK gangs remain a contested issue that is variously denied as mythological; or partially admitted as conceptually misread, 'overblown' or the result of 'moral panic'.[3] Echoing the critique of Simon (2007) and Garland (2001), who caution that increased fear of crime provides opportunities for increased executive control, Hallsworth and Young caution against 'agents of control' who might benefit from increasing public anxieties about gangs. Critical of the 'series of conjectures' they believe sits behind the thesis of gangland Britain, they mount a sharp attack on the evidential base and academics who, they contend, 'misattribute' the gang label. Simultaneously describing gang violence in the UK as serious (Hallsworth and Duffy, 2010), they profess gangs to be the new 'folk devil' of UK society. Critically assessing the role of the 'gang-obsessed media' through 'gang talk', they argue that coverage retains 'many of the hallmarks of a full-blown moral panic' (Hallsworth, 2013) and is central to the 'construction of what they would term the gang myth' (Hallsworth and Young, 2008). Rejecting positivist US traditions/definitions, while calling for UK practitioners to be sceptical of administrative surveys or empiricist approaches that misread the evidence, Hallsworth cautions researchers not to concede to the gang any importance it does not have.

This perspective is dominated by the argument that gangs, if they exist, are defined by social disorganisation; that 'control agents' of the 'gang control industry' (Hallsworth, 2011; Hallsworth and Brotherton, 2011) talk up gangs and mythologise street life. For Hallsworth, gangs are a 'collectively induced fantasy' (Hallsworth, 2013, p 8) whose novelty is significantly overstated.

Latter-day labelling theorists/Left idealists

A different perspective on gangs is held by gang researchers working in Manchester including, Aldridge and Medina (2008, 2010); Aldridge et al (2008, 2009, 2011); Medina et al (2009, 2012); Ralphs et al (2009). While acknowledging the existence of violent street gangs, their views are linked to those of Malcolm Klein. Leaning heavily on labelling theory (Tannenbaum, 1938; Becker, 1963) and social reaction theories of stigma (Goffman, 1963), this perspective acknowledges that the UK has a gang problem, and that UK gangs differ from those in the US. These Manchester based researchers argue that the 'so-called emergence of youth gangs in the UK over the past few decades ... represents a change at the discursive level: a new label to designate the – not radically changed – experiences of marginalised urban youth' (Medina et al, 2009, p 4).

Following extensive investigation in what Aldridge and Medina refer to as *Research city* (Aldridge and Medina, 2007; Aldridge et al, 2011), Aldridge and Medina argue most gang violence comes from interpersonal disputes and intra-gang issues rather than turf issues; that some gangs have no street presence; that territoriality issues are often individual rather than group; that desistance is a gradual maturation process; and that young people in gangs operate 'cafeteria-style earnings', both licit and illicit (Aldridge and Medina 2007; Medina et al, 2009).

Many practitioners agree and indeed some findings from this perspective do resonate with recent research in London, notably that gangs are largely ethnically mixed and reflect the ethnic composition of their neighbourhood; that gang members often retain strong family links; that having criminally active family members indicates future gang involvement; and that the term 'gang member' may be misleading for the gang involved (Aldridge and Medina, 2007).

This perspective supports the Klein contention, however, which can be summarised as being that gangs exist, but that they are less well organised (Aldridge and Medina, 2007) or indeed as criminally sophisticated (Mares, 2001) as people think.

In a retrospective glance at *Research city*, Medina and colleagues (2009) refer to the emergence in the late 1980s of a 'new informal economy' of drugs operated by specialist gangs. The authors note that gangs in *Research city* have become entrenched over the past 20 years due to 'intergenerational transmission of gang identities', development of a 'gang culture' and the 'fragmentation of existing gangs into amorphous unpredictable networks and less organised little factions' (Medina et al, 2009, p 6). They contend that, since being broken up, drug dealing is now undertaken by 'individuals trading as free agents'. This finding seems to be more in line with the views of John Hagedorn and seems a curious fit with a theoretical position suggesting a change at the discursive level. The link between drugs and gangs in Manchester was researched in depth by Bullock and Tilley (2002), who pinpointed gangs as responsible for escalating firearm violence. For them, drugs was only one element of a wider pattern of offending and gang 'conflict was endemic and easily triggered' and spatially concentrated, (Bullock and Tilley, 2008). Given such findings, notably linked to drug-related violence, it is surprising that Aldridge and colleagues fail to reconcile Bullock and Tilley's position regarding drug-related gang violence with their own position that drugs are not controlled by the gang. Similarly, Bullock and Tilley (2002) found that gangs in Manchester have differences in composition, origin, activities and organisation, and include recruits. For Aldridge and colleagues, these differences remain unexplored. Aldridge and Medina (2008) maintain a clearer position regarding joining gangs. Here they align with the US literature, citing 'self-protection, labelling and taking advantage of illegal opportunities' as key motivations. In this perspective, gangs are 'informal friendship networks', which are 'fluid, loose, messy'; gang rivalry is 'more complex and interwoven' than it appears; and violence is often symbolic or rhetorical. Given such wide-ranging generalisation, there is considerable scope for greater clarity and precision in the gang's debate.

The Left realist perspective

The contemporary Left realist perspective can be summarised thus: violent youth gangs exist and pose a real threat to local communities, specifically to young people (Bullock and Tilley, 2002; Palmer and Pitts, 2006; Matthews and Pitts, 2007; Pitts, 2008a, 2008b, 2011; Toy, 2008; Centre for Social Justice, 2009; Palmer, 2009; Densley, 2011, 2012a, 2012b, 2012c, 2013; Harding, 2012). This view is arrived at via extensive field research in gang-affected communities in London, which identifies hierarchies and levels of gang organisation (Pitts, 2008a,b; Toy, 2008); increased embeddedness[4] (Hagan, 1993; Hagedorn, 2008); networked links to older career criminals (Toy, 2008); and significant levels of violence (Pitts 2007b, 2008b).

A recent practitioner's perspective supports the evidence of organisation in London gangs; Toy (2008) notes the recent emergence of 'organisational gangs [which] are well structured, profit-led businesses ... led by entrepreneurial, dynamic individuals' (p 30).

Common to this perspective is a belief that violent youth gangs have evolved to fill the vacuums in deprived and contested communities left by executive authorities that are increasingly disengaged (Hagedorn, 2008) from residualised and vulnerable communities (Pitts, 2008b, 2011). Acknowledging that youth gangs are not themselves a new phenomenon in the UK, this perspective argues that the type of violent youth gangs now operating in the UK is indeed a new phenomenon and it is one that continues to rapidly evolve (Densley, 2013).

Pitts (2010) argues that restrictive methodologies and 'correctional' (Matza, 1969) ideologies have narrowly prescribed gang research inhibiting examination of the social field of the gang (Bourdieu 1984, 1998c; Martin, 2003; Fligstein and McAdam, 2012; Bourdieu and Wacquant, 1992). I argue that social field analysis is deemed important primarily to give clarity and precision to the many rationalised generalisations, but also to fully understand the concept of gangland (Thrasher, 1927). Moreover, analysing gangs by employing social field analysis provides improved understandings of the interface between organised criminal networks and the gang-affiliated young people who share the same social field (Gordon, 2000; Pitts, 2011).

One point of consensus among UK gang researchers is that US contextualisation and framing of gang debates establishes unhelpful preconceptions as to what a gang is, and thus a UK-specific framework of reference is required.

Having acknowledged these different theoretical perspectives and before I myself join this conversation, I want to further review US and UK academic literature to identify consensus, disagreements and gaps within contemporary thematic debates that will hopefully help establish a new research agenda. To do this, I have grouped this review under the following headings: joining a gang; gang organisation; gang characteristics and boundaries; gang behaviours and offending; respect and reputation; and becoming a competent actor in the gang.

Joining a gang

The motivations for entering the gang are a good place to start. Here the US literature is situated within the enduring theoretical paradigm of the Chicago School. Frederik Thrasher (1927) observed how gangs thrived in 'interstitial areas' in inner-city deprived constituencies with transient populations. He found gangs to be fluid and dynamic, under constant change. He identified an evolutionary process from early diffusion, through 'solidification' to 'conventionalisation' (the adoption by members of legitimate societal roles). Thrasher noted the isolation of gangs and the effects of intra-group bonding and cohesiveness. This cohesion allowed for internal social control through gang rules (sanctions) and the emergence of 'collective representations', such as symbols, signs and language, which enhanced a separate identity. I shall return later to consider the concept of sanctions and gang rules from a field-analysis perspective. Despite criticism of Thrasher for failing to highlight issues of racial segregation and political corruption, nonetheless, many of these issues – notably territory, evolutionary processes, symbols and 'integration through conflict' – remain highly relevant in contemporary studies of gang development.

Gang development, for Shaw and McKay (1931), arose from delinquency and normalised behaviours. For them, criminal behaviour is learnt from other offenders, and members graduate from initial stages (where fun is the primal motivation) to more serious crimes. This concept of graduation (Tannenbaum, 1938) or movement through the gang remains a strong element of all gang research.

A handful of researchers have tried to identify the latent functions (Parsons, 1937) of gang affiliation and Zorbaugh (1929) from the Chicago School was an early advocate of the theory that gangs were the labour pool for the Mob. More recently, Chin (1996) notes that Chinese gangs are used as 'entry-level employees' in illegal businesses, and Hagedorn (2008) suggests that the testing of members in criminal activity equates to a latent function of auditioning and apprenticeship for higher-level, more serious crime.

Tannenbaum (1938) reported that gangs become 'street-corner families', bonded through loyalty and in conflict with the local community. For him, societal responses to the gang push young people to affiliate and criminal associations help young people to move up the criminal hierarchy. Edwin Sutherland (1947) furthered these ideas through concepts of differential association.

Gang cohesion identified by Thrasher (1927) continues to be a central focus of gang research in the US and UK. Later, attention shifted towards class theories, notably strain theory and social opportunities (Cohen, 1955), strain theory and anomie theory (Merton, 1957), and differential opportunity theory (Cloward and Ohlin, 1960). Miller (1958), on the other hand, offered a cultural interpretation, viewing gangs as emanating from the cultural values of working-class life.

In terms of gang genesis, Moore and Vigil (1989) identified gangs as developing 'oppositional cultures', where social rejection bonds members through greater cohesiveness. This introspective dimension can lead gangs to develop what Moore and Vigil term a 'victim status'. In her work *Homeboys*, Moore (1978) noted that where there are few opportunities for young people to engage and connect with wider society, gangs can take on an important role.

Societal estrangement was later developed by Hagan and McCarthy (1997), who suggest that young people become extenuated from wider society and socially embedded in relationships that transfer criminal knowledge and skills via 'criminal capital'. This echoes Sutherland (1947) and social learning theories as well as Hagedorn's arguments that gangs have the potential to become embedded.

Looking at Chicago gang cultures, Hagedorn (2007) locates their genesis within a local history of ethnic segregation, political corruption, mass incarceration and economic segmentation. Such pervading conditions represent a localised expression of similar macro-socioeconomic and structural problems, which in the US is leading to an expansion of street gangs and increased 'embeddedness' in large cities (Sampson and Laub, 1993). Hagedorn warns of the potential for such environments to endure, to be increasingly violent, to create informal spatial monopolies and, in places, to become 'institutionalised'.

Entering the gang could, however, include members being 'drafted' into the gang through coercion or threats of violence (Yablonsky, 1962). Such themes are echoed in contemporary UK research (Pitts, 2008b). Once in the gang, new arrivals face unique challenges (Taylor, cited in Huff, 1990) and have to learn gang attributes quickly and demonstrate cohesion.

Meanwhile, in the UK these concepts of intergenerational traditions and social learning theory are also cited by academics who argue that parental involvement in gangs predisposes some young people to gang affiliation (Shropshire and McFarquhar, 2002).

Deuchar's research findings (2009) mirror Thrasher's, namely that people join gangs through intimidation and a need for protection. Protection from rival gangs is a recognised dynamic across all UK gang research, though is best expressed by Pitts in *Reluctant gangsters* (2008b) acknowledging a legitimate fear of sanctions by those seeking to disaffiliate.

For labelling theorists/Left idealists, joining the gang involves factors of 'self-protection, labelling and taking advantage of illegal opportunities' (Aldridge and Medina, 2008, p 17). Leaving school is viewed as a critical moment in gang involvement (Ralphs et al, 2009, note 10, p 498).

The Left realist perspective argues that schools and colleges are part of the social field – arenas where gang-related violence is reproduced with internal peer conflicts then replicated outside school boundaries. Conflicts are exacerbated by rumours rapidly spread via mobile phone texts ensuring that tensions are introduced constantly into the learning environment (Pitts, 2007b, p 38). Recognising that gang behaviours may have an impact in schools, attempts were made to address such issues by the Home Office (2008) and NASUWT (2009).

More recently, concepts of social capital have been identified as motivations for joining gangs, (Deuchar, 2009), for generating reciprocity (Horowitz, 1983) and as a way of filling the void if social institutions become depleted (Putnam, 2000).

Gang organisation

Levels of gang organisation are hotly debated on both sides of the Atlantic. Yablonsky (1962), drawing on Thrasher, identified three gang types: delinquent gangs, social gangs and violent gangs. The violent gangs form in response to threats to safety, offering protection to members, a 'collective structure' situated on a spectrum between totally disorganised groups (such as mobs) and well-organised groups (such as delinquent or social gangs).

A different view emerged from Walter Miller in the late 1950s. Following this up in a later work (1980), he also identified three types of gang: territory- based gangs, fighting gangs and gain-oriented gangs. Taylor (1990) argues that gangs evolve from less to more organised units over time. Both these findings appear closer to the UK research findings in terms of broad groupings.

A key contributor to US gang studies, Malcolm Klein argues that gangs are disorganised (1971, pp 109-23). Writing again in 2006, Klein argued that little has changed from his classical description in 1971 (Klein and Maxson, 2006). Decker and Curry (2002) also concur that street gangs are not well organised. In a recently updated work, Decker and colleagues (2008) reiterate this finding while noting that even marginal increases in gang organisation lead to increased offending and victimisation. Somewhat contrarily, they further note that recent research showing gang organisation to be weak (Klein, 1995) failed to consider 'the influence of different levels of gang organisation or the influence of gang organisation on behaviour' (Decker et al, 2008, p 169).

Klein identifies street gangs as 'more a loose collection of cliques or networks than a single coherent whole' with individual membership lasting one about a year (Klein and Maxson, 2006, p 164). Thornberry and colleagues (2003) argue such high levels of turnover challenge suggestions of any stable structures. While this finding differs considerably from my own, I did find agreement with Klein's view that transformation from one gang form to another was more common that dissolution. What Thornberry and Klein crucially fail to acknowledge is that in a structured social field, the structure endures even though the personnel may change. In many ways the social field is analogous to a football squad – the players may change but the roles, rules and pitch are pre-established.

Klein argues that US debates are often distorted by a dominant academic argument, which says gangs have a tightly bound, organised structure. Arguing that they are more often leaderless and disorganised

(Klein and Maxson, 2006), he has developed a five-point typology relating to this variable structure. This typology is the basis for his recent gang research in the US and Europe focusing largely on gang intervention programmes. Hagedorn (2007), however, rejects Klein's Eurogang (Klein and Maxson, 2006) definition as overreliant on narrowly defined US research, commenting that it fails to account for individual city dynamics and issues arising from globalisation.

In the UK, gang organisation is also hotly debated. The labelling theorist/Left idealist perspective echoes Klein, suggesting that gangs are typically fluid, with 'messy structures', porous boundaries and 'far less organisation than expected', and that young people are largely engaged in low-level criminal and antisocial behaviours (Aldridge et al, 2008). One might argue that 'messiness' is an untidy sociological phrasing suggesting that researchers have failed to identify, separate and test the interlacing lattice of gang networks, age bands and functions. Research by the Jill Dando Institute similarly found membership to be 'fluid', but found concepts of 'membership' highly contentious.

The concepts of 'elders', 'youngers' and 'tinnies' are recognised terms (Toy, 2008) and are daily realities for practitioners working with gang-affiliated young people. Despite this widely recognised point, Hallsworth (2013) contests such terms, and Hallsworth and Duffy (2010) conclude that these terms are generic to young people in London and warn against 'gang-obsessed individuals' using them to 'construct the fantasy of a criminal gang' that replicates corporate structures.

Hallsworth and Duffy (2010) refute any sense of organisation as a division of labour, referring instead to organisation as characterised by 'relations of domination and competition between members' and arguing that 'the gang typically exhibits more pack-like behaviours' (p 8) (this suggests that gangs only act in concert and never alone, which denies agency to its component parts). They argue that gangs are dangerous because they lack structure and coherence and it is the volatility of members that leads to lethal outcomes. What motivates this alleged volatility remains unexplored. The authors do, however, offer the notion of a violent street world consisting of a core of older organised criminals surrounded by a 'street periphery' of volatile young people, which is where, they argue, gangs are to be found (bearing in mind that Hallsworth does not believe in their existence).

Hallsworth (2013) rejects attempts by so-called 'gang talkers' to 'corporatise the street'. He describes such organisational descriptors as arising from Western 'arboreal' or tree-like thinking, which searches for patterns and hierarchy in social structures. He argues instead that 'informal organisation of the street is fundamentally rhizomatic', exclaiming that 'rather than read gangs as a command structure shaped in the image of a tree, let's capture them [as] a glorious species of weed' (Hallsworth, 2013, p 113).

Medina and colleagues (2009, p 7) found the gang has a 'strong territorial identity [which] is a key factor in explaining the persistence of group identity despite individual "members" turnover'. In the football team analogy, while the home turf has its dedicated fans, for others it is the performance of the squad that matters, whether playing at home or away. Social field analysis, however, tells us that players, coaches, officials and spectators change over time, and that what endures is the structured social field, a belief in 'the game' and a belief that 'the game' is worth playing (Bourdieu, 1991, pp 22-5).

Conducting gang research by social field analysis provides fresh opportunities to break free from the 'organised/disorganised' binary preoccupying much of the UK gang research. It offers the prospect of considering the field in its entirety, of identifying obscured correlations or foregrounding elements previously considered incidental. Moreover, it forces the researcher to unravel 'messy' structures, explain complex rivalries and bring into focus clouded generalisations. It demands a confrontation with the contemporary realties of the field as it presents, rather than the Hallsworth approach, which selects low-hanging fruits and squeezes them into ideological boxes.

Gang characteristics and boundaries

Moving on from the thorny issue of gang organisation, we arrive at the thorny issue of gang behaviours, characteristics and boundaries. What are the characteristics of the gang and how do they behave/offend? To whom is territory important and why? How do gangs define their boundaries? What help does US research offer to these questions?

Klein notes that recent US studies are either behavioural or structural (Klein and Maxson, 2006). Sub-cultural theorists such as Albert Cohen maintained that people are socialised into criminal sub-cultures, whereas strain theorists and structural functionalists argued that offences such as robbery were committed by 'utilitarian innovators'. Cohen (1966) believed that young men rob for fun as they reject dominant middle-class value systems; to address their 'status frustration', they adjust their structural position in society by undertaking non-utilitarian, deviant, negativistic behaviours.

Behavioural studies largely focus on predominant non-conformist behaviours and cultural adaptations (for example, Cloward and Ohlin,

1960), while structural studies tend to focus on race, ethnicity, gang size and role differentiation. I suggest that this methodological divide potentially excludes or complicates attempts to consider the interplay of both elements, inhibiting any holistic approach. Only recently have US gang researchers such as Huff (1990) called for more gang research into the 'context of social and economic milieu', or for more research on measures of social capital and collective efficacy (Short and Hughes, 2010). This call for different approaches to gang research was echoed by Dwight Conquergood (1994), who cautioned researchers not to consider gang members as 'others' but as spatially transformative, active 'cultural agents' functioning within their own social field. While insightful, this clarion call largely fails to engender fresh perspectives.

Recent UK research has focused on the spatiality of opportunity for young people (Ball et al, 2000), often restricted and mediated by place, which develops into differentiated social horizons leading to 'geographies of exclusion' (Sibley, 1995). Similarly recent research identifies parameters and boundaries to gang activities (Bullock and Tilley, 2002), but largely fails to explore how these are established, governed, crossed or revered. Territoriality, 'postcode wars' and restricted movements of young people have been a recent contribution from spatial geography rather than sociological theory. This research hints at, but does not develop, the explicit relationships between urban street gangs and how they view/use territory. In a useful pointer for my own analysis, the authors call for further research to consider links 'between low-level territorial behaviour and the formation of criminal gangs' (Kintrea et al, 2008, p 7).

Aldridge and Medina (2010) found no fatal shooting incident in *Research city* related to territorial disputes and while members were fearful of 'straying' into rival territory, they found that such fears were linked to previous individual conflicts rather than gang rivalry. Vendettas linked to previous unsolved murders from 20 years ago were also identified as a key source of violent conflict.

Hallsworth and Duffy (2010) locate gang violence in four spatial arenas: territorialism; the street drugs trade; visiting leisure centres; and perceived disrespect. While failing to qualify the role of the gang in violence, how violence is enacted or why these localities are significant, they argue that peer groups and individuals equally engage in violence in these locations. Such views discount or mis-recognise the role and agency of independent operators.

Gang behaviours and offending

Almost all gang research reports criminal offending within gangs to be versatile rather than exclusive (while acknowledging that some speciality gangs do exist). This broad range of versatile criminal offending is referred to as 'cafeteria style offending' (Klein, 1995a, p 68). However, this broad self-selection grouping fails to take into account differences between expressive and instrumental crime, age ranges, favoured specialisms, motivations or manifest/latent functions. This suggestion of a 'self-selection menu' requires further scrutiny.

Within this broad range of versatile criminal offending gangs engage in violence. However, both Klein and Maxson (2006) and Thornberry and colleagues (2003) argue that it is inaccurate to describe a gang as a 'a violent gang'. Why violence is used in some situations and not in others, or why, in this 'cafeteria of offences', violent offences are being selected more frequently, remains unexplored.

In the UK, academics argue that gang affiliation increases offending behaviour for some young people while escalating the level of offending behaviour for others (Bennett and Holloway, 2004; Smith and Bradshaw, 2005). For US gang researcher Terence Thornberry (1998), the gang acts like an escalator, slowly elevating young people to more serious forms of offending.

The link between gangs and urban violence in the UK is disputed by Hallsworth (2008) who over the years continues to argue that 'much of the violence blamed on gangs is not gang-related. Many of the crimes blamed on gangs can be explained in ways that do not require evoking gangs at all' (Hallsworth, 2013, p 14). Similarly Hallsworth and Young (2008) question whether UK violence has increased in any meaningful way.

Aldridge and colleagues (2011), while offering no clear insight into the detail of offending behaviours of the gangs in *Research city*, identify that 'violent conflict rarely derived from disputes over territorial drugs markets and/or protection rackets', but arose from 'jealousies and rivalries over illegal acquisitive opportunities (which) tended to occur within rather than between gangs' (p 80). Medina et al (2013), however, identified that 'gang membership increases the chances of offending, antisocial behaviour, and drug use among young people' (p 3)

Toy, offering a London practitioner's perspective, says that crime data 'supports the theory that there is a growing chaotic nature to serious youth violence caused by personal conflict and territory based feuds, fuelled by illegal drugs markets and robbery' (Toy, 2008, p 20), and that the current spiralling of street-based violence is due to 'fear and glamour', with young people seeking protection by joining gangs that are glamourised by the media. He supports Bullock and Tilley (2002), acknowledging the increasing role of illegal drugs markets on gangs, and supports the view that violence is increasingly being used at a younger age (Schneider et al, 2004).

Notions of 'gang culture' and 'gun culture' in the UK are rejected as theoretically weak with little explanatory value by Hallsworth and Silverstone, who argue that 'gun use "on-road" is much less instrumental and planned and far more erratic and situational' (2009, p 366). They paint a bleak picture of 'outlaw' young people manipulated by elders into carrying weapons, using guns to wield power in a self-destructive manner. This view, however, denies agency and strategy to young people and fails to accurately account for how firearms are accessed within the gang, as I shall show later. For Hallsworth, 'it is rather the volatile, febrile nature of the violent street world which gangs inhabit that creates the context which provokes their formation and persistence' (Hallsworth and Duffy, 2010, p 19) that generates the violence and allows gangs to endure. This suggests an overarching social field in which the gang is only an actor and inhibits potential exploration of the internal dynamics of the gang, which may itself generate such behaviours.

Densley, however, takes a more realist perspective, viewing the gang as 'rational organisations' and members as 'rational agents' (Densley, 2013, p 3). Stressing the evolution of gang life and gang careers (2012a,b,c), he identifies gang life as a liner progression of four stages, from recreation to crime, enterprise and then governance (2013, p 43). For him, these are actualisation stages through which the gang progresses. Gang are therefore 'a rational adaptation to the perennial threat of violence' (p 20) in the community.

Respect and reputation

The causes of delinquency and gang involvement have long been considered by academics. Delinquency for sociological theorist Albert Cohen (1966) arises from 'status frustration' by working-class young men repudiating middle-class values. For Cloward and Ohlin (1960), these common societal values lead to blocked opportunities. However, a deeper reading of older gang texts, such as *Street corner society* (Whyte, 1943), suggests that building social capital is a key function. Suttles (1968) similarly identified the importance of a network of community relationships used to support the gang. More recently, Vigil (1988a).

noted how gangs can develop a 'group esteem' instead of self-esteem. This observation again tilts towards notions of bonding social capital, but gangs as a vehicle for building social capital remains overlooked by US gang researchers.

Social capital and social disorganisation have been explored successfully by Puttnam in *Bowling alone* (2000) and while social capital is seldom addressed in gang research, the absence or evaporation of social capital within communities has been documented by Sampson and Groves (1989) and most notably by Elijah Anderson in *Code of the street* (1999). Their observations, however, beg the question: As the social capital in the wider community frays and disintegrates, what function then does the gang have as an arena where social capital can be acquired or rebuilt?

Issues of respect and reputation are understood to be central to gang studies, but quite why violence based on respect and reputation is so crucial in a gang context often remains unexplored. For Hallsworth and Duffy (2010), UK gangs are highly volatile because 'reputation and honour can never be presumed', as gangs operate within a chaotic and unpredictable street world. This oversimplified account of street justice adds nothing to our understanding of how a gang creates its own codified social norms. Our understandings of UK gangs, community norms and masculinities has, however, been deepened by Sanders (2005) and Winlow (2001), and Palmer (2009) has articulated well the black experience of youth culture with the emergence of youth gangs.

The clearest exposition of 'life on the road' is by Elijah Anderson in *Code of the street* (1999). While located in US street life, these cultural street codes clearly resonate in UK street life. For Hallsworth and Silverstone (2009), street codes are shaped by the demands of the informal economy, for example the drug trade, and young people beholden to these conduct norms 'remain locked within [a] mythic order' (2009, p 371). While acknowledging the 'hothouse world' of rumour and violence, they offer no explanation of why 'imagined injustices' have such a profound impact within this social domain, or why retribution is critical or how oral histories are woven into gang identities. Unsurprisingly their limited perspective dilutes both experience and reality of daily gang life, in which perceived injustices are not 'imagined' but real.

Referring to UK gangs, Hallsworth and Young (2008) argue that 'in a disorganised street world the networks into which people enter are typically messy and rhyzomatic, very rarely organised and hierarchical' (Hallsworth and Silverstone, 2009, pp 368-9). Here the centrality and importance of the gang network and its interface with street gangs remains unexplored, its roots unearthed. Indeed, both community and gang networks play a distinct role within the gang. Pitts (2008b) argues that only through triangulating street-level accounts with higher-level career criminals will the full picture emerge. Social field analysis of the gang (Pitts, 2011) provides just such an approach.

Becoming a competent actor in the gang

Though expressed in a different narrative style, the older works of Whyte (1943) and Yablonsky (1962) are two of several behavioural studies that offer insight into what it takes to be a competent actor in a gang. For Whyte, young men are attracted to gangs as they realise group strategies can achieve more than individual strategies. Finding gangs more cohesive, enduring and organised, he acknowledges the centrality of leadership and the importance of networking and information.

In a later echo of Thrasher's work, Miller (1958) identifies two key concepts for young men in street-corner gangs: belonging and status. The former is achieved by conforming to group norms, the latter by demonstrating qualities and characteristics that resonate and fit the social milieu of the gang. He further identified a range of focal concerns and values for working-class youth, such as trouble, toughness, fate, autonomy, excitement and smartness. These values, he argues, lead to increased delinquent behaviour and gang involvement.

Miller also usefully suggests an early focus on masculinity and character traits of street cunning and shrewdness for those seeking to achieve status. I shall revisit this theme of agency for personal advancement later in my own theorising. Miller also provided a useful definition of a gang that retains much contemporary currency.

Cloward and Ohlin (1960) believed violence is a currency used by young men to rise above their peers. Antisocial behaviour, they argue, arises from young men seeking to exhibit their ability to commit crime and thus overconform to the delinquent group values.

Yablonksy, in *The violent gang* (1963), considers character traits in relation to specific behaviours that generate status. He identifies personality types and socialisation as pertinent factors. While criticised by Klein as offering a narrow depiction of gangs, this ethnographic work offers an early insight into the very contemporary themes of spontaneous emergence, core and marginal membership, individual status, 'rep' making, the sexual exploitation of girls, personality and the individualistic sociopath. Such issues retain contemporary resonance and are further advanced in my own theorising.

The UK view on gang actors and leadership is again mixed. While decrying any suggestion of the 'American stereotype' gang in London (with a command structure, leaders and lieutenants), Hallsworth and Duffy (2010) then defer to such a stereotype by arguing that gang leaders have achieved dominance because they are 'ruthless' and 'hard'. Such views lack explanatory value of complex internal gang dynamics, the role of individual agency, and what is required to be a competent actor.

Talk of being a competent actor is usually highly gendered. In terms of gang involvement, Klein (1971), Moore (1991) and Miller, W. (2001) estimate that almost a quarter of all US gang members are female. Campbell (1984) found that girls could act as members of female gangs. Miller, W. (2001) found female gang membership to be more integrated than previously thought and Klein (1971) reported that girls carry out auxiliary functions. Jody Miller, however, reported strong gendered hierarchies clearly biased towards males. More recently, Jody Miller progressed this work (Cobbina et al, 2010), identifying alternative gendered narratives, namely that men interpret gang violence as necessary, instrumental, essential and dangerous, and that women's roles interpreted by men are trivial, emotional and ineffective.[5]

In the UK, research into female gang roles is limited (Home Office, 2008). Although girls and young women rarely report victimisation, there is evidence of sexual violence, social control and exploitation within gangs (Firmen, 2010). Batchelor implores us to look beyond dichotomous portrayals of male/female behaviour, noting that the relationships between girls' violent offending and gangs is often obscured (Batchelor, 2009, p 3). In taking forward the gender discourse, it is important to view girls and young women as enacting their own agency and strategies within gangs.

As with gender, ethnicity in relation to UK gangs is often assumed or overlooked, although recent research by Pitts (2008b, 2011), Palmer and Pitts (2006), Palmer (2009) and Alexander (2008) has attempted to keep this issue in the foreground. Issues of gender and ethnicity still have a larger role to play in UK gang research, although some new works are emerging.

An emergent research agenda?

Having looked at the UK gang discourse historically, theoretically and thematically, can we identify what the UK research agenda should be? Hallsworth (2013) argues that we should be considering the wider street world and not the gang per se. Pitts (2011, p 168) notes that UK researchers overly focus on the easily accessible, mutable lower levels of street groups, thus presenting only partial landscapes and distorted views, which in turn produces findings that gangs are disorganised and have only slender linkages to drugs, for example the report produced by the Youth Justice Board in 2007 entitled *Group, Gangs and Weapons* (Young et al, 2007). But as Pitts (2011) observes, 'the absence of evidence gained through such restrictive research methodologies does not add up to evidence of absence' (p 168).

Marshall and colleagues (2005, p 31) anticipate my contribution to gang research by calling for research to address 'group dynamics, how groups develop, evolve and break down', alongside why some offending is disproportionately higher among some groups.

Despite differences between US and UK approaches, shared themes can be identified alongside specific omissions pertinent to developing UK research. Current US debates identify research gaps in the social processes of grouping and affiliations, micro-social interactions between members, the neighbourhood and social contexts of gangs, and the role of networking and social capital (Deuchar, 2009). UK gang debates identify numerous gaps regarding 'messy structures', fluidity, gang organisation and hierarchy; the role of territory; types of affiliation; gang boundaries; respect issues; member characteristics; the dynamics and criminal behaviours; issues of age, ethnicity and gender. It is these issues I wish to now consider.

In addressing these issues, I acknowledge the influence of Pierre Bourdieu and Loic Wacquant. Although they are not 'gang researchers' as such, their sociological theories offer a valuable, but hitherto underdeveloped, perspective. Their concepts of social field, habitus and cultural capital present exciting opportunities for gang research.

I also believe the history of gangs in south London is linked to the cultural, social and political dynamics of London, and that this is primarily a function of wider macro- and micro-level socioeconomic factors, namely: globalisation, educational polarisation, de-industrialisation, structural youth unemployment and income polarisation (Pitts, 2008b), alongside concentration of crime (Hope, 2003), inequality (Hagedorn, 2008), disadvantage (Pitts, 2003), a retreat of the state (Castells, 1998) the emergence of discredited communities (Baum, 1996) and social and economic marginality leading to 'hyper-ghettoisation (Wacquant, 2008).

Having identified gaps and neglected areas in the UK research base, I began to formulate these gaps into a series of research questions and to develop an inductive methodology through which I seek to answer these questions.

In the following chapter I expand on the field-analysis approach devised by Bourdieu drawing on the key sociological constructs of social field, habitus and agency and concepts of social capital, to explain how violence is generated in the social field of the gang.

Notes

[1] Multiple marginality, i.e. the relegation of certain persons or groups to the fringes of society, where social and economic conditions result in powerlessness' (Vigil, 2010, p 6).

[2] The Five Boroughs' Alliance was a multi-agency programme set up in 2006 to develop long-term, effective solutions to serious violence, including gang-related issues. The programme brought together the Metropolitan Police Service and five local councils – Croydon, Greenwich, Lambeth, Lewisham and Southwark – alongside the Home Office, the Probation Service, local Crime and Disorder Reduction Partnerships and the Government Office for London to deliver schemes in partnership.

[3] Interviewed by Justin Parkinson for the BBC in March 2005, Hallsworth describes the gang culture threat as 'overblown'. Following research in Hackney, east London, Hallsworth concluded there was no 'gang culture', adding "we've had these panics before with Mods, rockers, Goths. This is the latest" (http://news.bbc.co.uk/go/pr/fr/-/hi/education/4308945.stm, accessed 13 July 2013).

[4] Pyrooz and Decker refer to embeddedness as 'individual immersion within an enduring deviant network, restricting involvement in pro-social networks' (Pyrooz and Decker, 2011). In Decker and Pyrooz (2011, p 6) they measure embeddedness by grouping six measures: involvement (wearing gang clothes/colours, participating in gang fights, having contact with gang members, friends in a gang); status (position in the gang); and identity (importance of the gang to you).

[5] They also note that young women use violence more commonly than previously believed and that similar to men, this relates to issues of status and respect, while the overall situational context differs.

THREE

The game, the stakes, the players: key concepts

The magnet may cause the field, but it is the field that has the effects on the iron filings.
Martin, 2003, p 23

In this work, the starting point is the recent rise in serious youth violence in the London Borough of Lambeth and the need to explain why it is happening. In this chapter, I present the formal theory underpinning my study. I identify the factors influencing my approach and the valuable insight gained from using tools developed for domestic violence training and counselling. I continue by illustrating how this insight then led me to consider the gang agenda through the lens of Pierre Bourdieu and the concept of space and social field. I then move on to a formal exposition of field theory as applied to the youth gang and in particular the valuable contribution of his concept of gaming theory. I conclude the chapter by applying field theory to the social field of the gang, establishing my key concepts of street capital and its acquisition through the gang repertoire.

From my professional work in London SW9, it was evident that the violence perpetrated in the name of 'gang activity' had several noticeable but contradictory features: it was not random – but appeared to be; it often appeared chaotic, but was in fact targeted; it was increasingly violent – but arose from seemingly minor issues of respect; it had a profound impact on key groups – leaving others relatively untouched; it involved only certain young people – yet others often knew what was going to happen; it occurred in specific locations – yet many denied it was geographically based; individuals concerned changed over time – yet the same issues persisted; girls were reportedly peripheral to activity – yet were clearly central to it; gangs were rivals – yet some members were linked to both; some gangs existed for several years while others dissolved; academic studies claimed an absence of hierarchical gang structures – yet gang affiliates claimed structures existed; local tensions could rise or fall quickly. There was a need to make sense of this confusing and paradoxical picture where violence occurs in different spaces, seemingly random, yet often predictable.

These 'random/predictable' patterns of violence evoked scenarios of domestic abuse where violence is a constant threat and women adopt survival techniques for each day and each environment. It appeared that by considering violence in a domestic setting, parallels and similarities with violence in gangland settings might be elucidated. This led me to re-engage with an illustrative tool I had often used previously while providing domestic violence training: the Domestic Violence Power and Control Wheel. The Duluth Model, (as it is commonly known), pioneered by the Domestic Abuse Intervention Project in Duluth, Minnesota, in 1984) (see Appendix C) is a useful conceptual model for counselling and education. It lists the most common abusive behaviours or tactics used against women experiencing DV and is characterised by patterns of action used to intentionally control and dominate both the individual and the situation. The wheel schematic demonstrates the connectivity between actions, patterns and intent. Importantly, it illustrates that intentional control and domination over women in a domestic violence scenario is ascribed to several different spaces or environments: home; public spaces; social spaces; physiological space; economic space; physical space; and reputational space, including cyberspace.

The model offers several possible examples and a mixture of techniques ranging from intimidation to physical and sexual violence. It further illustrates a range of tactical choices available to the abuser, from authoritative power to direct personal control. These tactics include active use of sanctions. In each scenario, the abuser selects from a range of possible techniques, previously tried and found to be effective. Intriguingly, different forms of violence are used in different social environments to different effect, with the abuser selecting from a personal menu or repertoire of favoured tactics. I shall return to this later; however, the concept of control in social environments provides an interesting discursive avenue of thought.

The learning evoked from the Duluth Model suggests a concept of differentiated spaces providing a template for considering how gangs might actively control a neighbourhood – the unifying theme of male violence being recognised. To take this further, I required a better understanding of how violence can occur in different social environments and spaces and frequently only occur to gang-associated or gang-affiliated individuals. I also needed to better understand how such issues worked when multiple actors were involved, often changing over time. Sociologists have struggled for years to understand how people act and build relationships when they are constrained within social structures outside their control and yet do so in spite of social constraints and overwhelming social controls. Giddens (1984) suggests we underestimate how everyday life is reproduced by social actors.

To address all these questions, I turned to field theory and its proposition that social order and social change can be understood by considering how actors act within their social domains. In particular, I turned to those writers who have considered issues of stability and change within social fields and their internal dynamics, in particular, Bourdieu (1969), Bourdieu and Wacquant (1992), DiMaggio and Powell (1983), Martin (2003) Scott and Meyer (1983) and the more recent work of Fligstein and McAdam (2012).

Field theory

From its origins in physics, electromagnetism, Weber's 'spheres of value' (Weber, 1915, 1946) and the psychology of perception (Lewin, 1936, p 14), field theory has now been usefully embraced by the social sciences and by organisational theorists. Field theory provides a useful lens through which to consider how social actors build relationships and act to produce, reproduce and transform their social domain; more importantly, it helps illustrate how this is done via both individual and collective action and within a set of social orders. This terrain of action where collective actors strive to advance is called the social field (Bourdieu and Wacquant, 1992). Organisational theorists have interpreted this for the corporate world as 'sectors' (Scott and Meyer, 1983), 'organisational fields' (DiMaggio and Powell, 1983) or strategic action fields (Fligstein and McAdam, 2012). The goal of actors within the field is to overcome their unequal allocations of skills and resources to achieve advantage that will lead ultimately to success. In this way, the field, or social domain, exists as 'an ensemble of relationships between actors antagonistically oriented to the same prizes or values' (Turner, 1974, p 135). Thus life is geared towards winners and losers all operating within the social order or 'rules of the game'.

Furstenberg identifies social fields as locales for possible social climbing determined by 'interrelationships between the ascending individual and the current social environment' (Furstenberg, 1969, p 52). These social environments provide opportunities for aspiration and social trajectory (concepts furthered by Bourdieu). Both Furstenberg and Bourdieu emphasise the social field as 'fields of organised striving' (Martin, 2003, p 20).

Actors sharing a social field, then, must share an understanding about the purpose of the field and why it exists, why actors present, who they are and what they are trying to achieve. There must also be certain rules governing what constitutes legitimate action in the field. When this understanding exists, actors can identify what it takes to get to the top and what is required to get there. Operating within their field of rules, and highly attuned to those around them, they work to reproduce their social order while constantly making minor adjustments they hope will give them slight advantage as they try to advance. This introduces incremental change into their social world. Thus, change is a constant dynamic in the field as actors struggle to improve their strategic position or to defend their privileged position. If actors can reproduce their field over a long period of time, the field is said to be stable.

Importantly, each social field operates its own internal logic (Swartz, 1997, p 128). Within the field, any actions, decision and behaviours generated by actors assume a logic and importance (pertinent to the field) that is amplified by and reverberates within the field. These actions or behaviours have scant significance to those outside the field, for example, the issue of respect for young people. Events generated outside the social field operate outwith the logic of the field. As such, its significance may be overlooked, downplayed or unrealised until its purpose is translated into the internal logic of the field – 'what does it mean for us' (Swartz, 1997, pp 128 and 215). As noted by Martin (2003, p 23), this is 'akin to the principle that the magnet may cause the field, but it is the field that has the effects on the iron filings'.

Within each field there exists a variety of different domains, each interconnected and each possessing autonomy while remaining interconnected (Bourdieu, 1969, pp 161-2). For Bourdieu, this creates a social landscape or topology that lends itself to analysis of actors and interrelationships. It is this conceptual framework that was developed by Bourdieu into his theory of practice centring on relationships between individuals and society, notably advanced in his studies of the cliquish domains of French art or literature.

The field then provides goals for the actors within it but importantly it operates as a 'structured arena of conflict' (Bourdieu and Wacquant, 1992). For Bourdieu, social groupings develop their identity through opposition to other groups. He argues that sociological character evolves from the internal struggle for scarce resources that occurs within each social group or field. Each field is, however, also located in a wider landscape dominated by class and power. Bourdieu's' theory of the social field contends that actors are in conflict and convulsive struggle towards mutually agreed goals and are guided by the rules of the game and the habitus.

The habitus

For Bourdieu, striving within fields is coordinated by the habitus. In the social field, actors are strategists linked to social structures through internal 'blueprints', which he terms the 'habitus'. Habitus is early socialisation of social conditions that, over time, have been internalised into a series of mental and bodily dispositions that then govern our actions. Habitus leads actors to assess what actions are possible or not possible within their social conditions, or field.

Those sharing similar social conditions and opportunities in life will share the same habitus, thus giving them similar outlooks on life and on occasion the same life trajectory or social fate. For many, this presupposes a general acceptance of social conditions and their perceptions of how they might advance in life. The habitus acts as an internal compass orienting those actions and behaviours that, based on previous experience, are most likely to help people succeed (Swartz, 1997, pp 104-6) in their social field.

Bourdieu believes that action is generated by social opportunities/ constraints interfacing with the dispositions of the actor, namely learned past experience, history, habit and tradition. This perspective differs, however, from straightforward rational-action theory, as Bourdieu believes these internalised dispositions lead actors to be 'strategic improvisers', working to a set of 'deeply internalised master dispositions that generate action' (Swartz, 1997, p 101).

Habitus allows for actors to employ actions or behaviours that serve to elevate or distinguish themselves from their peers (Bourdieu, 1984, p 166). This dynamic potential of the habitus confirms Bourdieu's actors as strategists who employ actions, not through conscious choice, but 'as a tacit calculation of interest and pursuit of distinction' (Swartz, 1997, p 290). The predisposed actions of the habitus relate to what is a credible or possible course of action within any field of strategic actors.

The settlement and the players

For a field of strategic actors to emerge, several key factors have to be agreed in what Fligstein and McAdam (2012, p 88) term 'the settlement':

- first, a shared understanding among actors of what is happening and what the stakes are for all involved (Bourdieu and Wacquant ,1992);
- second, a set of recognisable actors whose different levels of status and power are defined by other actors in the field;
- third, a shared understanding of the rules governing the field, and which tactics are legitimate and possible within the field (including a cultural understanding of legitimate forms of action and their likely meaning);
- finally, a 'broad interpretive frame that individual and collective strategic actors bring to make sense of what others with the strategic action field are doing' (Fligstein and McAdam, 2012, p 88).

It may take time for a field to emerge with this understanding. It may even be conflictual and drift for a time in an unorganised way before settling. In addition to having a shared interpretive frame, each actor will have their own strategic frame depending on their position in the field. Thus those challenging the status quo have the strategic perspective of a challenger. If the majority of actors share and understand this 'settlement', and then act to reproduce it, a stable strategic action field has emerged and the majority of actors will conform to this as their 'default position' as this suits their interests (Fligstein and McAdam, 2012, pp 92-6).

In any field, not all actors possess equal skill and resources. This provides some actors with greater power; they then dominate and set the rules. In this way, the social field is hierarchical. Those who are in positions of power and are advantaged by the 'settlement' will seek to keep this favourable status quo; they are termed incumbents. Those who are disadvantaged by the settlement or disadvantaged relative to the incumbents are termed 'challengers'. They occupy less privileged positions in the social field and thus may only wield slight influence over operations in the field.

To obtain any slight advantage, actors constantly try to adjust their own field position by 'jockeying' for a better one, leading to 'constant low-level contention and incremental change' (Fligstein and McAdam, 2012, p 12), which then becomes the norm.

The type of field interactions among actors is also determined by their field position in the hierarchy. In this way, struggle within any field occurs between those in dominant positions and those occupying subordinate positions. Bourdieu stresses that position in the field hierarchy is determined by the unequal distribution of relevant capitals rather than by the personal attributes of their occupants. In this way, class background and habitus will be mediated through the structure of fields (Swartz, 1997, pp 117-23).

This internal field hierarchy pitches actors against each other in an internal struggle for power and dominance, between these different hierarchical positions and between orthodoxy and heterodoxy. Thus, to advance within the social field, actors employ 'investment strategies' to achieve goals. Bourdieu illustrates three types of field strategy (Swartz, 1997, p 124):

- conservation – mostly pursued by those in dominant positions of seniority;
- succession – generally pursued by new entrants seeking to reach dominant positions;
- subversion – pursued by those who expect to gain little from dominant groups.

Bourdieu devised these subsets to explain the dynamics of power struggles within any field, for example, academia, sports or education. Crucially, all positions within the hierarchy are interrelated; thus, a major shift or change in one position will alter the boundaries of all other players. Fligstein and McAdam (2012, p 13) view fields as composed of 'incumbents', 'who wield disproportionate influence within a field and whose interests and views tend to be heavily reflected in the dominant organisation of the strategic action field', and 'challengers', those who 'usually articulate an alternative vision of the field and their position in it'. However, most of the time challengers have to accept the status quo or prevailing order.

As this low-level 'jockeying' for position is normative, it can be said that fields are in a constant state of flux, with the constant pressure of change, adaptation and adjustment. Mostly this equates to low-level 'turbulence'. Incumbents or conservationists can weather this well, as they are better resourced and better advantaged. For example, they are better networked with information, conferring on them a 'house advantage'. Indeed, they may not even face any challenge at all if potential challengers hold to the belief that they are in control of events. What Fligstein and McAdam (2012, p 21) call the 'onset of contention' will only arise if those perceiving the threat/opportunity have the ability to control the organisational resources they need to take action. If there is any real contentious episode, new activities will be evident; otherwise, if challengers or subversives merely continue to press for change through traditional and established routes and mechanisms, no change or contention will result.

McAdam (2007, p 253) defines 'an episode of contention ... as a period of emergent, sustained contentious interaction between ... [field] actors utilising new and innovative forms of action vis-à-vis one another'. This, of course, includes a shared sense of crisis. This interpretation is important, because unless it is considered a serious threat to collective interests, it is unlikely it will ever be understood as a serious field crisis. Episodes can be very intense and last as long as the period of uncertainty regarding the field, its structure, rules or dominance persists. In short, this means that as commitment to the status quo frays or erodes, new challengers become emboldened and try to seize the initiative while incumbents appeal to the status quo. If the challengers are unsuccessful, it is likely the incumbents will still have to make some adjustments to the order. If challengers are successful, new rules might apply or wholly new groups might emerge from this 'crisis'.

Three further concepts in field theory are worth exploring before we consider how field position is allocated: coalitional organisation; social skill; and proximate fields. The first is the surety that to reap rewards incumbents must strive for field stability. This can be done by 'imposition of a hierarchical power by a single dominant group [or via] cooperation ... generally rooted in a combination of shared interests and a common collective identity' (Fligstein and McAdam, 2012, pp 14-15). In this way, actors must convince others that joining together will serve their collective interests – for example, the formation of coalitions. This perspective suggests that field order can be organised by hierarchy or coalition. To attempt coalitional organisation, dominant actors must possess the social skill to influence the opinions and views of other actors and to persuade them of collective action by compelling narratives. I shall return to this concept later.

The final concept regarding social fields is that no field exists wholly in a vacuum. All fields have relationships with other social fields, which in turn influence and shape the social field, for example, shared governance, access to resources, administrative or power relations. The nature and frequency of routine interactions will determine whether they are distant or proximate fields and the power relations between fields. Fligstein and McAdam (2012, p 57) identify that fields are 'embedded' in a 'dense latticework or system of interdependent fields that comprise modern society', for example, the state, the council, the department of education. Finally, the power relations linking different fields are of key importance: they can be 'dependent', 'interdependent' or 'unconnected'.

Actors' field position

Actors take position in the social field depending on the quality and weight of their skills, resources and capital. Thus, capital is unevenly distributed within any field, which is reflected in hierarchical power relations among those competing to accumulate it. In this contested spatial domain, actors develop exchange relations between those with capital and those without. I return here to Bourdieu's theory to explain capital allocation and distribution. Capital in social fields is not merely allocated but can be generated, earned, won, swapped or traded. In elucidating Bourdieu's central theory, Swartz notes that fields are 'arenas of production, circulation and appropriation of goods, services, knowledge or status and the competitive positions held by actors in their struggle to accumulate and monopolise these different kinds of capital' (Swartz, 1997, p 117).

In a social field, access to income and employment (economic capital) is dependent on educational attainment (cultural capital) and networks (social capital). Bourdieu contends that 'economic capital is at the root of all the other types of capital' (Bourdieu, 1986a, p 252). He argues that groups and individuals employ strategies of capital accumulation in order to maintain (incumbents) or enhance challengers' field position. This includes strategies for acquiring, investing and converting various kinds of capital. Bourdieu argues that the various capitals interconvert (while acknowledging that some conversions are easier than others) (Swartz, 1997, p 80).

Within any field, struggle may also occur over symbolic capital as well as material resources. For Bourdieu, 'symbolic capital is a form of power that is not perceived as power but as legitimate demands for recognition, deference, obedience, or the services of others' (Swartz, 1997, p 90). Thus, symbolic capital can be acquired and accumulated in much the same way as material capital. Although distinct from economic capital, it is also exchangeable or inter-convertible under the right circumstances.

Bourdieu believes social capital links more explicitly to power (Field, 2008, p 46), arguing that it is a product or asset that has to be worked on, built up and maintained (Field, 2008, p 18). Interestingly, the type of social capital arising from introverted 'club-type' networks (such as gangs) tends to support a struggle for increasing status. Bourdieu's concept of social capital largely relates to privileged individuals maintaining their privileged positions by using their connections with other similarly privileged individuals. I shall return to this later, but first I want to relate these concepts of field theory to Bourdieu's theory of gaming theory.

The game

In addition to being governed by the habitus, social action within a field is guided by rules. In life's game, distinction is the ultimate prize. Restated, for many this will read as celebrity. A number of points should be made about viewing the social field as a game. First, in social fields the key issue is much more than who achieves success or who wins the prize, but what type of player dominates and what kind of game is to be played in the future. This knowledge is key to those still struggling to rise to the top, as it may mean rule changes. However, 'the better established the rule (in the Game), the more advantage there may be in breaking it' (Martin, 2003, pp 30-4). Within the social field, therefore, 'the struggle is both over and within the rules' (Martin, 2003, p 31). By viewing the field as one of convulsive struggle, it is possible to view 'regularity' within the field as assumptions that can be overturned. Importantly, however, 'the game metaphor for understanding the field as a field of contestation may give us a better understanding of the regularity and irregularity in social life' (Martin, 2003, p 34). It again suggests a vertical social differentiation of winners and losers.

For Bourdieu, social field structure resembles not only the game of life, but a game of casino poker, where varying piles of game chips represent the unequal levels of the players' capital. This, in turn, illustrates the player's winnings from previous struggles and determines his future game-playing strategy (Bourdieu and Wacquant, 1992, pp 98-9). Advancement within the social field is achieved by maximising the number of chips available to the player; more chips equals greater power within the social field. Referring to the social field as a casino, Bourdieu identifies economic capital, cultural capital and social capital with black, blue and red gambling chips (Field, 2008, p 16). Actors take up position in the social field depending on the quality and weight of their chips.

The internal structure of a field is based on hierarchical positions, but also on shared principles, namely that all actors are competing for scarce resources and they all share the same 'doxa' (the value of the game) and 'illusio' – a belief or acceptance of the worth of the game (Bourdieu, 1991, pp 22-5).

In any social field, those with subordinate status have yet to master the rules of the game, or in the case of new arrivals, demonstrate an appreciation of game rules and values. These rules of subordination reinforce the hierarchy and ensure that those of lower rank play the game with fewer 'chips'. Their struggle for distinction and dominance is thus greater.

Critique of Bourdieu

Bourdieu's social actors tend to fend for themselves individually in a field possessing different forms of capital allocations using habitus, a cognitive blueprint to interpret others' actions. However, this individualising perspective might overlook the importance of collective action. Fligstein and McAdam, while supportive of Bourdieusian principles, suggest that collective action is just as important to field analysis, that is, actors must be able to persuade others of their compelling perspective of the field and moreover must convince that this perspective will benefit all. This account of collective action is common among American sociologists, whose views on field theory often derive from either organisational literature or social movement literature. While this perspective differentiates them from adherents to strict Bourdieusian principles, it is nonetheless a complementary view.

Fligstein and McAdam are further critical of Bourdieu in commenting that his work did not fully identify how new fields emerge or transform. They acknowledge Bourdieu's insight on the doxa (conventional wisdom) and his acceptance that if this is questioned by field actors, it might indeed lead to transformation or dissolution (Bourdieu, 1977). Bourdieu does not really take this discussion of collective action any further. Similarly, while acknowledging that fields are linked, he leaves field linkages and inter-field dynamics largely unexplored. There is room here for future research to fully explore these relationships.

Notwithstanding these criticisms, Bourdieu's concepts of gaming theory are a useful metaphor for illuminating gang organisation and development. Having considered gang organisation through the valuable lens of field theory and gaming theory, I shall now offer my reconceptualisation, drawing on both theories to illuminate the social field of the gang.

The social field of the gang

Having established the theoretical insights offered by social field theory and Pierre Bourdieu, I shall now formally apply this theory to my own study. I believe social field theory has a unique explanatory value for researching and analysing the internal mechanisms of the urban street gang. To illustrate this, I begin by establishing the concept of the urban street gang as a social field, illustrating how gaming theory, the development of strategies and capital acquisition all work within this social field. Having established this theoretical landscape, I introduce my central theory of street capital, arguing that it is the premium capital operating within this social field. In subsequent chapters, I explore these characteristics in more detail.

In line with Bourdieu's conceptual framework, I propose that the urban street gang in SW9 constitutes a 'structured arena of conflict' or social 'field' (Bourdieu and Wacquant, 1992). The key concepts of field and habitus posited by Bourdieu are central to this proposition; while essentially explanatory terms for social functions, they facilitate focus on conflict and competition within the urban street gang. Furthermore, in terms of gang research, they facilitate consideration of the contested, but often elusive, elements of hierarchy and power relations, which in the gang relate to organisational structures, rank, status and strategies for advancement. As such, social field and habitus form the theoretical backdrop to this study.

I propose that the socially deprived neighbourhoods of SW9 in Lambeth fit the framework of social field as 'an arena of struggle' (Bourdieu and Wacquant, 1992), where residents (actors) struggle to accumulate economic capital (money) and where opportunities for employment and advancement are also limited (Lambeth First, 2009). Moreover, within SW9, the urban street gang represents its own social field – a structured space with actors (gang-affiliated young people) competing to accumulate scarce resources, namely money, respect, reputation and status. Bourdieu refers to such contested resources as forms of capital. Within this space, actors struggle, often violently, to achieve distinction (Bourdieu, 1984, p 166). With distinction comes exciting opportunities for accessing a greater share of the contested resources, especially economic capital.

Within this highly contested social field, the actors (young people) develop strategies, both collectively and individually, to generate and maintain their levels of capital. Any strategies employed are undertaken within the rules of 'the game' and acknowledged by the shared principles of the doxa (Bourdieu, 1991, pp 22-5) (the field's deep structure, which dictates the forms of struggle) and the illusio. This means that for gang affiliates there is a 'tacit, fundamental agreement on the stakes of struggle between the 'dominant establishment' and the 'subordinate challengers'. This shared principle or imprint (specific to the field itself) is recognisable as a general acceptance that the 'field of struggle is worth pursing in the first place' (Swartz, 1997, p 125). Thus those within the gang social field all accept the rules of 'the game'; however, these rules and principles, and this logic, only pertain in full effect to those within this social field. The boundaries of this social field only relate to actors within the gang and its peripheries; it is here that the doxa and the illusio operate to maximum effect. Thus, any social field is bounded by the points at which its influence ceases. While those outside the field operate to different rules and different logic, within the social field of the gang, rules, logic and principles are *everything*.

In line with field theory, the internal structure of the social field of the gang is based on hierarchical positions. I propose that the hierarchal structure of a social field is clearly mirrored in the structure of the urban street gang in SW9, and is evident in the three separate tiers: elementary tier, (youngers, aged 13-16); mature tier (olders, aged 16-21); and advanced tier (elders, aged 21 and over).

In the social field of the gang, it is the longer-established elders who dominate (conservationists/incumbents) and it is they who determine what type of game will be played. In field hierarchy, they are accorded respect and status for having reached the top. Subordinates (challengers), however, especially new arrivals, must develop strategies carefully as they struggle up the ranks, as others may have a vested interest in preventing their ascendancy. The top-ranking gang elders largely control access to opportunities for conversion of capital by maintaining the hierarchy of the social field and setting the rules of 'the game'. This codifies the conditions of access and ascendancy within the gang, and also the rules for converting social and cultural capital into economic capital.

Importantly for this discussion, habitus retains several characteristics highly pertinent to any study of gangs. In the gang context, young people have internalised behaviours and 'ways of being' from their environment. Learned experiences determine actions they know are likely to bring benefits or advancement. This provenance is well understood by all in the social field, as all actors in the hierarchy share the same habitus. I address this in more detail in Chapter Four.

Following on from Bourdieu's concept of action within the social field, I propose that actors develop strategies within the gang (a club-type network) to achieve distinction by building status and reputation, expanding networks, increasing their social capital and rising through the hierarchy. Through such action, they are elevated to a new hierarchal field position they must fight to maintain in order to protect their newly accumulated capital.

The gang social field, while limited in economic capital, remains relatively well stocked in terms of interpersonal and family connections and community relationships. This community resource offers potential for capital accumulation – an opportunity frequently used by women in the social field. The key goal or objective for actors is thus to transform ordinary neighbourhood relationships into more useful 'social relationships' (Field, 2008, p 19).

For young people in SW9 with limited or no educational opportunities, the street gang perhaps offers the most effective and productive way to obtain the valued but scarce commodity of economic capital (Pitts, 2011). As with all fields, capital, in the social field of the gang, is distributed unequally.

Elementary-tier actors have had insufficient time or life experience to accumulate capital. Despite this, it is immediately evident to them that they must accumulate to speculate and to enter 'the game'. The elementary tier (youngers) want economic capital but cannot access it. To access opportunities, they must first demonstrate their investment to the ethos of the gang by gaining the trust of the next rank, the mature tier (olders). Trust is a valuable form of cultural capital in a neighbourhood where trust is in short supply. They must also build up their own unique stock of both social capital (connections, relationships and networks) and cultural capital (knowledge of 'the game' and trust), which can be later converted into the economic capital (money) they all desire (Coleman, 1994; Puttnam, 2000). Under certain conditions, symbolic capital may also be acquired through longevity and high status of leadership, or through conversion, for example, the symbolic power of displaying gun-shot wounds. It should be acknowledged that young people are members of several different social fields and the urban street gang represents only one of these. Also the type and the value of any social, symbolic or cultural capital are determined by the type of social field. In the urban street gang, having certain friendships, access to certain information and specific skills or knowledge is valued, possibly prized, differently from the way similar attributes might be viewed on a university campus. Traditional views of social, symbolic and cultural capital may be inverted; for example, knowing how to use a knife in a fight (street knowledge) is considerably more important to daily survival or advancement than having several 'A' levels. Practical knowledge of survival is generally elevated above educational achievement by working-class families (Bourdieu, 1986; Winslow, 2001).

Surviving street life within the social field of the gang presents similar necessities: street knowledge and skill regarding the 'code of the street' (Anderson, 1999), the golden rules of not grassing (Yates, 2006), and not helping the police and keeping your mouth shut (Evans et al, 1996) are established social norms. Acquiring this knowledge and experience greatly increases cultural capital and survival.

Gang periphery

Surrounding the gang repertoire and the social field is the gang periphery. This acts as a 'magnetic field' for some and 'miasma' for others. The boundary of the social field with its proximate fields is relational rather than physical. It constitutes a series of linkages and relationships. The gang periphery allows young people to engage with the gang through the blurred relationship boundaries of the proximate social field, such as school or social networking sites. Adults too may engage with the gang periphery, largely through economic activity or as professionals from the proximate field of the state. In this sense, the 'magnetic field' metaphor is perhaps a useful one, with the gang periphery acting as both attractor and repellent and 'push-and-pull' factors leading to differing degrees of involvement. The visual metaphor of iron filings surrounding a magnet suggests some filings move closer to the magnet while others circulate in the wider field, often changing and in flux. Those furthest from the magnet may never come any closer and may eventually enter the magnetic field of another magnet. Similar actions may be recognisable within the social field of the gang.

Within this periphery, the gang may share economic capital with the social field of the wider neighbourhood. Here linkages and relationships help to build and retain social capital at higher levels than operated previously. These relationships maintain access to wider community social fields for mutually beneficial relationships such as the buying and selling of drugs or stolen goods. Both activities will be permissible within their habitus.

Social capital

Before introducing my central theory of street capital, it is useful to consider how social capital operates within a gang's social field, variably described as the 'dark side of social capital' (Putnam, 2000, p 350) or 'perverse social capital' (Field, 2008, p 94).

Putnam (2000, p 315) notes that reciprocal obligations, 'such as being obligated to the hood', are indeed a form of social capital, and referencing his key academic work, suggests that they serve members' interests in the same way as social capital in a bowling club.

Gangs, it seem, embrace a form of bonding social capital to 'mobilise solidarity' and build strong bonds of reciprocity. As Putnam (2000, p 22) found, 'social capital can be directed towards malevolent, anti-social purposes', e.g. sectarianism. While building strong 'in-group loyalty, [bonding social capital] may also create strong out-group antagonism' (Putnam, 2000, p 23). He refers to this as the dark side of social capital.

Putnam and social capital theorists such as Bourdieu and Coleman have a contribution to make to gang research that is often overlooked or underplayed in terms of gang formulation and organisation but also in terms of excavating the underlying social interactions and dynamics of gangs.

Putnam focuses on the value of social networks, reciprocity and the importance of information flow and echoes Bourdieu by noting the value of maintaining reputations in 'dense networks of social exchange' (Putnam, 2000, p 136).

Putnam notes that while both bridging social capital[1] and bonding social capital[2] operate within the gang, bonding networks typical of gang loyalties may generate 'strong in-group loyalty ... and out-group antagonism' (Putnam, 2000, p 23).

Coleman's[3] (1994, 1999) broader view of social capital argues that cooperation is in the best interests of actors who otherwise operate independently. This suggests the development of group or gang strategies rather than independent strategies and supports the collective action and coalitional strategies suggested by Fligstein and McAdam (2012). Coleman argues that relationships build obligations, expectations and trust, opening up information networks and establishing social norms of communally agreed behaviours. Acting outside these norms will bring sanctions (Field, 2008, p 28). Bourdieu's contribution was to view social capital as an opportunity for people to manipulate their connections and thus employ investment strategies out of self-interest.

Meanwhile, Halpern (2005, p 10) usefully identifies three basic components to social capital theory that resonate with elements of field theory:

- a network – which in the social field of the gang will be high density with high 'closure';
- social norms – the rules, values and expectancies that characterise the community (network) members;

- sanctions – a range of mostly informal punishments used to maintain social norms.

Social capital theorists also maintain that social capital, its accumulation and components may have perverse effects or may be used for malevolent purposes (Putnam, 2000, pp 21-2).

Often it is the density of relationships within a 'durable network' that becomes important in a social field (Putnam, 2000, pp 315-6). Crucially, the value of an individual's network (or 'volume of social capital possessed by a given agent') is a function of his network breadth and reach, his ability to mobilise its support and level of cultural and economic capital (casino chips) held by his connections, (Bourdieu, 1980, p 2). In the social field of the urban street gang, the network component is critical, as it operates as the principal mechanism for establishing status and connections. I shall consider this in more depth in Chapter Six.

Street capital

Having set out the general introduction to field theory and established the centrality of capital to social fields and of capital accumulation to field position, I have gone on to explain how I have re-interpreted this in the context of the social field of the gang. I now seek to marry up the key field theory elements of 'strategic action' (investment strategies) with elements from social capital theory, to offer a more ambitious theory building that seeks to unite these perspectives. This process of collating theories and perspectives now presents us with gaps and thus unanswered questions.

Not least of these questions is how actors within the social field are able to recognise or acknowledge other actors as viable players in 'the game'. How does one become a competent actor in the field and be recognised and accredited by others? How do actors monitor their rise and fall within the hierarchy? How is field position recognised? There is no formal or empirical mechanism by which to do this. The closest mechanism is that of building a reputation, by which all in the field are bound. However, as a measure of available resources, either individual or group, it is insufficient. The measurement of these commodities – both qualitatively and quantitatively – poses a difficulty.

The absence of any such measurement, albeit one that is informal, creates potential difficulties in the field and also for the further exposition of my theoretical proposition. I am reminded of Bourdieu's concept of the casino, where economic, cultural and social capital represents gambling chips. This metaphor works for academic explanations of capital in contested fields but is limited if we seek to use it as a mechanism for informal measurement. Moreover, it relates to three different forms of capital rather than one.

To address the necessity of how actors measure, accredit and then exchange such capitals in the social field of the gang, there is a need to establish a broad unifying theory of street capital. Street capital is an aggregate of cultural capital (street knowledge and street skills), habitus, local history, family connections, networks (social capital), relationships, reputation, status and symbolic capital (available assets of recognition, honour and prestige), which form a resource of high value within the social field of 'the street', that is, the contested social arena of urban environments that function through informal but widely recognised rules and codes. Bourdieu notes that in Western societies economic capital has first ranking, but acknowledges that this is variable. I would argue that in street life, while economic capital remains the goal, it is street capital that operates effectively as the premium capital. It operates as a functional mechanism within the specific internal logic of the social field of the gang (Swartz, 1997, p 128). Outside this social field it is of little significance. The theory of street capital operates also as a broad theory for wider street culture; however, in the social field of the gang, it takes on critical qualities operating uniquely within the illusio and doxa.

As a concept, street capital represents more than simply street credibility.[4] It is a commodity easily recognised by those operating within street life. Crucially, the ability to recognise street capital in others becomes an important aspect of acquiring street capital. Street capital allows for more successful navigation and survival in a street environment. It is the equivalent of a road ranking – the totality of accumulated capitals and experience embodied by the individual operating within street life.

In their powerful ethnographic account of young black men dealing cannabis at an open drugs market called The River in Oslo, Norway, Sandberg and Pederson (2011) have also conceptualised street capital as 'the most important symbolic capital in street culture' (p 168). Similarly taking their inspiration from Bourdieu, Anderson and Bourgois, they have sought to use the concept to describe the embodied skills and competences of the drug dealers and to articulate how they operate and utilise a potential for violence within a violent street world. For them 'street capital refers to the knowledge, competence, skills and objects that are given value in a street culture. It is masculine in its essence, and values violence, retaliation, fashionable cloths and the attraction of females. Most importantly, street capital is a form of legitimate power that is relational and has the capacity to generate profit' (Sandberg and Pederson 2011, p 168). Here street capital is conceptualised as socially constructed symbolic power, 'masculine in essence' (p 43), not convertible (p 120) and acting as a form of resistance capital (p 60). In places, this is similar to my own conceptualisation, not least in the way street capital is visibly expressed and gendered by nature. Notwithstanding this, for Sandberg and Pederson, street capital appears to be an acquired vocabulary of street competence and symbolism which is then both skillfully and contextually deployed.

As a resource, street capital can be acquired and traded. Each individual and each group (or gang) holds and operates its own assets of street capital that fluctuate over time. Their acquired stock of street capital will rise or fall hourly or daily depending on fluctuations in the variables. As street capital is a tradable commodity, others can allocate street capital to you directly by boosting your reputation or giving you respect. Your accumulated street capital will count towards your overall rank within street life, as well as your overall rank or level of distinction within the gang. Levels of street capital (or more accurately the elements or variables) are openly discussed among other traders.

In seeking to allocate a total value, other traders will share views on all the variables of street capital pertaining to that individual before making a judgement on the level of street capital to be allocated to them. Thus, levels and value of street capital in this social field are often allocated by others through informal networks. Modal scores are generally accepted.

Field analysis provides us with a template of key elements that must be in place for a social field (the settlement) and for field stability. Table 3.1 illustrates these four elements of field logic and how they are interpreted with field properties. The concept of street capital does not replace the field properties of illusion, hierarchy and habitus, but

Table 3.1: Field logics

Factors requiring consensus for field emergence	Field properties	Gang social field
Agreement on the stakes and the nature of the game	Illusio	
Agreement on who are the players and field positions they occupy	Hierarchy	Street capital
Consensus on the rules governing the field	Habitus	
A broad interpretive frame		

rather complements and underpins them, offering a field abacus for measurement and calculation.

Any strategies employed are undertaken within the rules of 'the game' and acknowledged by the shared principles of the doxa (Bourdieu, 1991, pp 22-5) (the field's deep structure, which dictates the forms of struggle) and the illusio. This means that for gang affiliates there is a 'tacit, fundamental agreement' on the stakes of struggle between the 'dominant establishment' and the 'subordinate challengers.' This shared principle or imprint (specific to the field itself) is recognisable as a general acceptance that the 'field of struggle is worth pursing in the first place' (Swartz, 1997, p 125).

In this chapter, I have set out my main theoretical perspective of field theory, and how capital operates in the social field by way of 'the game', where players employ strategic actions from the gang repertoire to generate street capital and thus advance. The gang repertoire therefore acts as both a menu of tested actions/strategies and a rulebook of permissible actions. Its contents and how they are implemented – that is, the strategies employed – are determined and coordinated by what is possible within the social field, which in turn are determined by the habitus of the social field.

In the next chapter, I consider how actors in the gang social field develop strategies using the gang repertoire to increase their street capital in order to improve their field position.

Notes

[1] Essentially inclusive, bringing diverse people together and helping them to get on in society.

[2] Essentially exclusive, integrative and clannish, acting as 'superglue' to bind groups together; also clubs, ensuring reciprocity and solidarity.

[3] James Coleman offers a broader concept of social capital in which he believes individuals act rationally in pursuit of their own interests (Field, 2008, p 15). This differs from Bourdieu and is influenced by rational choice theory and Gary Becker (1968). For Coleman, social capital is generated by actors as they go along rather than setting out to create it and it is a means by which they cooperate (Field, 2008, p 29). It is this concept of mutuality that is useful in the context of the gang.

[4] Defined by the Urban Dictionary as 'commanding a level of respect in an urban environment due to experience in or knowledge of issues affecting those environments'.

FOUR

House rules, game rules and game strategies

'Nothing is more despicable than respect based on fear.'
Albert Camus

Neighbourhood rules

In every social field, social action is governed by the habitus. Social order is maintained both by field logic and field rules. This applies to the communities in the social field of the wider SW9 neighbourhood just as it applies to the narrower social field of the gang. In this way, the neighbourhood rules of SW9 act as the backdrop to the social field of the gangs embedded in SW9. Neighbourhood rules act as the predominant social order and the sub-field of the gang retains its own sub-field rules (see Chapter Five). In my metaphor, neighbourhood rules are 'house rules' and gang rules are 'game rules'.

The house rules for SW9 are in many ways typical of those operating in traditional working-class communities in the UK and include a suspicion of the value of education, wariness of the police,[1] self-reliance, and the cultural importance of violence.[2] These broad concepts are understood by all those living and working in the neighbourhood. These meanings and understandings are also determined by locality and local culture and the habitus. They are then passed down through the generations as an unspoken street code (Anderson, 1999) and what Vigil (2002, 2010) calls 'Street socialization' (sic). Vigil argues that in deprived neighbourhoods where families are parenting under pressure, primary networks of social control can be loosed leaving young people to be effectively socialised by street peers.

The influence of the habitus

Social rules and thus social action within the field are guided and coordinated by the habitus. Habitus functions as a regenerative repository of previous experiences and social conditions that subjectively frames future actions and decisions, that is, it leads actors to decide what is and is not possible within the social field:

> 'You learn it just by hanging around. You know what honour is and what isn't. You know what you are supposed to do and not supposed to do really. Just like what you are allowed to do at school. They don't even need to explain it.' (West African male older)

This 'bounded agency' (Evans et al, 2001, p 24) means those in the same social field often share the same social trajectory. Experience in this environment determines actions that are likely to bring benefits or advancement.

> 'You only get respect if you are a hard body. I hear things like my boy is the "best ratchet". If you don't talk about them quick and then don't act, you'll not get the respect you deserve. You've gotta be bad ... you know he done this, he done that. Then it goes through the community quickly, you know, he threw the petrol bomb through the window – he's cold! Then my rep starts. Then someone does wanna test you but until someone does then you've got respect. Y'know, don't mess about with him, he'll throw a petrol bomb through your window. And that's how you get respect. (African Caribbean male older)

Action in the social field is determined by how these subjective frames, both personal and social, interface with opportunities, meaning that for many, 'future possibilities' are bounded by 'past experiences' (Evans et al, 2001, p 25). Class, history, habit, experience and tradition thus determine the individual habitus (Bourdieu, 1997, 2004). In this way, any course of action is determined by what is perceived to be possible or credible; thus, for some, 'the game' becomes the only game in town. Thus actions within the social field are largely predisposed or constrained by the habitus, for example, by the code of the street.

In this social field, habitus dictates that educational achievement is not credible, whereas street knowledge and 'standing up for yourself' is:

> 'You can't get a job if employers know you are from SW9.' (West African female resident)

This translates to building and maintaining reputation and respect, or street capital, which is acquired by employing strategies from the gang repertoire. Maximising street capital helps achieve distinction and success.

Street code

A key element of the habitus operating within the social field of the gang, as in the social field of many deprived and contested neighbourhoods, is the unspoken street code. In his seminal work, Elijah Anderson (1999) identified and described a pattern of hidden cultural rules operating in many deprived communities. These hidden rules amount to a codification of expected and permissible behaviours that become established as the social norms and form part of the habitus.

Anderson notes that the code is understood by all in the neighbourhood and passed down from generation to generation. In SW9, all respondents understood this code:[3]

> 'There was one chap, if he hit you, you would fall over. He was a cage fighter and well known. You wouldn't hit him as he could take it and he has stamina. He had a certain physicality that I recognise. I can tell by the way he moves and just by his movement the way he conducts himself and what his street cred is. How, under the street code, he deals with himself is very important.' (African Caribbean male elder)

The transmission of 'street' knowledge from generation to generation is referred to by Sutherland as differential association (Sutherland, 1947). On the street, the code is viewed as a virtual survival manual underpinning the establishment of street capital and providing some basic rules for those in the game. It varies slightly from area to area reflecting the habitus of the neighbourhood and the social field in which it operates. There are some key tenets that are comprehensively understood and largely adhered to in such communities. These can be paraphrased as follows:

- no grassing or snitching;
- we sort out our own problems ourselves;
- limited interaction, if any, with authority;
- defend yourself and don't take any shit;

- violence is part of the 'hidden contract' of reprisals for any infringements.

In SW9, this means accepting, unchallenged, the dominant code of the street (Anderson, 1999).

> 'To these particular individuals that'll be enough for them to react. Code of the street says you must get your respect back or you will forever be thought of as soft. Yeah, absolutely so they have to act and live out the role basically. You can't just do the talk, you have to go and follow it up.' (Male police officer)

The social field of SW9 and that of the gang are defined and informed by their habitus and also by community history. In SW9, this includes several formative events for both the community and UK policing, including the arrival of the African Caribbean community; the 'Sus' laws[4] (Kennison, 2000); the Brixton riots (Scarman, 1981); deaths in custody; and widespread suspicion of the police regarding unfair treatment or racial stereotyping, including via stop and search, leading to stigmatising of the local community. This history finds visual form in the rapid emergence of the 'Brixton crowd' during any incident, and remains vividly contemporary in the form of the community's enduring suspicion towards police engagement and the maintenance of the street code 'wall of silence'. These experiences are now included in the habitus as part of the social field. The gang understands this fact and thus the street code defines behaviours, expectations and actions. It is used as a control mechanism for other gang members or those external to their immediate social field. This code operates as the 'social wallpaper' for SW9: the social field of the gang operates its own codes of behaviour.

Grassing

Grassing is viewed as abusing information with the intent of causing grief, by informing to the police, resulting in arrest, or by providing information to another authority in a proximate field. In his work on grassing, Joe Yates (2006) notes young people's early socialisation in life with regard to the social taboo of grassing via informal community networks. In the social field of the gang, this is codified in the habitus. Grassing illustrates individual strategies taking supremacy over a joint or collective strategy, that is, placing oneself first and above others for personal gain or advantage and thus stepping outside the gang. It shows disrespect and lack of allegiance to the gang whose reputation or street capital is violated by it. As a result, any group protection offered previously is annulled and withdrawn. Reprisals are sanctioned quickly, often resulting in group attacks as the gang reasserts its authority in the social field. All previous friends and peers are actively corralled against the guilty individual, placing him in considerable danger. The level of reprisal – fighting, stabbing or shooting – is calibrated to the seriousness of the incident.

In a social field where incidents are much hyped and exaggerated, individuals can suffer serious violent reprisals based on rumour, gossip or unverified and inaccurate accounts. In SW9, even young people who are seriously injured in violent incidents do not request police involvement. Younger people are afraid of being seen to talk to the police lest others interpret their actions as snitching. Arrests within the gang can also cause repercussions when accusations fly over who has snitched. Moreover, if anonymous police informants are involved, the gang may suspect the wrong individuals.

The code of no grassing is understood by both youngers and olders. Youngers can, through fear or enthusiasm to demonstrate loyalty, act as powerful guardians of this rule and they remain anxious not to impinge it. They will seek to increase their street capital by claiming excitedly, 'Yeah I'd go inside. I wouldn't talk.' They falsely believe their relationship with the gang will continue unchanged if they go to prison. Olders can exploit this belief, urging youngers to enact violent actions by proxy, knowing that they won't snitch and will get a lighter sentence than they themselves will if arrested. For some young people, this requirement not to discuss anything to their family or friends brings an almost unbearable burden. Trust and loyalty to peers is constantly under consideration. To build trust, many young members only go out in groups to minimise and monitor grassing.

Reciprocity

The habitus in SW9 demands a strict code of silence (Evans et al, 1996), achieved through fear and intimidation but also through gifts and the function of reciprocity. In this way, silence is 'bought' through community engagement in low-level criminality. The threat of potential repercussions to informers is widely understood, and actions, including physical violence, are widely advertised to both community and gang. Young people growing up in SW9 learn this as part of the code of the street. Both Coleman (1994) and Putnam (2000, pp 20-1 and pp 134-48) identify reciprocity as a central concept of social capital, describing it as a social norm arising from social networks and trust. In the social field of the gang, this contractual mutual exchange includes silence. As inducement for silence, the gang offers handouts such as food and cash to struggling families.

> 'They'll buy food for you … it's almost like a Robin Hood thing, so that if you are really stuck, they will buy you food, they'll look after the family a little bit. They'll look after the little ones, there is a sense of community in looking after each other, but then you have to pay back, don't you – you keep your mouth shut. So they are buying silence. I've seen that happen.' (Trident police officer)[5]

Such assistance may not always be repaid, although there is an unspoken acknowledgement that you have to keep your mouth shut. Flaunting the code indicates a challenge to be addressed through the sanctions repertoire. One example of how reciprocity works in this social field is through the buying and selling of stolen goods (Box 4.1).

Box 3.1: Buying and selling stolen goods

Buying and selling stolen goods is fully condoned within the wider community and forms part of the habitus of the neighbourhood as well as of the gang. This 'hidden economy' is linked to poverty and deprivation and is not unique to gangs (Bourgois, 1995). It is an example of Cloward and Ohlin's (1960, pp 161-71) 'integrated communities', where legitimate and illegitimate local economies co-exist. Sullivan identified the market for illegal goods as the 'most pervasive social supports for youthful economic crime' (Sullivan, 1989, p 119) and in Lambeth it represents a form of 'cultural adaptation' (Hagan, 1994, p 69), is 'not censured' by adults (Sanders, 2005, pp 43-55) and is locally 'highly valued'. All low-income areas have their local 'handler' who will buy and sell stolen goods. It is thus an established social norm for many both within and outside the social field of the gang.

In SW9, gangs are often central to the functioning of localised chains of supply for such goods. This activity is a further transitional element between the expressive and instrumental repertoire and an entry-level activity for those seeking to be introduced to the gang. Success in handling may result from family or personal networks. Those operating such networks are valuable as they help distribute goods quickly, create influence and goodwill, generate information and buy silence.[6]

In this way, gang members are pressured by both the field rules (game rules) and the wider neighbourhood (house rules). The habitus of the wider social field is well understood by all gang actors from an early age. Well before affiliation they are long skilled in the code of the street as it relates to SW9 (not to grass); they know who runs with the gang, and who to approach if they need to acquire money, drugs or stolen goods. They understand the role of violence in settling disputes and the imperative of respect. By the time of affiliation, they have been raised in the illusio of 'the game' and do not question it. What they must learn now is how to put all this knowledge into strategic action.

Developing game strategies and the gang repertoire

Once they are in the game, youngers must build their market share of street capital and establish themselves in the social field as players ('playas'). This is done by acquiring or building a reputation (or 'rep') (Anderson, 1999) and demonstrating 'street socialisation' (Vigil, 2002, p 2). A reputation is enhanced and expedited through the creation of a brand name and possibly a 'signature' (for example, for violence). Establishing a reputation in the social field permits entry into 'the game'. The overall aim is to acquire increased street capital in their social field, which can then be converted to economic capital.

   The youngers then begin their quest to raise their personal stock of street capital by employing individual strategies via their own agency. These strategies have three crucial goals:

* to maximise their personal market share of street capital;
* to maintain their personal market share of street capital by whatever means necessary;
* and to monitor closely any movements of their personal market share of street capital.

These strategies relate largely to social competition in deprived areas and are not unique to the social field of the gang (Winlow, 2001). However, within the social field of the gang, these strategies become imperative for survival. Strategies are about personal advancement, trying to succeed at all costs and not allowing others to take advantage of you or your situation. They are, in fact, common to us all. However, the strategies chosen by actors in the social field of the gang are determined by the habitus and the social field itself, that is, what are permissible, allowable, expected, normalised behaviours.

> 'So I developed a reputation for violence and acting quickly. You've gotta be harder, wilder and tougher than others to get through it.' (West African male ex-younger)

Actors in the field have developed a shared understanding of the rules and what is permissible. Stepping outside permissible rules is breaking the rules. Rules are therefore loosely codified as a range of tried and tested techniques. To achieve advancement, gang-affiliated youths must employ one or more of these techniques. I have called this the 'gang repertoire' – a series of possible strategies/actions for use by the gang, collectively or as individuals, to achieve the goals of:

- manufacturing street capital;
- maximising street capital;
- maintaining street capital;
- monitoring street capital.

These strategies include bullying and intimidation, robbery, burglary, physical violence, controlling public space, visual controls, revenge, abductions, controlling accommodation and so on. The development of strategies therefore operates as a series of mechanisms by which to acquire street capital and then maintain it. It is done hourly and daily by all in the social field.

> 'Nothing is random. Things are always done for reason. I'm not saying it's right but before they done what they done, whether it's rob a phone, smack someone's face – there has been a reason. It might not be a valid reason but it is a reason.' (African female younger)

How this menu of tested strategies or gang repertoire is constituted is determined by the habitus of the gang, that is, what is permissible from past experience (for example, the use aggressive dogs), social norms (enhanced physicality, levels of violence) and also by the wider habitus of the social class and community hosting the social field of the gang (for example, the tendency not to trust the police). There is thus variation from gang to gang and from one area or neighbourhood to another. Repertoire content is further determined by the characteristics of the social field. This menu of possible actions is acknowledged, sanctioned and utilised by the gang, with some aspects oriented to individuals and others having more impact on the wider community. The deployment of a particular repertoire component is determined by testing – or estimating its appropriateness and its effectiveness in achieving a desired outcome. Some elements will be used at different times depending on the objective – whether to manufacture or to maintain street capital. For example, physical violence may be used initially to manufacture street capital, while threats of violence may be used to maintain street capital.

Repertoire use is thus determined by both situation and by the tier operating the mechanism. For example, some activities and behaviours favoured by youngers, such as graffiti tagging, are not tolerated by olders, who instead tend to seek to exploit economic opportunities, such as armed robbery. Olders are likely to pursue strategies that favour the gang collectively; as incumbents, they seek to conserve the status quo. Youngers or newcomers (challengers) tend to adopt strategies that benefit the individual. Both groups and individuals pursue their strategies simultaneously. Gang members may operate an individual strategy and subscribe to the gang strategy at the same time. They may at some point clash, but until there is an episode of contention or a crisis, the gang strategy trumps the individual strategy.

As some gang repertoire actions are clearly more favoured by those at different stages of their gang involvement, this suggests a move from expressive to instrumental crime. This permits us to distinguish between the expressive repertoire (elements favoured and actively employed by the youngers) and the instrumental repertoire (those favoured and actively employed by olders). A third grouping of activities relates to sanctions used within the social field of the gang.

Through the repertoire, the gang effectively provides opportunities for individuals to collectively improve their chances of accessing street capital to achieve distinction. The three distinct components of the gang repertoire can be summarised as follows:

- expressive elements;
- instrumental elements;
- sanctions elements.

Each grouping constitutes a range of strategic actions regularly employed by the gang to increase and maintain street capital (building reputation and maintaining respect), and to access and engage economic capital (for example, through drug dealing or cash-in-transit robberies). Many activities are criminal undertakings, ranging from antisocial behaviour to more serious offences. Others provide a platform for offences to take place. Each element represents a strategy – employed collectively or individually – to achieve agreed goals that benefit either the individual or the group. Elements can be employed selectively and used singularly, individually, in parallel or multiple, sparingly or frequently. In this way, they become the modus operandi of the gang or the signature brand of the individual. The elements themselves are determined by the social field and the habitus. The gang repertoire is illustrated more fully in Table 4.1.

Table 4.1: The gang repertoire

Expressive	Sanctions and controls	Instrumental
Control of public space	Bullying and intimidation	Burglary
Control of access	Threats to family	Robbery
Visible presence	Religion	Handling stolen goods
Visual controls	Physical violence	Cash in transit robbery
Criminal damage	Revenge	Business take-overs
Intimidation of	Fear of retribution	Prostitution
professionals	Guns	Drugs
	Favours	Controlling accommodation
	Physical violence	Money lending
	Rumour	
	Rape	
	Abductions	
	Being outcast	

The expressive repertoire

The expressive repertoire represents forms of expressive crime. These activities, largely undertaken by the elementary tier ('tinnies', aged 8-12, and youngers, aged 13-16) provide opportunities for building reputation and branding to increase street capital. Actions are often aimed at the wider community, illustrating how at this level the neighbourhood becomes the arena for building street capital. Activities include controlling public space using aggressive dogs, grouping en masse, writing graffiti, carrying out criminal damage and controlling access to/from the estate – all highly visible and disruptive to local residents. As their individual street capital stock grows, so does their engagement in or access to low-level economic activity (for example, robbery or dealing weed). Youngers may seek 'fast access' to street capital by adopting the brand name of an established older (for example, 'Killa') with recognised stock market share. Youngers' strategies include controlling their postcode and territory, strategic action that operates to maintain and grow their street capital (through protecting friends and families from incursions) as well as to develop their economic base for selling weed (later graduating to selling Class A drugs). By building their 'rep' through violence (sanctioned by the habitus) and drugs (sanctioned by the gang), they will increase their reputation and thus acquire street capital. In addition, an elementary tier gang may operate an abbreviated gang repertoire that may expand over time.

The instrumental repertoire

The instrumental repertoire represents those actions or strategies favouring the acquisition of economic capital. This echoes findings by Venkatesh (2011) in his study of US street gangs, which refers to older members of gangs engaging in 'gang–gang' antagonisms that are overwhelmingly 'economically related' as opposed to 'gang–residents' antagonisms. Largely employed by olders or by individuals acting with individual agency, activities here include burglary, cash-in-transit robberies and taking control of accommodation or businesses. Some police officers may consider this to be organised crime. Robbery, and aspects of the drug trade, represent broad criminal spectrums and as such can provide entry points for youngers beginning to engage in instrumental crime. Here, youngers enter at the lower end of seriousness criminality, becoming involved in drug running or street robbery, before progressing to more serious crimes, such as cash-in-transit robberies or large-scale drug dealing.

The sanctions repertoire

The sanctions repertoire permits informal social controls to operate within the social field. Elements therefore include a range of informal punishments and controls utilised by the gang, or by individuals, to control social norms (Halpern, 2005, p p10).

> 'Many shootings and/or robberies are actually set-ups to address dealings.' (Professional)

Sanctions may be indirect or subtle (for example, rumour), or physical, interpersonal and dangerous (for example, acts of revenge, attacks, rape, abduction). They may be targeted at partners and family members, perhaps for tactical advantage in a revenge robbery. As reported by one gang member who employed this strategy:

'I would find out their movements first. I was smart. I wouldn't get random 'cos I could be hurt. I would get accurate information on them and their movements. This means you have to find out who's got info; who holds the info? Then access it; then hope this is accurate, truthful and that the person you spoke with is loyal and will not snitch to them that I am coming. It's a sneaky thing to do of course.' (Younger)

Some sanctions are mainly used by youngers or to specifically sanction expressive crime. The proximity of the young person to the social field and/or their field position or importance determines the frequency of use of sanctions; if respect or reputational issues are paramount, you will by default need to employ the sanctions more frequently to maintain your rep. Again, this explains why so many youngers are involved in fights and 'random' violence.

These sanctions/control mechanisms operate outside the social field of the gang in other communities, but within this social field they are highly effective and meaningful, acknowledged as integral and relevant by all. The sanction repertoire is employed regularly with other elements and strategies, each reinforcing the other, playing on the victim in different ways, as the gang determines the impact. Which technique works independently? Which works effectively or quickly? The answers are often held by olders or elders (incumbents), but may also be uncovered by employing a range of components in the repertoire to varying degrees. e.g. using a range of variables, such as increased volume, increased frequency or multiple techniques. If a different people are involved, all employing different techniques, the effect may be overwhelming for the victim.

Strategic action using the gang repertoire

The gang repertoire is an established menu of possible strategies, providing the gang with a teleological group of actions that over time and via differential association (Sutherland, 1947) have become accepted practice. Each component has been used before and will be used again. A decision to employ any specific component as a strategic action is situationally determined by estimates of its appropriateness and effectiveness in achieving strategic objectives. Employment is also contingent on other actions occurring within the social field at the time. Gang members are vociferous in their praise of components successfully employed, with the key planner in any such incident being accorded substantial street capital.

Once the gang, or individual, has decided on their strategy, for example, revenge, they determine how to implement it. Implementation introduces numerous variables. These depend on the individuals involved and whether the strategic action is to be carried out by the gang or an individual. As the core objective (revenge) remains the same, the outcomes are determined by interaction of variables. (Multiple variables lead to varying outcomes that are more difficult to control.) Thus strategic actors use varying degrees of dosage of violence, speed, stealth and so on, and this varies from incident to incident, providing a Popparian testing of the repertoire. The selected technique is then used until the police get on top of it, at which point the gang alters the variables, adapting the technique. Those members who conceive and execute strategic actions effectively achieve field advantage by demonstrating a good grasp of 'warfare skills' and leadership qualities. This knowledge is traded/exchanged and its possession, a favoured and valuable asset, is worthy of its own reputation. Those who fail successfully to implement strategic actions are most likely new to the social field and lack sufficient knowledge of the repertoire, or their attempts to implement its actions or variables are overly emotional in their application or execution.

In contrast to the teleological components sit a range of variables that determine the success of strategic action. Implementation of these variables requires social skills, usually acquired over time by older and elders. Some variables, such as timing of the action, can be controlled, while others (for example, the response from the victim) cannot. Variable selection and implementation of the gang repertoire is therefore often arrived at in a heuristic fashion – most often for the elementary tier. Strategic actors who are more agentic will have their preferred method of implementing the repertoire heuristically. The range of possible actions, variables and strategies adopted by a gang reflect the wide-ranging goals and objectives operating within the gang at any one time. The multiple uses of the repertoire, its variables and the sheer volume of its use, gives the impression that the gang is chaotic and random. The expected effects are learned through this process of testing outcomes, but this can change and vary depending on other multiples and variables. Thus there is a process of using social skill, constant learning and adaptation, as shown in Table 4.2.

A number of variables exist that alter/affect the way techniques 'play out' in the social field or are employed. Knowledge of these variables,

Table 4.2: Key skills in implementing the repertoire

Longevity and experience	Olders achieve rank through longevity and skillful testing of the repertoire. As knowledge and experience grows and becomes embedded, olders develop an intimate knowledge of street life and gang life, that is, what works, when, how and with whom; why to use the repertoire; how best to use it or to vary it; and, importantly, when not to use it. This is valuable street capital and builds reputation. Olders explain and demonstrate to youngers how to engage with the repertoire, then monitor their progress.
Adaptability	A person is either a key player/instigator in an incident or a secondary player/ follower. Key players have developed skills in repertoire usage. They may be omni-competent (skilled across a wide range of techniques) or a specialist in one particular element. Reputations are enhanced depending on the use of the repertoire. Youngers advancing in the gang become more skilled in its implementation. Indeed, advancement in the social field is partially determined by skill in implementing the repertoire. Those acting with individual agency are most likely highly skilled at employing the repertoire. Employing the sanction repertoire comes more easily to anyone well established.
Multiple uses	When to engage multiple elements of the repertoire is important, as usage depends on the objective and motivation for use.
Timing of use	Timing can alter the impact of the intervention; for example, when is the best time to rob or burgle a target?
Using rising tensions	If tensions increase, the gang can increase its influence over the actions of those seeking protection. For safety, more people will 'check in' with the gang with regard to their movements – more information is actively sought and checked. Tension can act as a recruiting tool resulting in increased requests to join the gang.
Ability to change or stop	A skilled player can identify when to stop using or change a technique, for example, when to move from bullying and intimidation to reward, or vice versa.
Emotional investment	Emotional investment affects outcome. It may be desirable, for example, when using violence. Youngers may get too emotionally involved, leading to reckless behaviour. Olders employ emotional investment sparingly. At other times, 'cold detachment' or emotional disengagement is required, for example, when a gang member is participating in a set-up of another person.

which can be grouped as either regulated or unregulated variables, again requires considerable social skill.

Regulated variables

Most regulated variables can be identified, planned for or regulated by the gang; others are more random. As shown in Table 4.3, variables and their relative importance alter depending on the element employed. For example, in the case of respect, the key issue is speed and timing of response.

Table 4.3: Regulated variables affecting the repertoire

Variable	Impact/example
Employment/use	Varies depending on level of involvement and length of time of involvement
Duration	Long-term harassment or short fight
Dosage	Heavy or light
Frequency	How often to use the same technique
Favoured usage	May equate to the creation of a personal repertoire
Motivation	Determines element to be employed, for example, money or revenge
Variation	A need to vary techniques and variables in response to policing
Location of deployment	May vary and be important, for example, in the case of a robbery on/off the estate. For set-ups, location is key; for steaming timing is key. Location is most easily planned for and can be surveilled in advance using local knowledge

Unregulated variables

A range of external variables also affects the execution of strategies. These lie beyond the control of the gang and cannot be regulated (see Table 4.4). These then act as unpredictable elements in the field and can seriously affect, disrupt or curtail strategic action by the gang or by an individual. Socially skilled players in the game will advance their street capital by recognition of these variables and their learnt ability to anticipate, manage and respond to these unpredictable and often inevitable interventions by those in proximate fields.

Table 4.4: Unregulated variables affecting the repertoire

Variable	Explanation
The repertoire employed by other gangs	Rising levels of violence may be ratcheted up in each gang repertoire. Successful techniques are lauded and then adopted. The reputation of these events will be important and the level of reputational 'traffic' will be monitored by olders
Media	Media influences, the breadth and reach of national stories, will influence the repertoire
Policing	Policing operations to disrupt, reduce or terminate gang activity affect how the repertoire is employed and the variables used

Unknowns and temporary suspension

Strategic action using the repertoire may also involve a number of unknowns, such as new gang members working with you for the first time who may introduce unexpected violence, fail to perform, or get caught. Victims are an unknown variable and 'ultra-violence' may be used against them to reduce risk.

The gang may temporarily suspend aspects of the repertoire until the situation cools down. The element may be slightly altered the next time it is used, via the process known as displacement (a change of location, for example). The five different levels of displacement represent the repertoire being employed differently as a responsive reaction to changes in variables.

Adaptations to the gang repertoire

What is permissible within a repertoire is guided and bounded by the habitus of the social field. While often durable, the repertoire will change slightly over time as new techniques are identified and tested. It is the variables and how they are employed that allow adaptations and changes to be made. New components are added or variables manipulated when a major incident lowers the benchmark of what works or what is permissible. Key 'trigger crimes' in gangland, local or national, have such an effect. For example, the execution-style shooting of Avril Johnston in front of her children by four men in Brixton in 1998 meant that similar future acts became 'permissable'. It was reported that the indiscriminate shootings of two girls in Birmingham in 2003 resonated within the social field of the gang and was widely discussed across gang communities.

A sensational incident considered universally impressive results in considerable discussion among the gang. This equates to 'reputational traffic'. Such incidents also register with the community and reverberate through families, churches and community forms. As the discussions continue, the offender achieves celebrity status and is eventually mythologised into local folklore; such was the case with the shooting of two young people in a crowded McDonald's restaurant in Brixton in 2006. Such incidents recalibrate the boundaries of the repertoire within the social field. Shropshire and McFarquhar (2002) argue that any firearm use in a school environment would similarly remove the taboo against guns in schools, leading to a dramatic increase in their use in schools.

The gang repertoire comprises tried and tested techniques employed by a gang. Should they fail in execution, fail to deliver successful outcomes, or fail to be employed easily and effectively, the variables will be altered, although in extreme cases failure can precipitate an issue of contention (such as a leadership challenge) or a crisis, such as the fracturing of the gang (see Chapter Five).

In the next chapter, I consider the hierarchy of the social field and how this relates to maintaining social order while providing opportunities for advancement.

Notes

[1] Parker (1974) in *View from the boys* noted that low income neighbourhoods 'can become "a condoning community" in regards to types of delinquency…. The hatred of "Authority" is implanted at all age levels. In their own way parents and sons feel the same way and protect each other against officialdom' (Parker, 1974, p 190).

[2] For further reading on this topic, consider Winlow (2001).

[3] Sandberg and Pederson (2011) are critical of Anderson's approach suggesting that it is unclear how the term code is being used, i.e. is it 'a logic of the street [or] a way to "read" the street'? Moreover its relationship to the subculture of violence or to the concept of street culture is also unclear (p 51; note 19).

[4] Sus is a popular abbreviation for 'suspected person', which in turn comes from 'suspected person loitering with intent to commit a felonious offence' – Section 4 of the Vagrancy Act 1824. This section was increasingly used in the 1970s and 1980s against the black and minority ethnic population in London and other UK urban conurbations generating discontent among these communities who felt they were being unfairly targeted by the police. In 1981 during 'Operation Swamp' in Brixton, London, large numbers of black people were stopped and searched under this section generating confrontation which resulted in three nights of rioting. In his subsequent report Lord Scarman (1981) identified this as a contributory factor to loss of confidence and mistrust in the police and recommended a return to more community-oriented forms of local policing. For more details see Demuth (1978).

[5] Operation Trident was established in March 1998 by the Metropolitan Police Service as a dedicated unit targeting gun crime within London especially within the black community. In February 2012 it was relaunched as the Trident Gang command unit with a new focus to tackle all violent crime relating to young people.

[6] For a more in-depth explanation of this issue see Harding (2012).

FIVE

Players, positioning and keeping order

'Innovation distinguishes between a leader and a follower.'
Steve Jobs

In Chapter Four, I examined how actors undertake strategic action using the gang repertoire. Before expanding the theory to consider further examples of strategy development in the social field, let us look in more detail at the field hierarchy, the actors (or players) and the rules of the game. These dictate how the game is played, how social order is maintained, and how gangs are structured and organised.

The structure of the social field

As identified in Chapter Two, there remains a rather unhelpful binary regarding gang organisation in the UK: gangs are not organised (Aldridge et al, 2008; Hallsworth and Young, 2008; Hallsworth and Duffy, 2010; Hallsworth, 2013); gangs are organised, (Pitts, 2008b; Toy, 2008; Harding, 2012; Densley, 2013).

Field theory (Bourdieu, 1969, 1984; Martin, 2003; Fligstein and McAdam, 2012) dictates that the social field is structured with actors placed by their 'relative location in the hierarchy of positions' (Swartz, 1997, p 120), reflecting capital distribution. This concurs with my own findings among gangs in SW9, where organisational levels, where perceptible, relate not to age, as some believe, but to capital distribution. Age is reflected in so far as young people starting out in the social field of the gang possess less capital than those already established.

I also found that in SW9 gangs are moderately organised at the lower level and more organised at the higher level in a common organisational structure that I have termed 'tiers'. These tiers represent more than capital distribution; they represent differences in use of the repertoires, strategies, types of criminal behaviour, levels of antisocial behaviour, ways of thinking, aspirations and group dynamics. Before further consideration of gang organisation, it is important to examine other organising concepts for the maintenance of social order in the field.

Reconstruction of social order

Social order in the social field relates to the internal field structure and mechanisms for its maintenance. In the social field of the gang in SW9, the evident social order is maintained for one overarching reason: there is no plausible alternative.

Returning to Bourdieu (1991, pp 22-5), we are reminded that the social field retains two key ordering principles: the doxa – the field's deep structure, which dictates the forms of struggle – and the illusio – the tacit understanding of a dominant establishment and subordinate challengers with an internal logic that confirms it is all worth the struggle. This organising principle is not only self-evident to all actors in the field, it is the basis for understanding the rules, the routes to distinction, how to demonstrate skills and abilities, how to test/audition for roles and how to acquire street capital.

This field logic is passed down to youngers by olders and elders, who, by virtue of their dominant field positions, employ strategies to conserve the status quo, as they believe this will be good for business. This established field hierarchy also provides clearly established routes for progression for all actors to advance to distinction. Were no such routing evident, chaos would ensue. Any new entrants to the field pursuing succession strategies (Swartz, 1997, p 124) will similarly have clear goals.

In addition to the doxa, illusio and field logic, the maintenance of social order in this field relates to several components:

- field rules (see Chapter Four);
- organising meta-narratives;
- gang organisation and hierarchy;
- the sanctions repertoire.

Organising meta-narratives

It is possible to identify several different organising meta-narratives in SW9: the gang as shield, as family, as protector, as business and as employer. Youngers often refer to gang life as 'a game', associating it with the key dynamic of fun and drama. Olders refer to it as 'the game', that is, a cynical recognition of the predetermined roles played by themselves and the criminal justice agencies in the social field.

Two internal gang narratives that emerged from my study and are often reiterated by researchers and youth workers alike represent the gang not as a gang as such, but rather as a group of friends. Here the gang is presented as a protector of young people, serving the community and protecting their territory from incursions. All narratives provide permissions and legitimisation (Sykes and Matza, 1957); for example, muggings in SW9 are often interpreted as, or excused as, legitimate by gang-affiliated young people on the basis that the perpetrators tend to be gang-affiliated visitors or rivals, not gang-affiliated locals.

This 'protection' narrative is often used alongside the narrative of gang as 'street family' (see Chapter Nine). The street family narrative permits affirmative, reinforcing language and positive 'framing' while again excusing behaviours and providing an organising principle where social order is maintained through allegiance to the family and family ideals. Common among youngers, it can be used as a way of rationalising their actions, and is associated with strong elements of excuse and denial. Behaviours are often rationalised through nostalgic perspectives that underplay the reality of those behaviours, the negative reactions of other residents and the actual outcomes. It also permits members to process illegal activity and assume the moral high ground for 'righteous' actions. For young affiliates, the 'street family' is a cogent metaphor, providing a rational interpretive frame for comprehending the complex rules operating within this highly bonded social group and social field.

Co-joined with both these narratives are concepts of poverty and legitimisation (Sykes and Matza, 1957) – in other words, young people are poor and do what is necessary to get by. Some youngers talked of pressure from their family to 'bring something to the table'. Robbing is permissible within the habitus, thus understandable, and those stabbed or killed in the process are deemed to have initiated or deserved their fate.

Such explanatory narratives, common among youth workers, often ignore the increased risks of gang affiliation, or deny the possibility of gang evolution from peer group to organised body. While neither narrative offers a true reflection of the social field, both all too often underpin debates on gang definition and organisation.

Gang rules (game rules)

The gang rules (or game rules in my casino metaphor) operating in the social field of the gang operate against the backdrop of the wider and more consensual neighbourhood rules (house rules in my casino metaphor) operating in SW9 (see Chapter Four). Gang rules establish how 'the game' of 'ganging' in SW9 will be conducted. They are thus a source of conflict and struggle between gang members (Martin, 2003, p 31) and are subject to variation and change.

Operating as a general backdrop to gang activities, gang rules are orally transmitted from olders to youngers. Some individuals or gang sub-sets (pods) retain their own rules or codes of action that act as shibboleths. Rules, in so far as they exist, are codes for operating and implementing the gang repertoire, setting boundaries on strategic actions and limits on variables – not to rob black people or pensioners, for example. For members they act as generalised credos that supplement the ethos of street life, as these examples illustrate:

> 'If someone troubles you, we deal with it.'

> 'We'll stand together, we've got your back.'

Such affirmations are often repeated as taglines when gang members are being recruited. They also send messages to members who view them as both support and license:

> 'That was appealing and meant I could do anything to anyone and I know that my boys have got my back.' (African Caribbean male older)

Gang organisation and hierarchy

The key component for maintaining social order is the field hierarchy, identifiable as gang organisation. Here the lack of consensus on gang organisation among academics is reflected in the conflicting views of professionals in SW9. In *Street boys* (Pritchard, 2008, p 255, an elder of the PDC gang known as Ja Ja (Elijah Kerr) argues that 'gang' is a pejorative term used by the media to trivialise and sensationalise, making members sound amateurish. He referred to the PDC as a 'crew, a loose affiliation of young black men like myself, almost like an umbrella organisation'. He notes that the PDC is 'much more sophisticated and complicated than that', with members often working freelance and together as a 'social network'.

Some professionals identify links between lower- and higher-end criminality:

'In general the Lambeth street gangs are "chaotic" in their
organisation and ability, but very violent. If the police
can't catch them with evidence for higher-end crimes they
will try and target them for lower-end ASB [anti-social
behaviour].' (male Trident police officer)

Others suggest a greater level of organisation, but struggle to articulate it:

'If you look at the make-up of the gangs and what the gangs
do without looking at any research then on the face of it
– you'd think these people are disorganised, a lot of ASB,
bit of cannabis dealing and random violence, but it seems,
especially the violence all has a purpose – it's all linked to
something else.' (White male police officer)

Residents on one estate argued that gangs were narrowly focused but
effectively managed and better organised than the local authority:

'It organises almost entirely by word of mouth and mobile
phones. That's as effective as any paper organisation. But
they keep track of things. There's a lot of brave and thought
goes into things. Gangs are better managed than Lambeth
council.' (White male resident)

Local professionals working more closely with gangs claim that gangs
only appear to be disorganised because of their antisocial behaviour,
but in reality are quite organised. Police officers working directly
with gangs have in fact identified clear structural levels of organisation
within gangs in SW9 but cannot agree on the numbers of young
people involved at each level. While it is important to acknowledge
that most young people in Lambeth are not affiliated to any gang, all
professionals agreed that number of gang-affiliated young people is
increasing, alongside levels of violence.

Taken as a whole, gangs in SW9 are undoubtedly organised, with
moderate organisation at the elementary tier and higher levels of
organisation at the mature tier. At the elementary tier, generating street
capital via the expressive repertoire results in highly visible territorial
violence and antisocial behaviour that appears chaotic but actually
represents strategic action. It is only the visible face and junior tier of
a more structured field that retains ranks, levels of entry, differentiated
roles, group and gang strategies, a series of repertoires for engaging
in both expressive and instrumental crime, marketing and publicity

strategies, recruitment, tactical manoeuvres, change, negotiation and adaptation, branding, opportunities for advancement, communication and information channels, networking possibilities and links to criminal business ventures. Those involved display intelligence and cunning, which clearly benefits them as they operate within their social field. This evidence is often difficult to reconcile with the views of senior police officers:

> 'When the police talk about gang problems in Lambeth they are really talking about young people aged between 13-20. Most of these guys are on bikes.' (White male Trident police officer)

While the behaviour described is evident in all the gangs I reviewed in SW9, there are variations within each gang. To substantiate the claim that gangs in SW9 are organised, I now examine the organisational elements of gang tiers, transitioning, and auditioning and testing. I then consider the social skills required by incumbents to maintain social order.

Tiers

Gangs in SW9 exhibited similar characteristics in terms of their organisational structure. The gangs comprised members in three broad age bands, which I have called tiers:

- elementary tier – youngers, aged 13-16; sometimes incorporating tinnies, aged 10-13;
- mature tier – olders, aged 16-21;
- advanced tier – elders, aged 22-30.

These tiers relate to the types of action and levels of criminal activity undertaken by members, as well as their use of repertoires. For some they represent 'terms' of affiliation to the gang. Table 5.1 shows how the tiers have evolved since 2005.

Table 5.1:-Tiers operating in gangs in SW9

1990–2005	2006–13
Olders, aged 16–19	Advanced tier: elders, aged 22 plus
	Mature tier: olders, aged 16–21
Youngers, aged 13–16	Elementary tier: youngers, aged 13–16
	Elementary tier: tinnies, aged 10–13

Elementary tier

Motivations for gang affiliation change over time. For youngers, the elementary tier provides opportunities for affiliation, building reputation and manufacturing street capital through the expressive repertoire. Their behaviour in the neighbourhood thus comes across as antisocial, highly visible and violent. Often fiercely loyal to the gang, they seek to enhance its brand as well as building their own. This loyalty extends to their local territory or 'endz'. They employ strategies, both at the individual and group level, to maximise their street capital and seek advancement. They are primarily brought into the gang via family, peers and olders for their skills, abilities or connections or because they seek opportunities for fun, money and protection. Their behaviour may appear chaotic and random.

Below youngers sits a more recently formed sub-group of young people aged 11-13 called 'tinnies' – gang 'wannabes' or younger siblings and neighbours. They tend to undertake short-term limited actions for youngers and provide youngers with opportunities to develop leadership skills and build 'rep'. For both groups, social networking sites and information flow is crucial to permit them to navigate this new landscape of risk. While youngers may affiliate to gangs with the expectation of minimising risk to themselves or potential victimhood, or for fun, drama or money, they often find the social field they enter is different from the one they thought they were entering.

Youngers operate to limited local boundaries with localised networks and mental maps and are thus caught up in largely estate-based 'beefs' or 'postcode wars', unlike older/elders, who are able to travel well beyond these local boundaries. For youngers, personal individual strategies – such as revenge, and building reputation and respect – are paramount. Fighting, and for some, a quest for violence, is a key imperative.

Within this elementary tier (youngers), peer pressure and potential violence are escalated rather than minimised, opportunities for accessing economic capital are at times remote and yields may be smaller than anticipated. The social field is violent and threatening, demanding constant vigilance of peers both within the gang and outwith the gang.

Affiliation demands loyalty and the expectation that you will act within the gang without question. This may require isolation from local social agencies or authorities:

> 'The smaller gangs that are trying to make a name for themselves won't work together and we have major incidents of violence or murder and it becomes impossible for them to work together.' (White male police officer)

In the elementary tier, members must adopt the gang narrative orally transmitted by olders before they join. Gangs believe that more affiliations bring greater protection and use social networking sites to try to widen their network. Increased exposure to the 'virtual' gang network leads to increased exposure to sanctions provoked by instances of disrespect, which, in turn, may lead to a downward trajectory of entanglement and gang interaction. Contrary to the narrative of the street family, so often repeated by young people and some youth workers, this social field is not collegiate, and is distinguished by back-stabbing, immaturity and volatile, shifting friendships, presenting a constant dilemma between individual and group strategies.

Olders offer inducements and guidance but use youngers to advance their own business deals or personal strategies. Youngers are tested for loyalty/skill, with any success in these arenas generating advanced street capital. Thus relationships between youngers and olders are both symbiotic and mutually exploitative. The balance of power, which used to favour olders, is increasingly being questioned and challenged by youngers keen to access economic capital more quickly than earlier generations, with some youngers believing it is they who are 'running the road'. Some professionals claim that increased levels of challenge contribute to increased levels of violence in the social field. Furthermore, the negative sanctions repertoire previously employed by some olders to keep youngers in line has begun to shift to one of affirmative sanctions to reflect this new dynamic:

> 'Half of them youngers didn't know how much these Brixton olders are affiliated with these Peckham olders but it's a money thing. The youngers in Brixton see that as wrong.' (African Caribbean female independent operator)

Olders recognise and accept that youngers may cause localised antisocial behaviour on estates, but they usually ignore it. Some olders get involved themselves to build allegiances. When such activities attract police attention, elders get irritated and, if the activity is too unruly, they may enact controls or sanctions, either affirmative or negative. Most of the time olders accept this as a social norm, even capitalising on such situations. Having only recently progressed from the elementary tier themselves, they recognise that youngers provide critical functions to olders wishing to advance by providing information, stolen goods and access to the network, as well as performing specified tasks such as drug shotting.

Failure to understand these social norms or demonstrating a lack of sophistication in the social field (for example, in misusing or mis-reading critical information relevant to the task or situation) often places many youngers at risk. Many youngers operate in a world of myth, anecdote, suspicion, rumour and gossip. For some, the gang is a concept mis-sold, where the small print remains unread. Others advance through violence or a reputation for 'madness', raising their street capital and reputation, building networks and specialising in elements of the repertoire. Eventually youngers become fed up with not making much money and seek other means of income generation – they are now ready to 'upgrade' membership to that of an older. Fed up with not making much money, they are now ready to 'upgrade' membership to that of an older.

Mature tier

Olders, often just a year or two older than youngers, have established reputations and are more interested in money. They school youngers in the social norms and the social field, setting tasks and testing both loyalty and candidacy for bigger jobs by using them as gofers and run-arounds. This relationships is essentially exploitative but also reciprocal as olders schools youngers in gang history, tips on how to succeed, the actors, the players and 'life on road'.

Crucially, olders influence youngers in terms of how to build reputation and street capital. Olders keep youngers in line, presiding over the affirmative sanctions repertoire of privilege, reward, inducement and advancement. Olders are needed and respected but increasingly come to be seen by youngers as potential barriers, or sometimes as braggers who 'over-claim' their ability and success. Whereas previously sanctions were largely negative, increasingly olders are also using affirmative sanctions towards youngers. It is widely reported that youngers are now no longer afraid to attack an older should they be disrespected:

> 'Most youngers would not be afraid to stab an older. They are realising if you cheat them and keep 'boying' them [treating them as a boy], it is safer and easier to take you

out than continue to be treated like this.' (West African male older)

As members reach age 16 or 17, life around them changes. They may have left school; started college; parented a child; begun accessing pubs and clubs. Personal, social and relationship boundaries expand. During this transition, some take the opportunity to drop out of the gang or reduce their involvement. For others it is a natural progression, as they move into the mature tier increasingly employing the instrumental repertoire and becoming more focused on raising economic capital. Reputations by now are largely cast, though they must be maintained with vigilance.

> 'As I got older the cost of living got more expensive, so my criminal activity got more outrageous 'cos I had to maintain my lifestyle. To keep up your reputation in an image sense – it costs money. So you might not have food in your system but you'd be clothed very well.' (African Caribbean male independent operator)

Many olders are more tolerant of individual strategies, such as having a family, going to college and so on. If they are still involved in the gang, their strategies become more collegiate, and gang strategies become more harmonised. They tend to use the expressive repertoire less and less, which results in decreased daily violence both within and between gangs, creating more opportunities for socialising and making money. At this point their individual strategies become more collegiate, and gang strategies overall tend to become more harmonised. Those still acting within the gang strategy become increasingly self-selective in their involvement, frequently matching strategic action with skill set, or linking up with others to form a specialist pod or group. They may be nominated by elders for specific roles or tasks based on their reputation and skill.

Olders now operate within wider personal, social and business boundaries. If they move outside the neighbourhood, they often remain affiliated to the gang. They tend to use the instrumental repertoire to develop new strategies, possibly liaising with hitherto rival neighbourhood gangs to expand business partnerships – Brixton olders with Peckham olders, for example. Many youngers viewing this connectivity from their elementary level consider it as wrong, and increasingly 'disrespect' olders, distrusting them or challenging them for leadership. Moreover, not all olders will be making money. Youngers are often disappointed when they discover this.

At this level, violence is now largely deemed to be aberrant and unproductive, except in unusual circumstances when the violence becomes more extreme. Violence is now used strategically as a last resort, aimed to end opposition once and for all – to draw a line.

At age 18 or 19, olders are either fully integrated into the gang or already negotiating withdrawal as other life chances present themselves:

> 'By 18, 19, 20 – it's money, it's not gang violence really, it's there. Maybe you have the beefs you had before, it's maybe still there, problems with other gangs but it's not as much as it was before. It's really all about money, you just want money. That's when I think you choose your pathways at 18/19 – either to try and get an education or carry on with the gang stuff. A lot of people, everybody chooses at about age 18.' (African Caribbean male older)

By the time they are 20/21, members are considered to be serious operators and able to start making more money. With street-level gang violence behind them, they can focus on networks and opportunities to move from bonding social capital to bridging social capital. Territoriality, often important in elementary tiers, is less important and can at least be minimised, increasing members' ability to traverse estates and neighbourhoods. Those returning from young offender institutions or prison can pick up ex-'birded' colleagues and put new, high-level, high-yield strategies into action that are less frequent.

If olders are connected to drug dealing, they will now manage a group of youngers on an estate, permitting the olders to develop new links with those further up the supply chain, including negotiating with elders operating drugs on other estates in other neighbourhoods. It is these network, business and family links that allow olders and those above them to interact with others in mature tiers. Thus deals are brokered and even ceasefires arranged. Organisation includes increased stratification and management of drug dealing, with energy going into locating markets; purchasing and mixing product; packaging selling and distributing drugs; and sourcing customers, even travelling up country if necessary. While some of these tasks will take place off the estate and be organised by elders, the olders are a key link in the business model.

In this tier, levels of organisation increased alongside quality and effectiveness. Olders often progress to cash-in-transit robberies, once the preserve of organised crime groups. However, the slightly chaotic, poorly planned and amateurish nature of these robberies sets this gang activity apart from that of organised crime rings. It is more common for olders to target drug stashes in transit, and to rob other gang members.

Advanced tier

Progressing from an older to an elder is not a given: "Only two or three hard and bad boys progress into the top element" as one respondent put it. Nor is this progression achieved simply by dint of age or 'staying the course', although both provide a starting point for acceptance. Elders have established their reputation by completing the transition, which may have involved a spell in prison. They are the street power brokers, often feared and admired in equal measure. They have leadership qualities, social skills and strong network connections, qualities that over time become important. Only a few 'hard and bad gang boys' progress to elders, either through madness, badness, contacts, stealth, availability or hard work.

Elders may be seen only rarely in the neighbourhood. Aloofness will add to their mystique. Others may be more involved in drug dealing locally and play a role in orchestrating and managing others from a safe house on the estate.

Police profiles identify elders with an impressive array of previous convictions from robbery and violence to drug possession, domestic violence and threats. Elders tend to range in age from mid-20s to mid-30s, although this varies across gangs and depends on how long they have been off the police radar. Peckham gang elders tend to be older than average, suggesting higher levels of organisation and setting them apart from the gangs in SW9. Members' longevity suggests fewer internal fractures in the gang. Peckham gangs also tend to have more members, and it is possible that a larger, more mature, group of leaders is required to maintain operations.

Elders maintain reputations in different ways, such as spending freely at night clubs (one SW9 elder reputedly spent £100,000 in 2010 celebrating his birthday at a West End champagne bar). Such stories, regardless of veracity, excite youngers, maintaining the reputations of elders more effectively than stories of reputed violence. Whereas money tends to come and go quickly for olders, elders may shift higher quantities of cash. Some may invest in small localised businesses such as barber shops and beauty shops to assist with laundering money. Others will have little to show and no evidence of a lavish lifestyle.

As privileged incumbents, gang elders can dictate movements in a member's street capital can both influence and dictate movements in a member's street capital. Youngers and olders know this, and seek personal links with elders to gain an advantage and give them an edge. Such links may confer:

- an ability to access high-level information more quickly and to tap into high-quality, first-hand information that is accurate and timely;
- an ability to develop deeper knowledge about rivals within the gang and in other gangs;
- an opportunity to gain higher levels of respect by association;
- an opportunity to build trust;
- an opportunity to develop bragging rights;
- a chance to be nominated for strategies.

Vigil (2010) refers to elders as 'veteranos', who, as 'developmentally delayed adults', have never matured out of the gang. A less pejorative perspective of elders therefore appears to exist in SW9.

Transitioning between tiers

Many professionals and academics assume that movement through gang tiers is dependent on age, but this is not the case. Movement is contingent on a transitioning period during which a range of internal and external factors affect forward movement to the next level.

The first transition period is from a younger to an older, and takes places at around the age of 16. For young strategic actors in the gang, opportunities, networks and relationships mostly prevail to create a bias towards continuing to run with the gang, especially as by now members would have invested so much time and energy in raising their reputation and status. Moreover, becoming an older presents greater opportunities for access to economic capital. For many youngers, the transition is a seamless one occurring over time:

> 'It was a natural progression for me to go from bullying to start smoking weed and that. To then work out that the people I smoke with they want drugs so let me sell to them – so I'm making money now. So it's a natural progression. I go into school and I'm leaving school with more money than I go in with.' (African Caribbean male independent operator)

When they become olders, their street capital will increase, bringing involvement in higher-yield activities as a result of having youngers running or shotting for them.

At this stage, other 'life' factors begin to impinge on strategic actors. For example, it is not uncommon for members to have a child at 15 or 16, and some use this experience to adjust their gang strategies or develop a part-time affiliation. Most gang-affiliated young people leave school at 16, or start college, often maintaining their level of involvement in the gang. Whereas at school they may have been exposed to one or two 'resident' gangs, at college they may have more opportunity to form links with other gangs. Affiliations may now have to change. For many, the transition from younger to older is normative, expected and easy, while that from older to elder presents greater challenges.

The second-tier transition

Most gang-affiliated youngers do not move onto be elders in the Advanced stage. Only two or three individuals (around one in ten youngers) move up to this level. Those who remain fully gang-affiliated as elders have not simply advanced overnight or because of their age; a great deal of work is required to get to this stage. Indeed for many elders, their personal or individual strategies may eventually be foregrounded presenting other options which may no longer include the gang. However for those who are extensively engaged in activities such as street robbery by the age of 15 or 16 and who then remain actively gang-affiliated, it likely that they will have moved on to bigger things (such as robbery of cash-in-transit vans, or betting shops) by the time they are 19/20.

Many youngers and olders have already entered the criminal justice system by age 18, often receiving multiple low-tariff sentences or no further action notices, or spending time in young offender institutions meeting peers and expanding criminal networks. This may prove to be a turning point for youngers; some may decide to leave the gang, find employment and lead a more stable life, while others will use their criminal associations to become more entrenched in the gang. Those seeking to leave often have to move out of the area and sever connections to the network. This is seldom a single definitive decision and usually involves a difficult series of decisions that occurs over time.

By the time they are 21, most active gang members have either been stabbed, had a baby or gone to prison – or, in gang parlance, been shanked, shelved or shackled. Being stabbed or having a baby is often a 'wake-up call', leading some to 'come off road' (Decker and Lauritsen, 2002, pp 51-67). For others, the mostly negative effects (both mental and physical) of constant violence accelerates this 'maturing-out' process (Vigil, 1988a) as members increasingly seek an end to the constant stress of gang violence.

Some loosen their ties with the gang because of other interests, while others are just a spent force after several years 'on road'. It may be possible for members to negotiate their role, reducing their involvement with the gang to become first part-time affiliates, then occasional affiliates. Finally, they will cease to run with the gang but remain linked to the network through family associations. Leaving the gang altogether requires significant changes to your network.

For those going to prison, the decision to continue with gang affiliation can depend upon the mentality you entered with, i.e. if you believe that going to prison will 'earn you stripes' and that this is somehow a strategic move which will increase your street capital. Thus the 'hardcore' element is often retained within gangs.

Those who are still selling drugs when they are 21 now tend to be more seriously involved in the business. Some olders may have expanded their patch through clever use of youngers. The 'postcode beef' is less of an issue for elders, so as new, high-yield business opportunities arise, elders move across boundaries more readily, keeping a low profile. Despite the enduring postcode beef between gangs in Peckham and Brixton, elders in the advanced tier regularly move drugs across both locations. Interestingly, a few Peckham elders even live with elders from Brixton. Thus connections and a strong network may help members progress to the advanced tier.

All gangs in SW9 have elders who by age 25/26 have extensive network contacts and act as overseers of activity. They can adapt gang rules, creating variations to the repertoire to boost cash flow and cash yields. Their role is covert, with business often conducted via telephone calls and oriented towards building partnerships to raise economic capital. Such a role may require particular characteristics.

As with leadership qualities (at any tier of the gang), achieving the distinction of being an elder depends on an individual's personal qualities, social skill and unique characteristics, for example, ruthlessness or an ability to direct and motivate. It will also depend on business ability and aptitude for hard work, alongside a determination to follow individual strategies or agency. Few gang members achieve this elevated status:

'I could tell you which of these youngers will make it to an elder – very few. Mostly cos of how they carry themselves, the position they are in; what they're doing; their road target, how they are doing it; how extreme they are willing to take it. You can be really wild on the road. But they not be good about money – you could just be reckless. That's not good for business. Or you could be really about money and really on top of this and no-one is taking this from you and it's dead evident that you are doing this by yourself – not cos you've got everyone else involved. But cos you're on it – it's about the money, making money, still holding yourself down and not disrespecting anybody – they're the ones who will end up there.' (African Caribbean female independent operator)

Auditioning and testing

Olders and elders manage the transition of younger members to a higher tier through auditioning and testing. This is essentially a conservation strategy on the part of incumbents in positions of field seniority, but it also maintains social order. Numerous examples were evident in my research in SW9, with olders testing youngers through involvement in violence. This further helps to test the workings of the social field. Testing is initially centred on developing particularised trust (Field, 2008, p 96), loyalty, a capacity to advance or emotional intelligence.

'Reputation? It goes back to when it's tested. So, it's either tested like, say, in a fight or tested by going to court and winning and tested by the fact that you keep schtum. So if you can hold on to those three, the word will spread. It won't take long for the word to spread.' (African Caribbean male elder)

William Foote Whyte recognised similar criteria in his seminal study of Italian corner boys in *Street corner society* (1943, p 107). Vigil reports that engaging in violent and destructive behaviour generates respect, which ultimately gives 'recognition as a dependable gang member with *huevos* (balls)' (Vigil, 1988b, p 160). Densley (2012b) also recognises testing and trust as key issues in London gangs.

Eventually, through testing, work increases in difficulty and importance. Those who succeed are given more responsibility and more difficult tasks to perform. As one member put it when discussing the drugs business: " 'cause it's not about the crime, it's about how you manage under pressure. So they want to see me under pressure." Or they are given work and asked, "Can you handle that? Deliver this parcel for me!"

> 'You are really being tested by these elders to make sure you can step up to the mark. It's not about how you do it, it's you've got to get away with it.' (African Caribbean male elder)

This testing process takes places across all tiers, illustrating the structural functionalism of the gang. For youngers developing strategies via the expressive repertoire (fighting, criminal damage and antisocial behaviour), the manifest functions (Parsons, 1937) are fun, drama and excitement, but the latent functions are generating street capital and opportunities to compete in the social arena. This competition is both observed and tested within the tier, by peers, as well as in the tier above, with olders testing youngers to establish their competence in the social field and assess skills, loyalty, trust and emerging characteristics. As olders begin to use the instrumental repertoire, elders now test their ability to maintain street capital while assessing their skill to chase money.

At this stage some participants may engage with the Expressive repertoire as they normally do but also now the Instrumental repertoire as they are increasingly tested by olders. While the different testing stages are not necessarily clearly distinguished from one another, the overall function is for elders to audition members for eventual transition to the advanced tier. The expressive and instrumental repertoires thus represent two stages of the auditioning process. This concept was aired in the 1920s by Zorbaugh (1929) and more recently by Hagedorn (2008). The auditioning process relates to all types of street gang activity. A member aged 21 who remains affiliated to a gang has established street capital, a pedigree, an extensive network, knowledge of life 'on the road', a specialism from the repertoire and a brand signature. Some members are viewed as long-term investments, receiving inducements and mentoring, while others fall by the wayside – collateral damage in a system of winners and losers.

Using social skill to maintain social order

Central to maintaining social order in any social field is social skill (Fligstein and McAdam 2012, pp 47-53). In the gang, social skill is central to group formation and structuring of strategic action. As it is often learned over time, the use of social skill tends to favour incumbents and conservationists, that is, elders and olders. It is essentially the gift of reading individuals, groups and situations, offering visions of the future, articulating actions and their meanings, and mobilising the emotions and actions of others. From its roots in symbolic interactionism (Mead, 1934; Goffman, 1959, 1974), the concept of social skill centres on 'meaning making' and communication. Some actors are skilled at social empathy and understanding others' social position, dilemma or feelings. In such ways they help construct shared meanings and identities, which in turn are used to generate collective action. Within the gang, incumbent skilled strategic actors use their skill to maintain group solidarity, to sustain and affirm shared identities that undergird the collective. Challengers will seek to identify and 'exploit emerging vulnerabilities they discern in their opponents' (Fligstein and McAdam, 2012, p 48). It is imperative that no weaknesses are discernible to potential challengers, even if violence is needed to maintain this position.

Action in the field depends on field position and opportunity, as well as an ability to mobilise others, to motivate, to provide meaning and to clarify purpose. The theory of street capital provides the framework for this, but it is the gang itself that provides opportunities for collective action, and when it does the rewards are multiplied and shared.

Leading and mentoring

The role of leader is of key importance in determining advancement within the social field and in maintaining order. Skilled leaders try to frame narratives that appeal to others (Goffman, 1974). Skilled social actors try to establish a 'resonant collective identity' where variant desires, ambitions and preferences are reordered and refocused into a 'common collective project' (Ansell, 2001, p 52). Indeed, these actors may have several different narrative versions on the go at any one time and only need to achieve success in one of them.

Leadership within the gang takes on different forms at each level. At the elementary tier, leadership often comes through popularity or ingenuity, while others rise to the top through a capacity for violence or fearlessness.

Members seldom identify themselves as leaders, but they will be recognised as such by others. Advertising the fact on Facebook will only attract police attention. Some members shy away from admitting that they are leaders even within the gang and are careful not to inadvertently create evidence and thus incriminate themselves. Those members who have been arrested have often gained useful insight into avoiding unwanted attention in their dealings with the police and criminal justice systems.

By the time they have been admitted to the mature tier, leaders are respected (a named brand), are well connected and are making money. They may be approached or nominated by other members to undertake serious high-value crimes such as armed commercial robberies.

Olders may mentor youngers in street socialisation and social norms, and in how to employ the network and the repertoire. The process strengthens trust between the two parties, while securing the older's position, allowing the younger to market his reputation for him and build his street capital. The younger also gains from the relationship, as the older is often the only adult who has ever taken an active interest in them, offering guidance, direction, support, discipline, leadership and parental advice. Such support and direction may be meaningful and useful.

Elders demonstrate an ability to judge situations and guide actions or responses, often exploiting opportunities to expand their network and links with families by offering support or protection. As Whyte notes, 'his capacity for social movement is greater' (Whyte, 1943, p 259-60). By designating an individual or a family as 'my people', the elder extends a protective arm. In return, he will be treated like extended family, receiving invitations to family events, and offers of 'help', such as providing hiding places for stolen goods or drugs.

Adaptability: social skill

Leaders are also skilled at the adaptation and reflexive use of strategies: skills they use to help maintain the social order of the gang, such as switching mobile phones, using discardable pay-as-you-go phones and changing SIM cards regularly. One older questioned by police on his estate was able to quote, in detail, aspects of the Police and Criminal Evidence Act. He also claimed to pass this knowledge on to his youngers so that they would know the law and their rights. Many police officers and professionals in this research identified examples of strategic action that signify considerable intelligence, organisation and skill. The police reported considerable adaptability, acknowledging that it is a 'very dynamic situation with these boys'.

Professionals reported examples of the ABM gang orchestrating their movements to tie up police resources in one part of the estate to distract from gang activity elsewhere, thereby allowing olders to shift drugs, cash or weapons unnoticed. This suggests strong links between olders and youngers. Another example of members controlling the environment in this way includes the use of continual antisocial behaviour so that residents become demoralised and less vigilant, and the constant flow of people to and from estates enables drug dealers to blend in more easily. Gang strategy is also determined by external events. If the police flood an area with officers after a murder or shooting, for example, the gang responds by lying low for several days; if the police alter their policing strategy, the gang alters theirs.

Harmonising and dialogue

Not everything occurring in the neighbourhood happens because of the strategic action of gang affiliates. Moreover, different individual strategies are in motion at the same time as gang strategies. Both these facts make the neighbourhood environment more chaotic.

Elders may therefore seek to maintain social order by harmonising members' personal strategies with gang strategies. For example, when an individual leaves home and moves into rented accommodation, a sudden need to raise funds for rent may coincide with the gang's desire to sell drugs. The efficacy of any strategic action is contingent on:

• the strategies employed by others;
• the variables employed for the strategy;
• the impact of the strategy on other actors (externalities);
• unforeseen events.

Strategies are thus often employed in a constant state of flux. This has the potential to weaken social order and possibly create chaos.

To address this potential for strategic action to go awry, the gang needs to constantly:

• re-evaluate all current activity via (informal) meetings;
• monitor street capital and brand profile (How big is the gang's name? Is there a buzz? Is street capital rising or falling?);
• ensure that the gang brand remains durable, fresh and alluring to new recruits. A strong gang history and connectivity to local history

and culture helps, as does brand recognition, strong leadership, opportunities for individual strategies, ability to change direction, flexibility and adaptability;

- reconsider alliances and gang/individual strategies by grading/assessing incoming information. This process may lead to realignment of alliances with an individual or group of gang;
- maintain close links into the network and maintain constant communication;
- update knowledge banks with new information about members, incidents, other gangs and external events.

This requires constant planning, strategy development and dialogue through regular meetings, something that the police in SW9 have described as 'a lot of dynamic movements here on a daily basis'.

New players, new rules and side bets

Change

As field incumbents, elders have an interest in maintaining social order and the status quo. Doing so protects their investment and generates lucrative business conditions. Despite attempts to maintain social order, however, the social field is in a permanent state of flux, as actors jostle to improve their field position. This low-level 'turbulence' (Fligstein and McAdam, 2012, p 21) permits actors to utilise their social skill to either 'weather the storm' or inch forward, i.e. to either maintain or improve their position. Challengers use different strategies partly to survive a situation that disfavours them and partly to improve their advantage while reducing the dependence on their superiors. Thus even in the most stable fields there is always turbulence and occasionally a crisis of contestation.

> 'Probably in a lot of gangs, there is always the main guy and under him, his best friend. There's always someone who wants to be the main guy. So this person will try and be the main guy but the main guy has too much respect. So he will try and form his own gang. A lot of arguments happen, a lot of falling out so they will set up their own gang and do their own thing. There is a lot of falling out within the gang.' (West African male older)

In this field of struggle, new entrants seek to reach dominant positions, while challengers, believing they have little to gain from dominant seniors, employ subversion strategies. This opens up the possibility that the social field of the gang is so volatile because the actors themselves are frequently and purposefully trying to generate advancement opportunities; it is in their interests to make the field as convulsive as possible. This can be seen in gang incursions (see Chapter Eight), which may cause convulsive moments in rival gangs while generating opportunities in the main gang for the perpetrators.

Fligstein and McAdam (2012, p 83) believe that real change only ever occurs within fields transformed through moments of crisis that have a destabilising effect, such as the arrest of a gang leader. Such events are often caused by external factors arising from outside the social field. Now the field rules will be up for grabs and those challengers who are innovators or entrepreneurs will make their bid for leadership and change. Fligstein and McAdam suggest that it is possible to detect when a social field is in crisis, with incumbents experiencing difficulty in reproducing their privilege as the rules either no longer work, or begin to change.

These 'convulsive moments' (Fligstein and McAdam, 2012, p 54) provide the potential for new innovative action with new opportunities being seized by challengers offering new visions and alternative solutions. This may result in new coalitions or even new social fields emerging. During convulsive moments challengers try to improve their field position. An aspirant young leader may break away to form a new gang that may or may not retain close links to the maternal gang. In such an event, the individual strategy of a forceful and dominant younger supersedes the gang strategy. The pursuit of such 'investment strategies' (Swartz, 1997, p 124) may lead to gang fracturing (Whyte, 1943, pp 78-86).

Fracturing

Fracturing is a notable feature of gangs in SW9, with clear examples occurring throughout the period 2005-12. Fracturing occurs following a moment of crisis, when a gang divides or breaks up into a collection of smaller, newer gangs. Allegiances are tested when members decide to create a new gang. This leaves others with the option to remain in a depleted version of the original gang, join in the newly created gang or merge with gangs already established. Three key factors appear to be involved: a trigger incident, a transition or a challenge.

A trigger incident is usually an action taken by or against a leader or leadership group. William Foote Whyte noted that 'abrupt and drastic changes destroy the equilibrium' of the gang (Whyte, 1943, p 263). Leadership may be 'decapitated' as a result of a key leader being taken into custody, a significant death or a strategic action by incumbents going badly wrong with dramatically unexpected outcomes, such as the wrong person being killed. This has a significant impact on the established gang, resulting in a 'general realignment' (Whyte, 1943, p 41). Fligstein and McAdam (2012, p 99) refer to this as an 'exogenous shock', noting that such events usually occur from outside the social field in proximate fields, for example, a police raid.

Following the crisis event, a challenge will arise. In his study of gangs in Italian slums, Whyte noted that 'the positions of members are interdependent, and one position cannot change without causing some adjustments in other position' (Whyte, 1943, p 263). A challenge may be triggered by a rising star who sees his moment to shine – a charismatic and 'wild' younger who has the support of several other youngers.

A neighbourhood gang may fracture if the leaders are unable to harmonise individual strategies to a common purpose. It is possible that the crisis event will open up the floodgates to generalised group dissent from youngers who are anxious to improve their field position and may view olders as having failed to deliver. At this volatile younger level, it is easy for gangs to split. Internal disputes, disappointments and disagreements generate alternative strategies that some youngers believe they can employ. At these moments of crisis, the social skill of actors becomes important – the ability to frame a new vision, to learn from failures, or to block or counter an opponent's vision or a detractor's comments.

A new leader or group of leaders will emerge, marketing a new brand, developing their own gang strategy with their own moniker, signature style and network. This 'new improved brand' often claims to be 'bigger, bolder and badder' than before. Indeed, the new gang may well quickly develop strategies to prove this point, thus increasing the possibility of further localised violence.

A trigger event may also occur during a period of transition, as a result of a bad decision by a key individual or leader or a failure to make a decision. Either way others within the gang may seize the opportunity to create something over which they will have more control.

Following a fracture, the new gang may negotiate with the original gang, perhaps acting as their youngers. There are possible benefits to both tiers here. The split allows youngers to engage actively in the expressive repertoire, building their own businesses and networks. Elders may seek to alter the direction of the established gang or to merge with another brand. Police focus on a newly established younger version of the gang allows members of the mature/advanced tier to recede into the shadow. Another possible outcome, as has reputedly been the case with the Roadside G gang, is that the mature/advanced tier will consolidate its older members and specialise in more highly criminalised activity that is less visible but more violent.

During such periods of change, uncertainty or transition, gangs may appear to go into abeyance or decline. This may be temporary until a new direction and energy is found. It may involve recruiting more members to build a new critical mass. New gangs or 'splinter groups' may appear and quickly develop a reputation, although a gang having 'downtime' may continue to promote itself via social networking sites. Appendix D presents a schematic diagram of how one local SW9 gang, Organised Crime (OC), has evolved and fractured over time (see Appendix E for approximate gang locations in SW9, and Appendix F for a timeline of known gangs in SW9).

Interestingly, fragmentation is a recognised downside to social capital's solidarity benefits. Brass and colleagues (1988) writing on social networks have observed that overly strong identification with a focal or sub-group can split the broader grouping as sub-group members become over-embedded in these relationships. In terms of gang dynamics, once such a sub-group has formed, loyalty is generated to this sub-group allowing for potential break away or fracturing.

If a new social field does emerge from the gang fracture, it will require a new settlement (see Chapter Three).

Changing tables

Gang membership and alliances are in constant flux when fracturing occurs and new gangs are formed (in the casino metaphor this can be viewed as changing tables). This inter-changeability occurs when players leave one gang to pursue strategic action elsewhere, perhaps prompted by a belief that they can no longer advance in their former gang or by a move to a new area of London. Some young people move around as a result of being 'snaked' or having sold out their friends and now believe that their individual strategy is best progressed through new allegiances in a different gang. They may have been 'rollin' on a job' on a couple of occasions and found a good fit with the way their new peers employ the gang repertoire. The most common reason for changing gang is falling out over a personal 'beef'.

Normally this occurs when one member 'disrespects' another gang member who then threatens serious violence. The member who has done the disrespecting may then mitigate his risk by moving to another gang. This however will now leave him vulnerable to victimisation from his previous gang members.

Some gangs share members on a regular basis, e.g. The Muslim Boys, OC and PDC, while all identifiable as separate, were also all closely linked through mutable members. This suggests that members were loaned out and shared proactively for mutual benefit. Mutability gives the appearance of disorganisation and this is often misread by casual observers of gangs. It is, however, the result of a logical pursuit of personal interest and represents a trackable investment strategy.

Side bets: quitting the game

Desistence from the gang operates as kind of 'side bet' (Becker, 1964). As members grow older, their individual strategy tends to become more important than their gang strategy and they are more likely to focus on other aspects of adult life – those previously ignored 'side bets' in the casino game of life. This leads members to re-evaluate their current situation, to risk-assess their current personal safety and to consider their future life trajectory. This often brings a realisation that they must reduce their involvement or sever ties completely. Those able to maintain this new strategy often have family support or have academic or sporting promise. Farrell and Calverley (2006) note that offenders may desist, i.e., leave the gang if they can identify a 'future me'. Essentially, this means a new social fate.

Leaving can be a difficult concept for other gang members to understand and it instantly breeds suspicion. Ebaugh (1988) notes desistance is problematic as others still expect you to behave in a particular way. Often this means those who express a desire to leave remain in the social field and thus continue to be viewed as players.

Those who do wish to leave will therefore find it hard to do so, partly because of threats from peers but mostly because if they are successful in following this strategy, there are many centripetal forces pulling them back in:

> 'A lot of people are still stuck in it. It's hard to come out.'
> (African Caribbean male older)

Moreover, incumbents keen to keep the status quo and maintain social order must manage those seeking to leave the gang. Confidences and trust must be maintained to avoid damage to the gang brand and reputation and this is best achieved by ensuring that allegiance to the gang endures. Many members are therefore forced to stay in the gang, unless they leave the city altogether. Network contacts and connections are so deeply intertwined and ingrained that it makes leaving not only difficult but sometimes impossible.

Most members who wish to leave do so by negotiating a different relationship or different boundaries with the gang, making clear what they are prepared to do and when. This can develop into a part-time approach to gang involvement which ultimately may allow them to 'leave' by inactivity. Some members develop a part-time relationship with the gang, perhaps when they are trying to move into education or employment:

> 'I've got a mate driving buses if he's not got enough money, he'll go back in short term to get money then go back in legit. He'd go back in just to get the money he needs or when he's struggling.' (West African male older)

If this strategy is interrupted or money dries up, the gang may again become an option. Throughout this period they remain networked to the gang, retaining links to the centre. Returning routes include selling drugs, buying and selling stolen goods, and hiding weapons. Continued residency on the same estate makes negotiating different boundaries problematic or even impossible. Even those negotiating different boundaries stay a part of the network and remain in close communication with remaining members.

In gang life, friends play a critical role in providing information that is imperative to one's personal risk management. According to some sources (MoJ, 2011), this creates many taboos around the issue of leaving, although Aldridge and Medina (2008) have found that 'generally, gangs did not oppose desistance from members'. Densley (2013, p 137) notes that desistence comes with maturation, but points out that 'retirees' are constantly monitored.

Some members find it almost impossible to leave the gang when the strategies of other players involve them in criminal activity. There are examples of members finding an exit route through youth work, although as one police officer from this research found, some tread a fine line between having left the gang and still being affiliated:

'I saw one youth worker with his arm round a 12-year-old saying, "Can you sort this deal out for me?", even though he's training.' (White male police officer)

Professional youth workers may advise young people in this situation to break all ties with the gang, but as one worker in this research noted, "Even though they want out there's often too much pulling them back in." Clearly many young people attempt to leave, but are drawn back in by a 'hook' – an issue of importance, sometimes serious, relating to current or recent friendships, 'bredrin' (breathren/brothers), emotional ties, feelings of honour or duty, family or extended family links.

In Chapter Six, I expand this theory further by considering how players play the game and in particular how they both generate and keep their street capital.

SIX

Playing the game: generating and keeping your chips

'First it's kicks, then it's money.'
West African male older

Playing 'the game'

The stages of 'the game' are readily understood by all in the social field. As determined by the habitus, the rules are firmly established and quickly become known to prospective players. Actors in the social field must first accumulate starting chips. They are then invited to join 'the game'. In the gang social field of SW9, those about to join the gang must first generate respect. They must then quickly manufacture street capital by developing a reputation. Establishing a reputation in the social field permits entry into 'the game'.

> 'When I was in my first gang, the older lot above me were the bruvvas of the group that I was in and then there was a younger lot behind me. And I'm not established in this group, I'm new. No-one knows who I am. So, what happened was something came up and everybody run and I didn't. I just stayed there and run at 'em, run at the crew. Everyone was like, "He's a nutter!" That was it, it was just like, that's it, the end of the line, man. That's it, I'm freelancing. I'm in the "cools" now. So now I'm working for the bigger group. So I've gone from here to working for the bigger group as I've established my leadership qualities amongst my peer pressure. So now, I'm working for the bigger group, getting bigger vibes and betting brought into bigger situations.' (African Caribbean male elder)

New starters will be severely tested during this process. They select from a range of strategies in the expressive repertoire. Initial strategies include personal branding and evidencing your new gang affiliation (for example, wearing colours) before graduating to strategic action affects the wider community. During this process, the players test the repertoire and also the boundaries of the social field.

Once this part of 'the game' has been successfully completed, players may then 'move up' to the next level. This is the stage of maximising street capital. Here players exhibit strong or profound attachments to the gang and its 'endz'. Goods acquired through strategic action may now be actively sold within the community to generate further street capital.

Once street capital is manufactured, it must be maintained through strategic action using the instrumental repertoire. Two key strategies – street robbery and drug dealing – act as entry points for those transitioning from the expressive repertoire to the instrumental repertoire. Here players cut their teeth with olders, generating low-level economic capital alongside street capital. Finally, all players must constantly monitor their street capital within the social field.

I shall now explore each of these strategy sequences in more detail.

Getting started in the game: earning respect

To become a 'playa' in the gang, you have to begin with your allotted handful of chips – your accumulated capital resources. The level and weight of your chips will initially determine the amount of respect due to you on the street. This is your starting hand of street capital – it will now be up to you to play the game and in so doing increase or decrease your street capital. Those with few starting chips must earn respect quickly.

> 'It comes gradually. For me my English was not strong so I affiliated with cool kids and I had to prove myself. It happened subconsciously for me. When opportunities presented themselves I jumped in – mostly fighting. I beat up one guy so much by next day it was – don't mess with that guy. They all knew. Then younger kids wanted to know me. If this happens in school imagine how much more this is on road – there are no boundaries on road, no one will exclude you for fighting or suspend you. You win, you lose, you carry on. So it could be a gradual building of a reputation – but if you do something extreme, then your reputation goes up in an extreme way. There is a replication or mirror effect. We always looked for a fight. Who can knock out someone with a first punch. But then I needed

a reason to do it; so you need to justify your actions.' (West African male older)

At the time of this research, professionals described the concept of respect as being a key issue: 'They are steeped in this; it surrounds them all the time.' Young gang members described it as a current issue: 'Yeah, it's a big deal right now at the moment' and 'Yes, very much. It's always been so. It is the key to it all.' It is widely acknowledged that people understand this concept from an early age (Anderson, 1999; Winlow, 2001; Yates, 2006).

Respect has to be earned, and some acquire it more quickly than others. Background, history and physicality increase one's chances of gaining and retaining respect. It is about both actions and attitude. Respect is temporal and needs to be constantly reinforced and re-established. The attributes that allow respect to be conferred relate directly to the habitus and social field:

> 'I'd respect him, but he'd have to have some attribute that would back me off. If he doesn't have that, he's gonna find it very difficult to get that street recognition. 'Cos street recognition is based on competitiveness, aggression, athleticism, physicality, the gait, you know, it's all part of it.' (African Caribbean male older)

For many, winning respect is a long process that occurs over time:

> 'There were people I grew up with whose name wasn't ringing back in the day, but their names is ringing now. But I know they always had it in 'em. They just weren't as popular as some others. A couple of people I grew up with would've done more wicked things, they always had potential – and they have rose to power now. Now they are there where they wanna be. It was always in them.' (African Caribbean male older)

Even once you are affiliated to the gang, the process of gaining respect must be carefully maintained. To get respect, members must:

• be well connected;
• be associated with an established elder;
• have a brand name;
• have a signature style;

- be loyal – "I could do anything to anyone and I know that my boys have got my back" (African Caribbean male older);
- be a hard man (a 'badman') – "There are people I know who are working now for years. But if they ever got in on the road thing, they'd make the papers 'cos they are bad" (African Caribbean male older); "Once you have a 'badman' reputation, no one will make a move against you, the worse you are as a bad person the bigger the rep" (police officer);
- be 'wild' – "You have to have that wild thing. Be wild. Be seen to be wild. Certain people just have that wild thing about them. You just don't care. It's all about the business. You don't care. Some people just see that in you. I don't care" (African Caribbean male older);
- have the courage not to back down/have stamina – "You know how people are built. But I've seen certain people rise to it. Certain people earn their respect. They've been the little prick, the donut at one stage – but no longer" (African Caribbean male older);
- be reputable in business – "You've got to be known for delivering when required and bringing it" (African Caribbean male older);
- be unpredictable – "Those who are difficult to read will always be viewed as unpredictable. Others will keep a lid on emotions until they blow" (African Caribbean male elder); "I've got friends who wouldn't have no gun around them. 'Cos they say, 'the way my mind works is just one little thing and I'd like blow-up', so it's best to keep it away bruv" (African Caribbean male older);
- be cool – "I can be cool, but there's a wicked side to me. Certain people may disrespect me but they'll be looking over their shoulder for me. There are some loose cannons out there now" (ex-older).

Failing to allocate respect to someone 'on road' indicates that you fail to appreciate his street capital and this indicates a challenge. It then becomes his duty to make you understand and appreciate lest you challenge him or take him for granted. Demonstrating your 'failure' to understand his street capital value implies limited knowledge of the street code indicating that you are 'green', new or unschooled. This marks you out as potentially 'soft' and likely to be targeted. Thus the social skill of conferring instant and ongoing recognition of others' status is essential, as it quickly defines your ability to 'read' levels of street capital, demonstrates your street skill and sets the template by which you are 'ranked'. Alternatively, if you demonstrate an ability to 'read rank' and then wilfully display disrespect, you present a challenge. A key example of this is the 'visual bump' (Katz, 1988, p 110), also known in Brixton as 'screwing'[1] (Sanders, 2005), which can act as a trigger for violence.

Some elders claim that many young people want respect but have not earned it; this occurs both within and outside the social field of the gang. Conversely, social skill in managing respect opens up opportunities for those seeking to build bridging social capital. If one is considered to be well versed in aspects of respect and street code, one is respectful of both local and personal boundaries. Such people demonstrate social skill and become ideal candidates to deal drugs 'up country', as they are more able to recognise the boundaries of other social fields and act accordingly and respectfully.

In the gang, respect is often allocated for reasons that would be considered as perverse outside the gang social field:

> 'They have to fight too. They have to use all the right gestures and language, loud voice, frightening speech. It builds rep. Or two or three girls hanging around to show he's the daddy. Or wearing all the proper gear to show he's cool, trendy or he smokes the right things – stronger joints, always has some on him. Talks to girls like dirt. Girls will follow. Then they envy him and respect him.' (Turkish female resident)

This relates directly to the habitus and the tested repertoire that has proven successful in acquiring street capital. For example, shooting someone in a public place in an innovative or daring fashion, such as during a drive-by on a motorbike, will achieve kudos.

Violation (disrespect)

Showing disrespect is considered to be a 'violation'. Outside the gang's social field, violation is considered physical interference or even sexual penetration. Within the social field it is viewed as desecration of something sacred, a personal outrage or spoliation of street capital. Such transgressions are viewed as purposeful and deliberate acts because all actors in the social field are expected to know how the game is played. What may appear to someone outside the social field to be a minor infringement may be viewed within the gang as a major violation. Those operating in the social field will put their lives at risk to defend their reputation and prevent their street capital from falling:

'Dissing? From their gang member point of view they are interfering with how they can progress through their criminal ranks to earn more money and get higher status. If they are constantly disrespected, then they are not going to get their higher status.' (African Caribbean male police officer)

Members may also be seen to display disrespect by spreading rumours via the sanctions repertoire. This may include seemingly minor transgressions such as repeating another person's accusation that a member is 'moist' (a derogatory term meaning soft, or an easy target). This is considered to be enough to reduce street capital and warrant a confrontation or retaliation, which can lead to serious violence. Sandberg and Pederson (2011) identified similar findings in their study of drug dealers in Norway.

Declining levels of respect for olders and adults

During this research, older and ex-gang members in SW9 pointed out that over the past five or six years there had been a change in how respect was seen and used as a tradable commodity. One described the reaction that used to be caused by mentioning that you were affiliated to the PDC gang, compared with the one it would generate today:

'No one could talk to you or touch you. They looked up to you. Now you can't say to people I'm in this crew and expect them to leave you alone or to respect you. For these young people will say, "I don't give a fuck who you are, it doesn't mean nuttin' to me."' (African Caribbean female independent operator)

Some professionals and ex-gang members also noted a reduction in the level of respect shown towards older adults:

'You might have been terrorised by certain people at first, but you hold it in. Then you get bigger, older. Then you turn on them. Certain people have got pain 'cos of what they've been through and how they've held it in. And they just end up being wilder than the rest. There's a lot of man out there like that, a lot of one-man armies.' (African Caribbean male older)

The levels of deference formally held towards adults in the social field regarding their authority and community standing is now much more limited and conditional. Densley (2013) also identified a decline in respect for olders and adults. For those adults who operate outside the social field of the gang there appears to be no significant change, however challenging a gang member or remonstrating with them will make them viable targets.

> 'It's different now. They still do respect some adults sometimes but it is limited. It's not as it used to be. People are sliding. Now, if Mum pulls him away, you'd bring it to her – "Who are you to speak to me?" So that is kinda changing a bit now with respect to the elders.' (African Caribbean Female independent operator)

Street name and brand names

Adopting a nickname is part of youth culture and growing up. Within the gang's social field, it allows for the creation of a second self or second life (Presdee, 2000), possibly signifying 'on road' participation to peers. Once adopted, it permits any illegal activities to be ascribed to the street persona. Crucially, this persona enables entry to 'the game', or the pursuit of street capital. Your street name is the one you want others to recognise; it is something to market, to build a reputation around. Often chosen or allocated by peers, there are different types of name:

- early adopted names – a new arrival may choose or be given a name illustrating his character, for example, 'Sneaky';
- expressive names, signifying an individual's role in expressive crime, such as 'Blades' or 'Pulla';
- brand names, conferring protection and demonstrating links to contacts and networks;
- pre-fixed brand names that link into another brand name.

Most names are retained throughout a member's gang career, as they become synonymous with reputation:

> 'There are some names they can use and if uttered people will run off.' (African Caribbean male younger)

Youngers actively seek affiliation with known brand names:

'If you are Serious Guy younger, then you are cool. You are connected. A lot of people connected to them feel untouchable as well. So they'll join the gang to be untouchable in school. Certain people converted to Islam a year or two ago to prevent themselves from being robbed. For a time that was cool.' (African Caribbean male older)

Acquiring a brand name brings desired outcomes, notably being feared:

'My rep was always physicality and stamina. I would keep coming, keep coming, keep coming. That is where the reputation starts kicking in.' (African Caribbean male elder)

Achieving brand name celebrity maximises street capital while increasing demand for your services. Big brand names travel beyond the social field and network. They may reduce victimisation or increase challenges, bringing empowerment. For many they enhance the ego, implying connections, access to the finest cars, the biggest crib, the most beautiful women and the most money. These are the things that bring the most elusive element of street capital – 'cool'.

Prefixes

A prefix is often added to an established name, providing advantages for the adopter (younger) and the provider (older). It provides instant connectivity to 'street' or neighbourhood history, demonstrating high bonding capital. It confers street capital, establishing you in the street hierarchy, and giving youngers access to the fast track, permitting them to trade on olders' reputations – a way of saying, "I am connected so don't fuck with me." It may also bring unforeseen challenges if viewed as a lazy way of getting a reputation. For this reason, prefixes are often used by close family connections to strengthen the family brand.

For the provider (older), a prefix boosts status and field position, implying that his brand is worth buying into and his contacts desirable. It may even generate brand durability or dynastic aspirations. Prefixes denote an unwritten contract whereby olders extend brand designation, offering protection to youngers. This process defines the older's role as leader. The follower (i.e. the younger) now takes advantage of strengthened connections to the upper tier, including elders, for example, calling for assistance if required. Moreover, if providers are asked regularly to intervene on behalf of youngers, it becomes more difficult for them to leave the gang, thereby permitting the social field to replicate itself.

Prefixing also applies to girls and young women, permitting association with senior members and indicating connections. Male gang members describe this as being 'taken', with the girl becoming the 'property' of the name provider. This defined association provides a trade platform for girls that may improve the girls' access to goods and services or to higher-grade confidential information. Designations are valued, documented and reflected in social networking sites. Some names imply certain role, for example, 'Wifey'. Others, such as 'Lady' or 'Queen', aspire to street royalty.

Rented names

A recent development is for an older who is temporarily leaving the social field, or becoming less active because of, say, starting a family, to 'rent' out his name. This arrangement protects the adopter, while providing the older with a 'kick back' or some type of reciprocal 'payment', in the form of either goods or services:

> 'I look after you – but I want a kick back. This will be protection if you are troubled. I will get them. If I want to rob a shop or something, you could do it for me. If I need to get someone stabbed you could do it for me.' (West African male older)

For Bourdieu, this represents self-interest. Such 'gift exchange' may also represent deferred favours and actors may misperceive the objective consequences of their actions. Depending on the status and reputation of the rented name, this may also represent symbolic capital – the legitimation of power relations through symbolic forms (Swartz, 1997, pp 91-2).

Establishing a reputation as a 'playa'

Creating and maintaining a reputation ('rep') in this social field was uniquely singled out by all research participants as 'a massive issue', as 'very, very, very, important' by professionals, and as 'the key to it all' or 'everything' by youngers. The process becomes the first real test of the social field. It sorts those able to manufacture a reputation (street capital) from those who cannot. Having a reputation increases the likelihood of being approached to affiliate as a player in the social field.

It signifies your playing rights, allowing you to enter 'the game', to be part of something and to be accepted. This then allows you to play at a higher level, take control of your destiny and develop strategies to build your reputation. It reduces the threat of oblivion or victimisation as an outcast, and increases opportunities for advancement and distinction.

In *Street boys* (Pritchard, 2008, p 224), a biographical account of gang life in SW9, a 15-year-old younger called Tempman seeks to build 'his own name' by targeting boys with a bigger name than his: 'If other people had a name I took an instant dislike. I'd move to them and beat them up in front of their girlfriend and take money off them.'

Individual stocks of street capital are monitored by having a recognisable reputation in which you and others can invest. This will build on your street persona. It may be created and nurtured in both the virtual and the real world. As you invest more and more time and energy in maintaining it, it becomes indistinguishable from you. It embodies your character and persona, and gives life to your street capital. It signifies your bonding or bridging social capital, becoming a trademark extending well beyond the boundaries of the social field. It can even be your passport to celebrity status or your passport out.

If you fail to have a reputation, you will be victimised, designated an outcast, perceived as weak and ultimately victimised by 'everyone'. Young people in the social field are often challenged to account for themselves by listing their named contacts. A failure to know the 'right people' or the brand names that confer credibility brings the designation 'waste man' – someone who is dispensable, unconnected, or a wannabe. This designation invites victimisation for fun. Anyone seeking opportune moments to increase their street capital will view this as a free gift. It is therefore important to manage this risk by acquiring a reputation. This then acts as a defence mechanism that insures against future violence and victimisation.

Having a reputation also expedites offers of affiliation. To join the gang, you need a reputation. To be invited to join, you need a reputation. To stay involved, you need a reputation. To avoid falling or sliding, you need a reputation. Survival in the social field, and the demands of the street code, conspire to reinforce the imperative of a reputation.

As you ascend within the social field, olders might seek your association. Such an approach requires a reputation. Reputation also offers the benefits of establishing leadership. In this social field, a leader is determined by attributes other than age; he could be the youngest operative in the peer group. The role of leader is more likely to be determined by reputation and demeanour. If your name is out there, the offers will come, although it appears that reputation is no longer enough in itself, and that a potential leader must be a proven 'badman' (Anderson, 1999; Winlow, 2001; Hagerdorn, 2008). Once you have a 'badman' reputation, no one will make a move against you – as one respondent put it "the worse you are as a bad person, the bigger the rep".

Reputations for youngers

Most youngers build up a reputation gradually, often through violence. Yablonsky (1962), Whyte (1943), Pearson (1983) and Sanders (2005) all noted the importance of violence in establishing a reputation. For youngers it is fighting rather than the commercial activity of selling drugs that earns respect and reputation. Physical violence is therefore their principal strategy for earning street capital (Box 6.1).

Box 6.1: Physical violence

Physical violence is a common element of the social field of many deprived/ disadvantaged neighbourhoods (Winlow, 2001). However, in the social field of the gang, it is ubiquitous and normalised. Aldridge and Medina found that 'most violence emanated from interpersonal disputes, often about friends, family and romantic relationships ... jealousy and debt' (2008, p 19) rather than drug disputes. Aldridge and Medina (2008) also found that 'gang members did not specialise in violence, but that violence played an important role, particularly in symbolism and rhetoric' (p 18). However, they present no evidence as to how, why and when violence is used.

Similarly, researchers sometimes mis-recognise violent interpersonal disputes (Hallsworth and Duffy, 2010; Hallsworth, 2013) as evidence that most violence occurs outside the gang. Viewing such incidents through the lens of the social field clarifies that many such incidents *do* actually occur within the social field of the gang. I argue that violence is employed strategically by all tiers of the gang. Some strategies may be individualistic at the time, but they remain contextualised, bounded and determined by the imperatives of the social field. Violence is central to maintaining reputation, building name brands and maintaining respect. Violent rhetoric is ubiquitous and hyperbolic. This is most commonly seen on YouTube and social networking sites. Youngers struggling to build street capital employ strategies of physical violence more readily. For them it is both normative and casual.

One key factor in increased violence within the gang is that physical violence is the preferred strategy for building rep, raising street capital and employing sanctions.

The tripartite use of this strategy results in a social field where youngers describe violence as 'constant' and 'unpredictable'. To those outside the field, such activity is seen as 'random' and 'volatile', as in an incident in December 2010 when four young men were seriously injured in a drive-by machine gun attack in SW9 while tending to a man who had been stabbed in the street.

Violence can be, and is, used between young men and young women; the habitus permits its use. Previously held social norms that such action was not permissible have long since evaporated (Firmen, 2010). Physical violence is also the sanction of choice for those using the expressive repertoire, as one SW9 younger said: "There is a lot of stabbing in the bum – to me that's more of a warning than a deliberate act to take someone out." However slight this might seem, such actions will still generate street capital according to the logic of this social field. For those of us outside the social field of the gang such acts are characterised as random and senseless.

As a strategy, physical violence underpins all the verbal threats and intimidation offered by gang members. It is used as a strategy of first resort for youngers, more sparingly by olders and even less so by elders. It is said that 'olders keep violence in the hidden contract':

> "Cos they know they can't go to the police. 'Cos there is a hidden contract and code that everyone knows. You know you can get that vibe. People say to me, "How come your missus doesn't get any problems?" I say, "She keeps violence in the 'hidden contract." 'Cos what happens you get in a partnership with someone who thinks they understand the quid pro quo but when it becomes too difficult what they do is they call the police on you and then you go – "Hold on a second, that's not how it goes, you are not playing the game right!" So that is the hidden contract.' (African Caribbean male elder)

As youngers progress in the social field, olders may ask them to perform favours that, if successfully undertaken, designate them as assets. This reciprocal contract increases street capital for both actors, with the older now acting as PR agent to promote his new asset. This builds trust between the two (at least for the short term) and is acknowledged by gang affiliates. Favouring and gifting is thus a recognised and tested strategy from the sanctions repertoire (see Chapter Thirteen). Two further strategies to build reputation from the expressive repertoire are graffiti and criminal damage (Boxes 6.2 and 6.3).

Box 6.2: Graffiti

Visual controls such as colour, graffiti tagging and murals are used as branding to demonstrate and market gang existence. It is mainly youngers who use these methods via the expressive repertoire. Tagging provides opportunities to generate reputation, status and street capital using artistic flair. It is considered a non-violent way to create status, which accounts for its popularity in some areas (although it can also lead to challenge and attack). Profligacy and daring generate street capital. Tags may signify either individual or gang brands. Until recently, tagging was popular in SW9 to mark territory. Before the advent of social networking sites, tagging was also used occasionally to denounce snitches.

It is widely agreed that the use of graffiti and tagging is significantly decreasing, with brand-name marketing now almost exclusively carried out online via social networking sites.

> 'Graffiti is not such a big thing now. It was, but is not so much now. People also tend to know which gang is where. It used to be that tagging was used to mark the fact that you are entering this territory, but much less so now.' (Professional)

However, graffiti is still used to deface property by way of revenge, and to promote music and CDs made by the gang.

The creation of murals dedicated to the 'fallen soljas' of gangs is increasing. Some claim that this is the result of the influence of Somalian gangs, providing an opportunity for glorification of those 'killed in action'. Murals act a permanent reminder to rivals that the murder gang members will not be tolerated or forgotten and that 'vengeance is coming'. They demonstrate to prospective and current gang members that memories of their dead peers are being kept alive, and that the gang looks after its own, thus providing further marketing opportunities. Often used as gathering points for reflection, murals offer a platform for continuing to build status and street capital for the deceased, allowing them to enter gang mythology and the Pantheon of the fallen. In this sense, murals represent a form of symbolic capital for the gang – a landmark with symbolic value and utility. A Swartz notes, 'symbolic power is the power to "consecrate" and render sacred' (Swartz, 1997, p 47). It is possible that such sites are designated, either by elders or other members, as sacred. Their removal becomes highly contentious as they become places of local gang pilgrimage. Existing gang members who are close family or 'bredrin' will over time gain additional street capital through association to lionised names and by tending the site. Such murals are now increasingly evident in the cultural lexicon of the urban street gang.

Box 6.3: Criminal damage

Criminal damage is a key component of the expressive repertoire. Like many aspects of expressive crime, it is not solely the premise of urban street gangs. Criminal damage is deemed to be antisocial behaviour and is strongly associated with having fun (Katz, 1988); marking territory by 'wallbangin'', (Phillips, 1999); expressing involvement with Hip-Hop (Phillips, 1999); and with boredom or threatening rivals (Klein, 1995). Sanders (2005), working in Lambeth, found that none of his respondents thought that the tags used at the time were a means of warning rivals or communicating messages, suggesting instead that they were 'acts of transgression' (Katz, 1988). While professionals and residents often cite boredom as a key reason for gangs undertaking criminal damage (Downes, 1966), it is more commonly employed as a strategy to generate street capital. Several locations are frequently targeted for criminal damage:

CCTV

Criminal damage to CCTV and door entry systems is common on estates in SW9. On Moorlands and Myatts Fields estates the CCTV systems were shut down for many months on end. When first installed or commissioned, they are often targeted. Youngers are highly aware of how it works, the location of systems, the range, scope and quality of systems and blind spots are identified. This information is shared.

> 'Yes there have been issues in the past, with CCTV going up in Angell town – the contractors used to pay for police presence 'cos the young people were smashing the cameras and intimidating the staff and so on. So there was a problem there. It depends more on what that person is going to do when they are there. The gang would not be interested in a postman, for instance.' (Professional)

Youngers may also ignore the CCTV and act blatantly in front of cameras. Cameras may also be specifically targeted through the instrumental repertoire to facilitate drug deals and ensure client safety and anonymity in drug dealing. An estate covered in operative cameras will not be favourable to business.

Lighting

Gangs know that if the lights don't work then the cameras don't work either. Lighting wires will be pulled out and disconnected as gangs enter the lamp column covers. Youngers will smash lights and cameras to create a social environment that fits their social field. Criminal damage can be repetitive and persistent. Aside from motivation, such activities are highly impacting for local residents and increases fear of crime.

Door-entry systems

Many communal houses are secured by door entry systems which are often targeted. Key fobs are obtained to allow access to stairwells. Drugs may be stashed in stairwells or laundry drying rooms; however most access is required for youngers to smoke drugs and obtain shelter. Key fobs are often purchased from legitimate residents or they are intimidated into handing them over, leaving the local residents with little choice other than to compromise their own block security system in order to access their premises.

Fast-tracking reputations

In the crowded, contested field of struggle, players must stand out and quickly elevate themselves from their peers. This may be achieved by acting out of the ordinary, employing unusual strategic action outside the social field, or testing the variables of the repertoire. Kudos can come from incidents that may thus appear random. Often, however, these apparently random incidents are deliberate strategic actions aimed at increasing street capital, for example, randomly snatching chains or other accessories worn by other members. Other strategic actions may indicate skill, craft and daring: in one such incident in SW9, a gang obtained a CCTV disc from a control room. Such actions build trust within the gang and this is required to get closer to the top. Filming incidents on mobile phones helps to build the perpetrator's status and earn them street capital.

In a natural progression, violent or 'extreme' acts build reputation and mega-street capital. The bigger the scalp taken, the more kudos gained. Such strategies offer an opportunity to 'fast-track' to a higher tier in the gang. Examples of such violence include an incident in 2008, when a 15-year-old boy entered a McDonald's restaurant in Brixton and shot two young people in broad daylight, and another involving a multiple shooting at a club in Peckham with a MAC-10 pistol.

Youngers may also achieve notoriety by stabbing strangers without provocation. Some professionals or academics refer to this as 'gang initiation', implying that youngers are instructed by older members of the gang to carry out the attack. Such actions are just as likely, however, to be generated by the youngers themselves as strategic action to earn street capital or fast-track a reputation that has stalled. Many professionals believe young people add an extra element of violence to a situation or are 'over-violent' to maximise their reputation.

In the social field, members will know if you have a reputation for violence. You are then expected to act on it lest it be taken away. This also applies to a reputation for selling drugs, although a reputation for violence is more enduring and is tested less frequently. A reputation for extreme violence means you are probably less likely to be called on to fight. Those members reputed for 'craziness' or what Vigil calls the 'locura' (Vigil, 2003) will be given a wide berth. Fligstein and McAdam (2012, p 52) note that actors who are overwhelmingly disruptive or chaotic tend to be isolated, although some skilled social actors use such individuals by proxy to generate a disruptive event on which they can capitalise.

Reputations for olders and elders

Having advanced up the field hierarchy, olders are less interested in expressive crime than instrumental crime. With reputations established, their motivation is now money and generating business opportunities, with enhanced reputations based on economic returns. As one respondent put it, "I would say a 'face' is always based on the money they bring in." Some olders believe their reputation provides them with a passport to travel anywhere unchallenged. This, often false, assumption may lead to them being stabbed while on another estate. Alternatively, their reputation may lead a rival to instigate an attack to 'steal' their street capital and enhance his own.

Elders, as incumbents, command respect for having gained and retained respect. Their instructions are followed, their demeanours studied and copied. If an elder instructs a younger to refrain from a certain activity, for example, 'Stop *that!', don't trouble that house'*, the younger will pay attention and stop. Elders are rarely seen, which creates a certain mystique, thus compounding and enhancing their reputation. Seldom appearing with youngers, their role is mainly one of intervention: to have stolen objects returned; to liaise with the elders of rival gangs; and to negotiate ceasefires and high-level drug deals.

In my research in SW9, elders felt that youngers increasingly accorded them less respect, and that some gang members had 'names' for no apparent reason and were 'unproven', having failed to sufficiently develop their reputation over time.

Gang members moving 'up rank' by building a business and reputation may engage in serious violence to dissuade others from stealing their business or rep. They may also seek support by proxy, from friends or family. This enhances reputation, as does engaging in multiple strategic actions. The police report that some young people view participation in the gang as pursuing their chosen career (Densley and Stevens, 2014, p 17). Thus, anyone who chooses to show disrespect is viewed negatively as simply interfering with the career prospects of the young person and effectively interfering with their progression through the criminal ranks and thus their ability to earn more money and achieve higher status.

Manufacturing a gang rep

Building a shared reputation for the gang is also important in the social field. The gang as the common unit demands its own common identity. Building this identity and reputation becomes a shared experience, allowing group bonding and strategy development. A commitment to the gang demonstrates loyalty and builds bonding and bridging social capital. It also permits incumbents to reproduce their field advantage:

> 'We were definitely aware of building a rep for the gang. Everyone worked towards this. It was important to have a fierce rep 'cos you feel untouchable from other gangs. 'Cos they've heard about you and things you've done and have heard if they did do something to you, what would happen to them. We were working in partnership with other gangs from other estates. They liked what we were doing and wanted to be a part of it.' (African Caribbean male younger)

It is not uncommon for the gang to promote its reputation by shouting the gang's name during the altercation. This creates fear in victims and passers-by:

> 'They'll be happy to say the name of their group, GAS, when there is an incident or an altercation. Someone from GAS gang will shout GAS, GAS aloud in the street creating total havoc, so there is no hiding behind not wanting to be known.' (African Caribbean male, Youth Offending Team officer)

Such a strategy implies a desire to stamp authority on the incident as well as fearlessness and a causal disregard of the potential consequences, both clearly demonstrated in subsequent film footage of the incident on social networking sites. Shover (1996, p 91) notes that young men are 'judged' by their responses to challenges and that violence is 'condoned if not expected' and seen as a 'prime virtue' in this social field.

Such strategic action permits members to market the gang brand, increasing its visibility and affording members some control over its brand, strategic direction and reputation. This may be done to demonstrate ability, capacity, numbers or weaponry (indicating that 'we can do this to you') or establish a unique selling point ('this is what we are known for'). The reputation could be for an individual who will do anything, get anything, possess 'quality weed', or be fearless, armed, loyal, wild or crazy. Some reps, for loyalty for example, are common to many, while others are individualistic, such as a 'wild man' rep.

Establishing a gang as a recognised entity with a physical, virtual and reputational presence means the gang is a player among other gangs across a wider social field, for example, in the case of SW9 this would mean south London. Densley (2012c, p 132, 2013) suggests that signalling theory is used to reinterpret street codes.

A further example of strategic action to raise visual awareness of the gang is the use of designated gang colours (Box 6.4).

Box 6.4: Gang colours

Many people associate gangs with visual symbols such as hoodies, scarves and coloured bandanas (Decker and Van Winkle, 1996). Such signifiers provide a visual presence and shared meaning for the gang, representing key elements of the expressive repertoire. In the elementary tier colours can be important to gang identity. Visual presence maximises street capital, assisting branding and quickly becoming symbolic of gang affiliation. Often used to establish early reputations through a visual representation of 'otherness', colours, as with tattoos, may work to members' advantage or disadvantage. As reputation increases, there is less need to wear colours. Olders are not usually seen in colours, so colours tend to signify a junior field ranking.

Pritchard (2008, p 287) notes that the 'new generation was getting into "colours"'. However, the police quickly became wise to colour coding, leading to increased stop-and-search incidents involving young people. Black clothing is now the regular choice for all gangs and colours are only occasionally introduced. The visual presence of gangs is now the preserve of social networking sites, further reducing the need for colours. Most respondents in SW9 agreed that colours were a phase and 'very 2008'. Sanders (2005) also noted the absence of gang colours in Lambeth.

The increasingly territorial nature of 'postcode beefs' means that those wearing colours are at greater risk of attack. Colours are now mainly worn only during a mass event, an occasion for the gang to demonstrate its visual presence. Such events occur quickly and often involve revenge attacks on rivals or organised fights.

Under the rules of 'the game', the sanction of corrective action can be levied towards any member of a rival gang (a notion widely understood as a field rule). Minimising risk is a key reason for the reduction in wearing 'gang colours'. Gang tattoos are not a feature of the social field of SW9.

Manufacturing a neighbourhood rep

Creating a reputation for the 'endz' (neighbourhood) helps a gang become more established and develop more notoriety. This is similar for recreational gangs, i.e. where young people group together in a gang and engage in recreational violence often fuelled by alcohol (Kintrea, 2008). Many neighbourhoods become associated with or stigmatised by gang affiliations or violence:

> 'Back then, Brixton had a bullet-proof rep. If you came from Brixton, you didn't need a gun. People were in fear anyway. I'd go anywhere and rob a boy of his bike and know that he wouldn't come back on my people. They were scared. Back then I could go by myself anywhere 'cos of my rep. No-one could mess with Brixton.' (African Caribbean male ex-elder)

An established neighbourhood reputation supports a gang reputation. Often reputational branding for the neighbourhood is enhanced by those in proximate social fields, allowing stigma to be turned into emblem (Densley, 2013, p 128). Thus a reputation for the 'endz' provides numerous benefits:

- It implies that the neighbourhood is 'under gang control'. In reality, the gang is bounded by its own social field.
- It recalibrates the social norms where aberrant or extreme behaviour is now 'to be expected', acting as a permissive reputational cloak, permitting behaviours and activities to occur within the neighbourhood that would be out of place elsewhere. When normative behaviours are modified, this supports the gang's 'claim'

that it 'controls the neighbourhood'. For some young people, this becomes a formative narrative.

- It enables gangs to claim responsibility for neighbourhood notoriety, allowing them to lay claim to non-gang-related actions. This is furthered by lazy media reports that blame the gang for all problems within the neighbourhood. In this way, the general public often assumes gangs to be larger than they are.

- It acts as a protective shield for gang affiliates by reducing the number of rivals entering the area, thus reducing potential confrontations. It also alters the way the neighbourhood is policed. Casual police patrolling and community policing is likely to be reduced or withdrawn in favour of targeted intelligence-led swoops that the gang then views as easier to monitor and respond to. Police absence or reluctance to enter the neighbourhood is viewed by gang affiliates as confirmation of the gang's authority or its strategy of reputational dominance.

- It enables expansion into proximate communities, spreading fear and facilitating easier control over some individuals or areas.

- It supports criminal activity, for example, creating an open drugs market. If maintained over time, a reputation may develop its own gravitational pull, for example, for drugs in the case of SW9 (May et al ,2007).

- It means neighbourhoods can become irrevocably associated with the gang's reputation and stigmatised themselves,(Hanley, 2007), as in the case of Angell Town and PDC (Pritchard, 2008).This stigma leads to a flight of business (MacDonald and Marsh, 2005) and contributes to a spiral of decline, increasing further concentration of crime and poverty (Hope, 1998), and of disadvantage (Pitts, 1998). Such circumstances may benefit the gang, providing unchallenged opportunities for it to expand its social field.

For many members, a gang rep or neighbourhood rep is the same thing. Once a reputation for their endz has been established, the gang then views any incursion or violation as intensely personal.

The virtual nature of the rep transcends the boundaries of the social field, potentially blurring them with the boundaries of other social fields. Individual 'reputational reach' depends on one's profile. In traditionally close-knit communities like SW9 and Lambeth, this reach could be considerable and may also stretch into networked contacts elsewhere in London. While residents in the wider community (outsiders) are aware of gang members and their reputations, they are not directly affected or influenced by them unless they enter the social field of the gang.

Strategic action in the wider neighbourhood

Gang members, as strategic actors, are continually developing their reputations and generating more street capital. Actors increasingly seek to expand their visibility or to control public space, by, for example, gathering in groups on tower block stairwells. These highly visible activities are often viewed as threatening by the general public. Several strategic actions in the expressive repertoire allow street capital generation in this way. Examples include control of public space (Box 6.5), use of dogs (Box 6.6) and controlling access to and from estates (Box 6.7).

Box 6.5: Control of public space

For elementary tier gangs, the control of public space is an important strategic action from the expressive repertoire, providing an arena for gangs to demonstrate power and authority locally and market themselves visually. Gangs also assume territorial rights over public spaces adjoining their endz, treating them as localities in which to safely employ strategic action. Public spaces are usually:

- open spaces within or on the estate periphery;
- public shopping streets and quasi-private areas such as shopping malls;
- parks.

Open spaces, public areas and sports courts on or adjacent to an estate are deemed to part of the endz of the peer group or gang affiliated to that estate. This assumed ownership gives local boys rights over usage. Others may visit such spaces, but may not 'take liberties'.

Local shops serving an estate are almost exclusively deemed part of a gang's endz. Beyond this 'front line', public spaces are freely available to all, although some are associated through postcodes with other gangs. It is not uncommon to see groups of ten to 30 gang-affiliated young people hanging out or moving through an area. In this case, low-level antisocial behaviour including littering, play fighting and expressive crime such as criminal damage, is to be expected.

Parks outside an estate are considered to be public areas, although young people from estates may regularly decamp to a park and 'claim' it as their own. Parks further afield are either assumed to be 'open territory' or 'watering holes', where rival gang violence is temporarily suspended, for example Brockwell Park during the Lambeth County Show, or battlegrounds, for example, Larkhall Park in Stockwell, known as the 'killing zone'.[2] Few parks are deemed to be fully 'neutral spaces'. Gang-affiliated young people seldom use such public spaces individually or in small numbers. Some view parks as locations for violence, although altercations may occur seasonally or by chance, when someone is caught 'slippin''. Serious planned violence may also occurs in someone's house, hang-out or recreational venue. The sheer volume of people and noise in these incidents make these gang appearances intimidating, effectively offering the gang 'control' of the space.

Some gangs use public spaces to progress gang or individual strategies, for example, fighting with individuals or groups. Public spaces may also be the arena for large-scale fights among school peer groups that may or may not be gang-related. Brixton High Street has increasingly been the locale for serious acts of violence, including stabbings and fatal shootings. Such events 'raise the veil' surrounding the gang for the general public. Such events are likely to generate fun (Katz, 1988), adrenaline (Presdee, 2000), gang myths[3] and opportunities for filming on personal electronic devices.

Box 6.6: Use of dogs

One fast-track way of acquiring street capital is through the acquisition of large, aggressive dogs that are seen to convey increased status – hence the term 'status dog' (Harding, 2010). While this phenomenon occurs on social housing estates and in parks and high streets all over the UK (RSPCA, 2009), in the social field of the gang it has a particular resonance. 'Tooling up' with an aggressive dog provides opportunities to maximise street capital or to develop strategies to dominate, physically or visually, the open space. This self-evident fact is apparent to gang members. This, and the fact such dogs provide a range of important manifest functions for the gang, has resulted in a recent proliferation of status dogs in SW9 and in Lambeth in general.

> 'At one point it was like everybody on the estate had an ugly dog, a pitbull. I thought my God, you could not go outside. You could not go outside, seriously.' (Turkish female resident)

Fitting both the expressive and instrumental repertoires, dogs are used for street fighting to gain credibility and resolve gang conflicts (Ortiz, 2010). Similarly, 'chain rolling' (i.e. fighting dogs while still kept on the chain or leash) of dogs is evident on estates across the UK (RSPCA, 2009c) and in the social field of the gang in SW9.

Dogs signify a credible threat of violence to others (Daly and Wilson, 1988), while supplementing the physicality of a gang member through its amplified musculature, or what Wacquant called 'crude body capital (Wacquant, 1992). For young men seeking to demonstrate their individuality (Jacobs and Wright, 1999) or to 'get a rush' (Katz, 1988), such dogs act as the perfect foil. To dominate public space as a member of the street elite (Katz, 1988), young men may use dogs to complete their 'cool pose'. In the social field of the gang, dogs now form part of the habitus (Harding, 2010).

In Lambeth in 2009, police targeted known gang members in Operation Navarra. My subsequent analysis of the offending profiles of those gang members who owned dogs (Harding, 2014) illustrated the correlation between ownership of an illegal dog and a history of criminal offending.

I examine this issue in more detail in my book *Unleashed: The phenomenon of status dogs and weapon dogs* (Harding, 2014), in which I identify different motivations for gangs using aggressive or dangerous dogs (see Table 6.1).

Dog fighting also occurs in Lambeth (Lambeth First, 2011) and in SW9, and is recognised by both police and residents:

> 'Oh yeah, dog fighting takes place. We know there's dog fighting going on in the borough – in open spaces and underground garages.' (West African female resident)

In Lambeth, reports of illegal dog fighting rose from eight in 2006 to 118 in 2008, while seizures of dogs involved in dog fights rose from three in 2004 to 64 in 2008 (Harding, 2010). This proliferation has implications for public space. The *Streatham Guardian* (2009) reported that more than 1,000 people were injured in dog attacks in Lambeth in 2008, with 924 injuries occurring in public places. Dog fighting provides strategic action for young men to gamble and build street capital. Recent police activity has driven dog fighting underground and all agree that this activity is now less evident.

Box 6.7: Controlling access to and from estates

Elementary tiers may control or monitor access to and from local estates. A common sight on all estates in SW9 over the past 20 years, this practice has recently altered as a result of 'postcode beefs'.

The practice involves youngers acting as watchmen on balconies, stairwells, walkways, rooftop vantage points and perimeter exits of estates to identify and challenge other young people and provide early warnings of raids and police operations. When warnings are shouted, whistled or sent via mobile phones, and gang members run to prearranged locations – homes, hidden areas, hang-outs or underground garages – where weapons may be secreted. Internal checkpoints within an estate, such as stairwells, may also be used as congregation points for the gang.

If unknown individuals enter the estate, they are challenged and possibly subjected to violence. Controlling access may be covert or overt; it may be done in shifts or only at key times, for example, during a drugs stash or gang 'beef'. Such activity is intimidating for local residents and is the subject of many complaints to the police.

Police incursion on to the estate is considered to be a violation of territory and gang members may retaliate by throwing missiles and so on. Violence is sometimes directed at other people entering the estate, adding to the general atmosphere of intimidation. Such strategic action fits well within the expressive repertoire and is considered by youngers to be great entertainment as well as a gang duty.

In SW9, controlling access to the estates has sometimes been described as the gang patrolling their 'drug patches'. This is a basic mis-recognition of this activity. Patrolling the estates is essentially a risk management strategy to provide early alerts to incursions from rivals and to police activity. Their presence is thus largely related to 'postcode beefs', and only then when a beef is in play or is expected (see Chapter Eight). Access is now mainly controlled through reputation. In relation to drugs, watchmen are only occasionally posted temporarily to oversee the safe transfer of drugs or money.

Table 6.1: Key motivations for gangs using dogs

Motivation	Comment
Protection	In deprived neighbourhoods, dogs are used to provide protection and empowerment alongside risk reduction. Dogs are also used to reduce the risk of victimisation or the threat of attack. Often they are used to intimidate others without a need to be used to attack.
Drugs	Dogs are used to protect dealers, and to guard drugs/money fortresses and places where cannabis is cultivated hydroponically. In the SW9 research, police reported that most known dealers of middle rank retain aggressive dogs.
Breeding	Illegal or irresponsible breeding provides entrepreneurial opportunities (Merton, 1968) for those on benefits. A breeding pitbull can produce 12 puppies, each of which may be sold for £300 to £500. However prices vary with market conditions.
Weapons	Aggressive dogs may be used to attack rivals or the police. Young people in the SW9 research reported that for some young people the crackdown on knives contributed to increased use of dogs: "Sometimes they won't have a gun or a knife 'cos they'll go to jail so a dog is the next thing. Then they let them off the chain."

These strategies allow young gang members to manufacture a reputation. The examples given are the strategies favoured by those new to the gang. These often highly visible strategies generate street capital each time they are employed, establishing the new affiliate as a 'playa'. Having manufactured a reputation and some initial street capital, members must develop strategies to maintain them. Chapter Seven illustrates how this is done.

Notes

[1] Deliberately holding the stare of another individual without looking away. Vigil (2002) refers to this as 'mad dogging'.

[2] It was here in April 2009 that 16-year-old Seyi Ogunyemi was brutally murdered, having been chased and savaged by local rival gang members using their dogs. For a full account of this murder see the Introduction in Harding (2014).

[3] Felson (2006) in his 'big gang theory' argues that gangs deliberately construct myths in order to make themselves appear more ruthless and violent than they actually are. For a discussion of gang myths see Howell (2012).

SEVEN

Staying in the game – and playing to win

Once a gang member has manufactured their reputation and become a player in the social field with its variable economy of street capital, the demands on his reputation must be monitored so that he can stay in the game. Some players seek to maximise their street capital and then play to win.

Maintaining your street capital: 'being tested'

If creating a rep is the first big test of the social field, maintaining and defending it is the second. Those in the social field quickly become aware of who is serious about their rep and who is not, who will act and who will not. Failure to act quickly with sufficient force damages your rep (Matza and Sykes, 1961; Anderson, 1999; Messerschmidt, 2000;) and diminishes street capital. Having established your market share of street capital, you must now strive to defend it at all costs, preventing it from being destroyed, diminished or acquired. This is referred to as 'respecting your rep'. Any attempt to interfere with this rep is a violation (disrespect or 'dissing'). Those outside the social field refer to such incidents as 'respect issues'. Here young people develop strategies to increase their own street capital by diminishing that of others. As street capital represents tradable market shares, this is achievable by simply 'disrespecting' someone, or by failing to act when the code of the street demands it. An attempt to diminish or acquire another person's street capital is known as 'being tested'. Similar issues are identified in US gang research. In an account of membership of an LA gang, Monster Cody talks of building respect to the status of ghetto hero, a position that ascribes the benefits of walking the neighbourhood unmolested. However, he notes how such a high rank marks you out as a target, as others try to take your place and thus gain status themselves (Vigil, 1988a).

Testing is carried out regardless of age and gender. One young woman who acted as an independent agent in SW9 dealing Class A drugs was regularly tested by young men, including being threatened with a gun to her head, physical assaults and fighting and subjected to physical assaults and required to defend herself by fighting.

> 'Everyone wants to test the theory of how hard I woz. Boys would test me – I'd say, "Do it!" I would not back down. Once I got into a fight with this guy then later at a party he put a gun into my face. He said, "I could take your life right now." I said, "Do it! And do it twice!" Then we tussled and the gun fell to the floor. Then friends came over and he ran off. But similar things have happened. Then you get pushed to do things you don't wanna do.' (African Caribbean female independent operator)

It is unclear in this case if the testing was for business or reputational reasons, or because of the victim's gender.

Testing often takes one of two forms: an immediate provocation in a group or social setting or a virtual provocation. In face-to-face settings, the victim must act quickly to challenge the offender and any retaliation would be expected to involve violence if it were to be taken seriously. A provocation may arise within the gang or from a rival gang, or from someone outside the social field. Virtual provocations take place on social networking sites and are usually targeted towards another gang or specific members of another gang.

The purpose of destroying or disrespecting someone's reputation ('dissing') is to diminish their street capital and thus acquire it for yourself: "I reacted quickly. If someone took the piss, I'd hit him straight away" (West African male younger)

Reputational testing may happen anywhere at any time. Youngers and new arrivals to the social field are commonly tested by incumbents with established reputations or street capital. This puts gang-affiliated young people under pressure; they get locked into responding even though they do not want to (Anderson, 1999; Winlow, 2001). Some aspire to having a 'badman' reputation so nobody will challenge them: "It's all about maintaining your rep – once it starts you can't back down or back off. Yes, it's like a spiral" (white female professional).

If a gang member is hit, stabbed or shot, speed of reaction determines their reputation and ability to retain their street capital. Most will not let it lie: "You have to show what you are made of, otherwise you won't ever be able to come back" (male African Caribbean police officer). For most, reputation is heavily linked to violence and how they react to violence. Many young people express anxiety over the pressure to maintain their rep. This is understandable, as any decline in their personal stock of street capital will reverse or stall personal advancement within the social field, leading to increased victimisation. Maintaining one's level of street capital is therefore both a strategy for advancement, and a strategy for survival.

Transitioning from the expressive to the instrumental repertoire

Having established themselves as 'playas' with a recognised reputation, youngers expand their use of the gang repertoire, moving from the expressive to the instrumental repertoire – from fun to money. Robbery and drug dealing both offer opportunities for transition from the expressive to the instrumental repertoire (Boxes 7.1 and 7.2). Both offences offer an opportunity to progress up the internal social skills ladder to a higher level where criminal activity becomes more organised. A third strategy, handling stolen goods, complements the other activities. Each can be undertaken as an individual or group strategy.

Box 7.1: Robbery

Robbery is usually the earliest form of instrumental crime attempted by youngers making the transition from the expressive to the instrumental repertoire. At the expressive level, it accompanies physical violence, enabling early manufacture of street capital – in the school playground, for example. It may be employed within the sanction repertoire. As a strategic action, it is easily used in multiple locations – schools, colleges, local streets, the estate. It is even used regularly within the gang itself – and often has multiple victims. Robbery offers instant returns of street and economic capital, and coupled with its ability to be employed frequently and repeatedly, it is not only ubiquitous in the social field, but is also the ultimate activity for gang-affiliated youngers. It offers:

- numerous opportunities to test the gang repertoire and its variables;
- choice of gang or individual strategy;
- opportunities for peer bonding;
- extensive bragging rights;
- opportunities to add to gang folklore;
- opportunities for hype, fun and exaggeration (Katz, 1988);
- instant returns of stolen goods that allow trade/exchange;
- financial returns;
- generation of social capital.

> 'Everyone wanted to join in the robbing crew. It was fast money!
> Everyone knows you are a phone robber, so they'll put in an order for
> an iPhone. You know who you'll sell it to already. A lot of foreigners
> or phone shops will take it – they don't know if it's stolen. So you get
> rid of it quickly.' (African Caribbean male older)

Moreover, robbery is policed only in a limited fashion and reporting levels are
famously low. By using this strategic action, gang members can hone personal
skills in fighting, emotional control or physical violence. It provides access to the
latest technology and, when the theft involves mobile phones, to information.
Actors within the social field already tend to have considerable experience of
robbery at school and accept it as part of the habitus. In short, as a strategic
action, it almost always guarantees success.

Robbery also provides an opportunity to employ a secondary strategy –
humiliation. For example, a gang member may purposefully humiliate his victim
after winning a fight by stealing his chain. This enhances the street capital of
the victor while diminishing that of the loser. Such is the universality of street
robbery as successful strategic action within the social field of the gang; it may
be employed in a very casual manner: "You see, if your phone broke, you'd just
go and get another" (West African male younger).

This casual acceptance of robbery as normative within the social field of the gang
may also extend to some households. According to respondents in SW9, when
a parent asks a young person to 'bring something to the table', there is a tacit
understanding on both sides of what this means. This casual approach relegates
stealing phones to the realm of lesser transgressions, such as bullying and 'taxing'
(robbery of, for example, dinner money, as payment of dues). In police parlance, it
is not necessarily considered to be a crime or recorded as such by them. Robbery
takes a number of different forms, as shown in Table 7.1.

Olders and elders will engage in cash-in-transit robberies once they have become
more confident and skilled in robbery techniques. They may be either planned
activities or undertaken impulsively:

> 'Sometimes there is planning involved and lot of the time it is just
> instinctive or impulsive. You'd go to somewhere with a lot of back-
> roads – like off the main road away from any CCTV, West Norwood
> used to have a lot of back-roads – and then go to the estate and bust
> it open with a blow torch or what you'd use to open it. Sometimes
> it would be impulsive – you know, you'd be parked round the corner

up by Barclays Bank and you'd see the transit van and the driver and the ringer, so it would be hoods up, let's go take this ting and go. Then sometimes it would be planned – you'd start to clock that they came by every Monday between these times and you'd go and do it.' (African Caribbean male independent operator)

Table 7.1: Robbery strategies in the instrumental repertoire

Strategy	Comment
Individual or group robbery	Individuals either employ their own agency or 'group up'. It is the 'apparent' individual agency that leads to confusion as to whether street robbery is an individual or group activity, and whether it is organised or not. Some members may specialise in this strategy, testing variables until they build their own personal robbery repertoire.
Initiation robberies	Street robbery is often used as an early initiation rite for gang affiliation. By age 13 to 15, many boys in the social field of the gang have been robbed at school. Youngers are told to rob to prove their loyalty to the gang. Their approach, style, and the levels of threat and violence they use are assessed by peers and olders.
Sanction robberies	Sanction robberies are targeted towards individuals for reasons of revenge, punishment or control, and are seldom reported. Victims may be targeted more than once from such events.
Specialised robbing groups	In the more organised mature tier, the robberies may be more coordinated. Here tasks may be allocated to specific individuals to maximise their previous experience and their unique skills and abilities. In this way specific groups might be formed so that the diverse skills will be more effective.
Stash-in-transit (drugs-profit) robberies	Gangs target the movement of drug profits if the stash, usually crack cocaine but occasionally skunk, is over £1,000. Olders undertake these big jobs and proceeds are seldom shared. Some olders in SW9 reported robbing another dealer of their stash as a 'rite-of-passage' activity.
Pack robberies (steaming)	This expressive form of instrumental crime may involve up to 20 people, and sometimes more. It is used effectively on public transport where victims are corralled. Pack robberies are planned carefully, and timings are precise. Pack robberies provide opportunities for group bonding and fun. Yields are high, but gains divided widely.
Cash-in-transit robberies	Part of the instrumental repertoire, cash-in-transit robberies represent the higher end of gang criminal activity. Often undertaken by olders/elders, but increasingly involving youngers, they may be opportunistic or planned. As a strategy, they are often high in violence and low in yield.

Box 7.2: Drug dealing

Drug dealing provides an excellent strategy for maximising street capital. The selling of drugs is an integral element of the social field of the urban street gang in SW9 (Sanders, 2005; May et al, 2007). This differs from the findings of Aldridge and Medina (2008), who argue that drug sales in Manchester are undertaken by individuals rather than by the gang.

Drug dealing is both a transitional part of the instrumental repertoire and an entry-level activity. In SW9, it is also a long-established social norm which is widely recognised via several open and closed drug markets, e.g. Loughborough Road, Coldharbour Lane and central Brixton are all known London-wide as localities for purchasing drugs (Ruggiero and South, 1995). In the search to make money, both youngers and non-gang-affiliated young people view drug dealing as both 'employment' and 'enterprise' (Hagedorn, 1988; Bourgois, 1995). The higher end of the market is highly organised, although it is also well organised at the local street level.

'Yeah, and that is how the game'll work out. So the ones on the road are the soljas. They knew the rumours, the things, etc, they maintain the reputation and listen out for the gossip. They are behind that will be the second in command. He will know where the stash is, cut[s] the deals and he won't be dealing pocket deals at all. If he deals, it'll be a couple of ounces, two ounces. If it gets any bigger – the deal – then you bring in the next man up, who knows where the warehouse is now and talking to the main people themselves and so if there are any really big deals then you go back to the main man.' (African Caribbean male elder)

The SW9 postcode area has long-established historical links to drug leading in Lambeth (May et al, 2007) with market demand from areas all around London (Sanders 2005). Dealing in weed or skunk is a familiar aspect of community life, and not just the realm of the gang.

Certain types of offending, notably drug dealing in SW9, have been traditionally associated with the Caribbean community (Sanders, 2005; May et al, 2007; Pitts, 2008b). Ruggiero and South (1995) noted that selling crack, smack and weed was an activity that occurred among a greater proportion of young black men in Lambeth than in other London boroughs, and May et al (2007) noted that 'Brixton has a well-entrenched reputation as a place where drugs can be readily bought' (p 2). Drug connections between the Lambeth African Caribbean community and the West Indies (notably Jamaica) are locally well recognised but under-researched.[1]

Toy (2008) and Pitts (2008b) also note that in recent years the traditional sources of cocaine have shifted from South America and the Caribbean to West Africa and Nigeria. Many respondents in this study noted that several years ago youngers began selling drugs for cousins at age 16/17, whereas now they were doing so at the age of 12/13. In addition, whereas youngers previously started smoking weed at age 18, they now began when they were 13 or 14.

Youngers act as shotters and runners for both cannabis and cocaine. When police stop youngers they may have several wraps of crack cocaine on them. As one respondent put it, "Starts with weed then you work your way up to rocks."

As gang members age and move from the expressive to the instrumental gang repertoire, the allure of being a recognised drug dealer becomes more attractive and more normative. For youngers, dealing is seldom a big commercial scheme; rather, it is 'money on the side'. It is also fun and helps them to learn the ropes of the neighbourhood business and access information. Olders develop strategies by exploiting vulnerable people to run drugs for them and paying them 'peanuts', allowing them to maximise their personal economic capital. Such strategies permit the olders to cleverly transfer risk downward to junior gang members:

> 'People who get caught by the police are the people who are sloppy, we leave that to the pawns. That's what I used to do, I used to manipulate people. If I thought this was a bit risky for me to do, I would say to someone who looked up to me, "There's this little ting ... just a quick one ... don't worry about it, it'll be fine." The little runner would go off and do it and whether he got caught or not caught, that is his risk. It's not my risk. It's not coming back to me.' (African Caribbean male independent operator)

> When youngers become olders, they are unlikely to be pressurised into selling on behalf of others, and more often choose to deal in Class A drugs directly. Olders may sell drugs in nightclubs or at college or casually on the estate or to other gangs, 'just to get by'.

Youngers sell drugs largely within the confines of their own estate. When they become olders, the turf for selling widens, and members are less dependent on the estate. By the time they reach the mature tier, drug patches extend even further; they are not the same as gang patches or turfs, but are wider, often encompassing several estates, and economics is now the main motivation. Elders may supply drugs to two or three different gangs across a neighbourhood irrespective of the fact that gangs may be rivals and engaged in a 'beef'. This stratified dimension to the spatial distribution is often confusing to professionals, but to summarise, youngers deal on their own estate; olders travel more widely; and elders supply a range of gangs in different neighbourhoods.

Olders, and only very trustworthy youngers, may transport drugs from SW9 to other parts of the UK, in a process known as going 'up country'. Toy (2008) confirms similar findings in Southwark. Popular destinations include Cardiff, Nottingham, Coventry, Luton, south coast towns, university towns and East Anglia.

Earnings from drug dealing vary depending on age, rank and reputation. Youngers may make £50 a day (a lot of money to them) from only five buyers. Youth workers report that youngers often make very little money. Olders aged 16 to 18 could potentially make £25,000 over several months. Cars are used to transport drugs, stolen goods and money. Girlfriends are used to hire cars and evidential documents for car rental verification are changed weekly or falsified. Information is central to operating a solid business. It is crucial for the olders and elders involved to know the customer base and have long-standing contacts in the area.

Larger sums of money in circulation around SW9 are not uncommon. During one police pursuit of olders in SW9, one boy dropped £7,000 from his pocket. It is highly unusual for youngers and even olders to have bank accounts. A police raid on a property in Brixton revealed a teenager with a gun and £70,000 in cash.

Before being 'cut', large quantities of product are stashed in what is known as a 'fortress' – often a house or flat on or off the estate – along with the drug profits. Some elders use their home as a fortress, with alarms, 'emergency points' and strategically placed weapons as protection. Others use dogs to sit on the stash:

> 'You have your dog there as well, a key-purse safe to make sure that if anything goes wrong you can rely on the dog, maybe 'cos you can't have the gun. ... It's basically another way of having a weapon without having a weapon.' (African Caribbean male elder)

Business take-overs

As olders increasingly take to the instrumental repertoire for their strategic action more profitable ways of raising money come to the fore. This might include intimidation of local business and demands for money whereby businesses are pressured into 'buying protection' from intimidation or 'trouble'. This is only likely to occur when the gang is well established with a strong local presence.

A different and more common form of activity is taking over the running of door management and the club security of local businesses. Elders will use youngers to establish a premise of constant disorder and fighting in the venue. Subsequently the olders will present themselves as able to calm the situation and thus provide the necessary security for the venue. The youngers are then told to stop the violence, which allows the olders and elders to give the impression they have brought the premises under control. The new set of bouncers will control all door security, thereby permitting total control over the movement of clientele and drugs. As one professional noted:

> 'The older ones will get involved in taking over door security. They will get the youngers ones to cause problems which they then sort out. Certainly the older ones do this. There's been a bit of move in Brixton to try take over security. Running the security for the venue is key, 'cos if they run the security for the venue they can get whoever they wanted, they can get weapons in there, drugs in there etcetera, obviously it's worth a lot of money. That'll be the older ones who control this. They will set sights on a place they want to take over and if the owner won't play ball then they will get the younger ones in to cause problems, and in the end the others leave saying it's not worth all the hassle.'

In this way the gang extends its local presence and control. It also expands information networks. This strategy provides regular opportunities for gifting (permitting entry) and sanctions (excluding entry), building local loyalties, and strengthening gang bonds and bonds with the local network.

Playing to win: maximising street capital through reputation

Once members have established their reputation within the social field, they must maintain their street capital in order to continue to advance and to stay safe. Those gang affiliates who are impatient to advance more quickly may choose to maximise their street capital through two key strategies:

- promoting and marketing their individual or gang brand;
- becoming involved in group violence and gang incursions.

These two strategies are critical to understanding the reasons for increased violence in the social field of the gang. Both strategies offer new adaptations to existing strategies and have only recently become a tried and tested part of the gang repertoire. Importantly, they also represent a gamble within the social field. They may go spectacularly well and bring instant and enduring street capital or they may go spectacularly wrong and bring future grief and victimisation. In a social field where social competition is increasingly fierce and achieving distinction increasingly challenging, it is possible that young people resort to these strategies more frequently. This increases tensions in the social field leading to increased violence.

The frequent use of these strategies attests to their efficacy. The inherent nature of these strategies dictates how and when they are used, and any response is likely to be similarly violent and emotionally charged. Such strategies are used on purpose to antagonise, goad and humiliate rivals by causing their street capital to diminish in spectacular fashion. By definition, then, these strategies are:

- highly provocative;
- intensely personal;
- innovative and creative;
- designed to highlight weaknesses;
- highly public with huge visual impact;
- recorded, widely broadcast, archived and repeatedly aired.

These strategies may be employed on the spur of the moment or planned in advance, either in person on the estate or through online forums.

Promotions and marketing

An established 'rep' quickly becomes a vehicle for increasing street capital and a passport to advancement and distinction. Once rep has been established, it becomes easier to strategise to maintain and maximise it through:

- word of mouth via the gang;
- word of mouth via the network;
- a willingness to act on your reputation;
- social networking sites;
- linking into music;

- hype and myth;
- visual presence.

As one gang affiliate noted, "YouTube can have a large effect. Music is a big part of it – it helps get the gang known, nowadays" (West African male older). Most affiliates have an online web presence and some brand names will be 'trending', or rising in popularity. It is important for youngers to market their rep immediately and get their name discussed on social networking sites. Websites are the perfect medium for illustrating and reinforcing the core nature of expressive crime (a show of nature and character).

The principle medium of expression is art and the demonstration of artistic skill. Such 'art' used to be the preserve of graffiti artists. Until the arrival of social networking sites, graffiti was the medium for posturing, challenging and 'dissing' rival gangs. Social networking sites have now almost completely taken this over.

The most straightforward way to market a reputation is to broadcast your actions visually via social media, thus providing cast-iron proof of involvement. The more your peers view your presence online, the more your reputation increases. Visual representations of your actions are transmitted as high-grade evidence of your reputation, which garners further respect. Such 'visual copy' is highly prized because of this evidential factor, and because it can be easily transmitted and 'lives forever' online. It enables members to build reputation and earn street capital in same way that physical actions would garner 'royalties' on the street.

For those seeking to maximise their individual reputation, gang reputation or street capital, a simple web presence or website is considered insufficient and technically too low grade. Provocative, high-quality video productions are essential to enhance street capital (Box 7.3).

Box 7.3: Use of video

The more provocative the film, the greater the street capital accrued. Footage usually includes a lyrical rap, culminating in a free-style monologue, often containing provocative claims denigrating rivals with multiple terms of abuse and mocking language, such as "You are not as brave as us, you pussies." Gangs boast of being 'untouchable' and 'invincible', while illustrating their gang policy and rules. Individuals openly boast about their exploits – "I cut him, I shot him" – listing names to provide evidence of the gang's numerous branded affiliates and designate assumed territory and authority. Confrontations and challenges are proffered to rivals. Gang affiliates, rivals and the local police all monitor the use of social networking sites to identify the profiles of those accessing the sites.

Videos containing high levels of violence, both real and threatened, are posted on social networking sites. Recent video footage shows the Peckham Young Guns fighting the South Central Gang in Croydon, while another example shows a large gang fight in the Whitgift Centre in Croydon.

Gangs will deliberately enter the turf of a rival to produce film footage, which is then used to denigrate rivals:

> 'But people go on to estate and make video footage on their estate. They go on the estate and make a video by phone – "Look, look, look, I'm on Angell town." It's all mouth, all for show. Now that's a violation. "I thought no-one could come on Angell town, but here I am. It on YouTube now." They call you everything. It makes the others look rubbish when they've said no-one can come here now – but we can. Evidence!' (African Caribbean male older)

Gangs telephone their rivals to advise them when a new video has been posted. This taunting is considered to be extremely provocative and represents an electronic version of 'throwing down the gauntlet'. This instantly diminishes the street capital of those challenged. Such diminishment can only be prevented by the rival gang 'picking up the gauntlet' and either posting a retort or taking revenge. Gang affiliates with specific IT skills are used to spread the word quickly. Incidents can be deliberately manufactured to obtain good visual copy that may even include council CCTV footage. Such footage is highly prized. One website, entitled Fear and Fashion, was recently taken down following complaints that it glamorised guns and was a crucible for violence.

Marketing reputations via social networking sites generates considerable hype and myth. A buzz is generated and young people feed off the buzz, hoping to 'give action and get reaction' (Katz, 1988). As one respondent in the SW9 research put it: "Certainly with the youngsters it's all caught up in a big hype. That's why we say the levels of violence has gone up" (white professional female). This buzz is complemented by opportunities to produce video footage on the internet and many reputations are made here. Some active gang affiliates are disparaging of those who only appear in videos, terming them 'YouTube gangstas', and implying that their role is lightweight and insignificant. Those peripheral to the social field will find it easy to claim association, saying, 'Yes I'm part of that.' Others find the buzz addictive and hard to ignore, while those peripheral to the social field may find that social networking sites enable them to claim association with members who have an online presence.

A further reason for increased violence in the social field is that youngers and new arrivals to the gang can easily get caught up in online provocation and posturing without fully realising the significance and danger of doing so. This may lead to a proliferation of provocative postings, with youngers seeking to maximise their street capital. The high emotional content of such postings often leads to swift and extremely violent retribution.

Central to manufacturing and maximising one's street capital is the role of hype and exaggeration in storytelling or trading of information. Herman and Julia Schwendinger note that young people use different moral rhetorics when in discourse with peers. Sandberg and Pederson (2011) identify Gangster discourse as the dominant linguistic practice in street culture. This discourse offers the wide appeal of suggesting that those involved in street culture have more rewarding and dynamic lives than those outside street culture. As such it is used to create both fascination and fear in order to gain both self-respect and respect from others. These rhetorics may support the criminal activity and utilise hyperbole (Schwendinger and Schwendinger, 1985). This is done by way of developing strategies to maximise street capital. Such stories recreate the member as central protagonist in their own heroic narrative, demonstrating through oral tradition their ability and social skill in controlling situations and using 'street knowledge' to outwit, survive and thrive. This includes using social networking sites to describe incidents more violently than they actually were when they occurred. Police records corroborate these findings; in one example, where officers connected the stories being broadcast on social networking sites to an actual incident, the gang members claimed that a victim was in an intensive care unit when in reality the rival had received only minor scratches. David Matza (1964) refers to this process as 'sounding' – originally inferred as teasing, insulting or imputing negative qualities, which leads people to take offence and then act accordingly. In the social field of the gang, however, 'bad' is a revered quality. Moreover, both victim and perpetrator in the example cited will have acquired street capital through such hype. This is further maximised if the story is repeated multiple times.

Group violence and gang incursions

In addition to personal/gang marketing and promotion, group activity offers numerous potential ways for members to advance up the hierarchy and acquire street captial. These activities also perform additional functions:

- facilitating group bonding;
- permitting members to test strategies from the repertoires;
- providing a platform to demonstrate trust and loyalty to peers and to the gang.

The two favoured strategies are group violence (see Box 7.4) and group incursions into rival territory. Both strategies are permissible within the gang habitus, and have been tested and proven effective. Both strategies are also responsible for the increased frequency and level of violence within the social field. These increases occur not least because of the frequency and repetitive nature of such events, but also because of the sheer numbers of participants. Critically such incidents involve multiple players, all developing strategies independently and as a group, simultaneously. This means that gang repertoire variables are frequently used in a variety of different ways by different people at the same time. As a result such events are difficult to control. Group activity may be organised and controlled at the outset, with an agreed group plan of action, but individual strategies soon take over, with individuals employing different variables in different ways. This often results in plans going astray and in unexpected outcomes. Witnesses to such events may report violence to be random or chaotic. The violence that is permissible is guided by the habitus.

Two further elements crucially determine the level of violence of such incidents. First, those seeking to maximise their own street capital may suddenly and dramatically increase the degree of violence used. Second, in any group attack, all those involved must be seen to participate, as all wish to increase their street capital. This may result in multiple, often frenzied, stabbings. The locality of the stab wounds inflicted further increases street capital – newcomers to such violence may seek to stab in the legs, arms or buttocks, while those seeking to maximise their street capital may stab in the chest, throat or heart. Police report that stab wounds are sometimes inflicted after the victim has collapsed or died, suggesting that members who have not initiated the violence may get involved once the damage has been done in order to seek to claim bragging rights by showing that they have acted in concert with the gang.

Box 7.4: Group violence

Police and professionals in SW9 have reported a recent increase in joint enterprise attacks, where several perpetrators act in concert. The degree of permissible violence as dictated by the habitus of the social field has changed since the shooting of two young people in a McDonald's restaurant in 2006.

> 'People have this mentality, they are ready to do anything. They all know it's illegal so that doesn't come into it. Doing something bad or illegal is easy, it is doing something legal that is difficult. Also the younger people don't care about the consequences.' (West African male older)

Revenge attacks now tend to involve several assailants instead of just one. This further increases the level of violence in SW9. There are a number of reasons for the increase in group violence:

- With whole groups being 'dissed' on social networking sites, more gang members feel violated and seek retaliation. Moreover, being 'dissed' online, in the public domain, triggers a highly charged desire for immediate revenge. This is often compounded by the immediacy of the online event, i.e. a sense that it is happening now rather than a week ago. In this way a high level of emotional involvement is sustained and not dissipated.
- As a strategy, group violence offers opportunities for group planning, excitement and buzz.
- It offers opportunities for group validation and bonding.
- It gives the gang a reputation for acting 'as one', demonstrating cohesion and organisation (although any action may in fact be chaotic).
- It provides elders with the opportunity, in private, to take the credit for apparently orchestrating the action.
- Group violence dramatically increases the fear factor for the victim. Attackers expect the victim to carry a weapon, and group rushing or mobbing the victim as a group reduces his ability to retaliate effectively.
- Gang affiliates claim that youngers have 'no fear' of just one person armed with a knife.
- It plays out better – either on video, or after the event, in terms of myth making.

- It maximises fear and street capital.
- It increases the likelihood of success, with affiliates eagerly 'opting in' to participate in what they consider to be a sure-fire 'hit'.

Group violence may occur spontaneously, but may also be planned if an incident triggers a gang strategy response. For example, in 2010, a TN1 (Trust No-one) gang younger from Tulse Hill was stabbed outside Brixton police station by a GAS gang member. Two days later, ten TN1 olders visited a local 'chicken shop' (i.e. a fast food outlet) in recognised GAS turf. Within minutes, approximately 25 GAS members arrived from different directions to surround the shop. Police intervened, breaking up the potentially violent incident. Such instances demonstrate a certain amount of gang planning and fast tactical response.

The issue of territoriality is complex and frequently misread or misidentified by practitioners and academics alike. In Chapter Eight, I expand my theory of social field and street capital to offer a unique and fresh insight into the issue of territoriality.

Note

[1] Pitts (2008b) highlights the Caribbean connection.

EIGHT

The game in action: habitus, street capital and territory

'Every time a friend succeeds, I die a little.'
Gore Vidal

The game in action: playing on my turf

Social field theory and street capital theory bring a new understanding to the issue of territoriality, revealing it as less about spatial dimensions and more concerned with reputation, metaphor and field dynamics. Territoriality is useful in examining how the concepts of habitus and street capital interrelate within the social field, especially through gang incursions. This chapter examines these concepts to illustrate how 'the game' works in the social field. First, however, it is useful to consider how academics and the media have previously misinterpreted the issue of territoriality in relation to gangs.

Misreading territoriality (the game board)

The concept of violence relating to a spatially defined area has been the subject of much gang research (Cloward and Ohlin, 1960; Spergel, 1964; Klein, 1971; Hagedorn, 1988; Vigil, 1988a; Taylor, 1989; Kintrea et al, 2008). Interestingly, Sanders (writing about Lambeth in 2005) noted very few, if any, accounts of young people protecting or controlling areas or of 'territorial rivalry'.

One example recently foregrounded by Ralphs and colleagues (2009) borrows from US social geographers Tita and colleagues (2005) and their discussions of 'gang set space' which has been defined as 'the actual area within the neighborhood where gang members come together as a gang' (p 280), that is, the streets, buildings and spaces where gang members congregate. In a later work, Aldridge and colleagues (2011) conclude that 'gang members understood, experienced and interpreted territory in complicated ways [with] considerable dissensus amongst gang members about what constituted "gang set space"' (p 10).

The concept of 'gang set space', which fits the quantitative geo-coded spatial discourse of Tita and colleagues, becomes considerably diluted when social field theory is applied. Although my research and participant observations identified several locations favoured by gangs, these were often highly temporally variable (for example, seasonal) and used functionally. They were also used by non-gang members. Social field analysis tells us such spaces are seldom exclusive and are usually shared with individuals from other social fields. They are functionally differentiated by actors operating in different social fields, for example, local parks used for recreational purposes by neighbourhood families may be used for dog fighting by local gangs, and housing estate stairwells used by the gang to smoke weed, discuss business or have sex are used by local residents to access their homes. These spaces are not habitual as implied, largely because temporal variables affect their spatial functions. My findings suggest highly variable use of social space determined by group function or current strategic action that is most likely functional and temporal. Social interactions among gang members occur in virtual spaces as well as physical spaces, e.g. underground garages, as reputations are built both online and via street presence, and gang-affiliated young people may live in neighbourhoods other than the one associated with their gang. The reputations of olders and elders, and gang-affiliated girls and young women, are not dependent on street visibility. The notion of 'gang set spaces' is therefore a gendered concept mostly pertaining to the elementary tier acting out the expressive repertoire; it relates to male rather than female activity. A focus on 'gang set spaces' risks obscuring the functions and strategies of girls and young women within the social field of the gang. The concept of 'gang set spaces' is not therefore used in this thesis.

Social field theory and street capital theory are useful tools for analysing the complexities and misunderstandings of territoriality. For example, Aldridge and colleagues (2011) found that fear of 'straying' into rival territory was linked to 'previous conflicts with particular individuals [rather] than to rival gang status per se' (p 7). Such dichotomous arguments between individually motivated and gang-motivated actions are better addressed through social field analysis. Utilising the concept of street capital, I argue that while appearing separate, such actions, i.e. individually motivated and gang-motivated actions are linked within the locus of the gang and the dynamics of the social field.

A further example of misreading territoriality, now clarified through social field analysis, is the claim by Ralphs and colleagues (2009) that young people (including those not identifying as gang affiliates) are given 'gang labels' and misidentified as 'gang associates' based 'on their use of place and space'. This leads to their victimisation by other young people, stigmatisation by the police, vulnerability as targets of police attention and exclusion by statutory authorities. Ralphs and colleagues argue that the 'less discriminate use of gang-status labels by both gang-involved youth and officials has severe implications for the personal safety and exclusion of those who live in known gang areas' (p 495). Social field theory clarifies this and suggests that it is not labelling by officials or gang-involved youth that puts them at risk. They are at risk already as young people and as strategic actors within the social field of the gang, whether they are gang-affiliated or not. Others actors in the social field assume that they are linked, networked or affiliated. As this chapter illustrates, the social field operates in conjunction with street capital to provide an imperative of risk analysis. This risk analysis operates an effective presumption that a young person is 'networked' if they share the same social field/habitus. Such assumptions are made peremptorily by other young people seeking to mitigate their risks and monitor their own safety. This is much more than the simple attachment of labels.

A further misinterpretation of territorial issues relates to so-called 'turf wars' over drug 'patches'. Some researchers have suggested that territorial disputes are based on fights over rights to sell drugs, with commercial gains to be made by expanding one's turf into rival territory (Toy, 2008). This narrative, often inspired by the media, portrays territoriality as 'drug wars', with youngers controlling access to estates to prevent rival drug dealers from entering to take over the patch (or market).

While drug dealing is central to the local economy on many estates in SW9, my research found no evidence to suggest that this is the causal factor in territorial disputes. Nor is it a causal factor in the so-called 'gang war' between Brixton and Peckham. Gang violence between SW9 and Peckham (largely the PYG) is essentially an issue of respect played out through territorial violations by youngers against youngers. Thus locally termed 'gang war' has lasted many years. At the lower level, drug selling is estate-based and often highly localised. We can therefore discount the theory that any prolonged dispute between the two areas of London is based on drug dealing, as Peckham is simply too far from Brixton for any 'war' to be about drugs. The commercial transactions of the drug trade continue to operate at a lower level undisturbed by this dispute. At a higher level, olders/elders profit from larger cross-borough deals. Market economy requirements soon preside over any disputes, forcing a resolution that favours profit. As a result, drugs do not fuel the 'war' with Peckham.

In Peckham, numerous gangs operate under the banner of the PYG with its rumoured ability to mobilise up to 300 people if required. Indeed, large numbers of PYG members do undertake incursions into SW9 and the GAS gang retaliates in return. PYG has its own gang social field and its own network, operating its own loose affiliations and alliances, currently united in their contempt for the GAS gang. This situation does not, however, amount to a confederation as it is loosely based and established on a variable and needs-only basis. It is not planned or negotiated and is unlikely to endure for any great length of time.

The origins of the 'war' are now largely lost in time. What is clearer is how it is perpetuated – by gangs on both sides maximising their street capital, minimising their victimisation and enacting group strategies to achieve this. Importantly, this includes the provocative use of social networking sites to diminish the reputation of rivals. An alternate theory for this 'war' is that Peckham and Brixton now host different communities that do not get on: Black Caribbeans in Brixton and Black Africans in Peckham. According to some survey participants, this, not uncommon theory, is supported by the fact that many young people who have been attacked or killed in the area recently have African surnames. Some claim that this reflects a rise in numbers of black Africans in south London. The theory of Peckham and Brixton as of two rival ethnic communities at war, however, is too simplistic and is not supported by the evidence. While some tensions are acknowledged between the two communities within Peckham, none were evident in SW9 or Lambeth. Some survey participants, however, felt that Black Africans were 'taking over' in both Brixton and Peckham.

A different theory suggests that the overrepresentation of Black Africans among the victims of gang violence relates to the fact they are new arrivals who do not understand the local gangs. While this may be true of some instances of victimisation, it is an over-simplistic interpretation. In Brixton and across SW9, African names are themselves common. There is no evidence to show that African young men are being targeted for violence because of their African heritage or name. Indeed, most young people of African descent living in SW9 or Lambeth have grown up in Lambeth, been schooled there and have UK cultural identity. In the social field of SW9, it is not country or culture of origin that is significant; it is where individuals reside now. Thus the ethnicity of the gang reflects that of the community.

It is, however, possible that new arrivals experience 'network poverty' (6, 1997). This would significantly reduce the level of knowledge and information accessible to a new arrival, and increase his risk status. As such, he may have unwittingly placed himself in situations or relationships of increased risk and potential danger.

Territory as habitus and metaphor

In any social field, the habitus guides action and determines which actions are permissible as social norms. Generated by neighbourhood history, the habitus is spatially as well as socially determined. It is this spatial dimension that links to the perception of territory. For many in the social field, the concept of territoriality therefore assumes great importance, often now enhanced further by an increase in the number of gang strategies using group incursions into territory perceived to belong to, or be controlled by, rival gangs.

The strategic action of group incursion into rival territory is a key element of the recently identified rise in violence among gangs in SW9, as it represents a calculated strategy allowing individuals as well as gangs to maximise their street capital.

For many youngers, territory or 'endz' is an integral part of gang and personal identity (Pearson, 1983), a fact recognised by other gangs who express similar feelings. Gangs use this knowledge to both generate and acquire street capital. A territorial 'violation' results in the immediate diminishment of street capital for the gang whose territory has been targeted. Often mislabelled the 'postcode beef' in London, this strategic action dominates the daily lives of youngers actively seeking to maximise their street capital. It leads to many potential hazards for those negotiating this social field as they try to avoid victimisation and violence, ultimately adding significantly to the landscape of risk.

This issue of territoriality has received a high public profile through media coverage. It is, however, a complex and nuanced aspect of gang life. For SW9 gangs, territoriality becomes significant in the early formative years through domain protectionism by youngers creating their own defensible space. Later as they grow older, such issues recede and criminal activity and the drugs economy are foregrounded. Within the dimension of protecting personal home territory are complex dynamics relating to habitus and social field. Younger and newer gang members are aware that their influence, 'control' and permissible actions (habitus) have limitations. However, they instinctively designate these actions as having spatial boundaries rather than relational boundaries. Relational boundaries are determined by proximity to the gang and its social field, and determine the degree to which members are influenced by issues of street capital, respect, reputation and violation. Within this localised and spatialised frame of reference, territorial incursions become a metaphor for personal violation.

The world experience of youngers is very narrow, their knowledge and 'world map' limited and bounded by their everyday experience, their locality, their school, the local high street and the local shops. The physical built environment becomes a metaphor for the corporeal – it is part of their life history. The spatial entity of the estate becomes the physical space of the group, giving youngers the opportunity of viewing the territory as more than just the domain of the gang. It comes to be viewed as an entity within the gang itself. It is the habitus. The neighbourhood reflects the habitus of the individuals in the gang and vice versa. They are linked to it and it to them. Of course, the territory is only really 'their territory' in their minds. For them, the neighbourhood retains the physical embodiment of their local history. To protect the estate is to conserve their history, albeit only for a short time.

Thus for younger gang affiliates the neighbourhood becomes a metaphor for the gang; as an entity it is allocated both domestic and intensely personal qualities. Any violation of this territory is viewed as a violation of the gang corpus. For youngers seeking to associate in group dynamics, this physical metaphor for the gang takes on supreme importance. The estate or neighbourhood becomes an entity over which they can quickly exert influence and then control, exercised through basic forms of intimidation, amassed numbers, visible presence and elementary forms of the expressive gang repertoire. It is 'control' formed and sustained by group activity. This control, albeit often more perception than reality, is their creation and has been achieved through their dedication and hard work.

Another way of looking at it is that olders 'pass on' the estate to youngers, installing in them a sense of manly duty to take responsibility for the space as they once did. This is often a false narrative. Having established control in the neighbourhood, they then consider it their responsibility to advertise the fact, manage the space, retain control over time and look after the space as if it were an actual gang member. Thus begins the very early narrative of the strong personal connection felt by a younger to their estate or neighbourhood. Now there begins a formative opportunity (especially for youngers) to build a relationship of trust and territorial attachment: they understand it, know it intimately, know where to hide, how to escape and how to move through it; they know the locations of key building, walls, fences, defensive positions and objects to use as missiles. By acting together as a group to defend and protect their neighbourhood, youngers develop trusting relationships with their territory and their peers. These territorial relationships become a binding and bonding contract, for both the individual and the group, upon which all agree, around which all rally.

Yet again, these concepts of territoriality are highly gendered. They relate to male privilege and assumed hegemony where male olders 'pass on' the neighbourhood to male youngers to defend. They are bound up in male narratives of defending honour (and street capital), of being schooled in defence techniques and fulfilling 'the man's role/ duty' – essentially 'doing' masculinity (Messerschmidt, 1993).

As the estate or neighbourhood is the habitus, and the habitus is the self, the desire to protect and defend the estate or neighbourhood is protection of the self. Applying this logic, the gang excuses any actions used to defend the territory from incursions. Incursion becomes a form of spatial violation, of disrespect to the habitus, in much the same way as a slap to the face. As one gang member in SW9 put it, "It is about being violated and disrespected and people doing things" (African Caribbean male older). Incursions are then regarded as reasonable provocation for any subsequent defensive action. For many, however, this just becomes a reason to fight.

An alternative reasoning for incursions is put forward by Martin Sanchez-Jankowski, who found that 'fear of organisational decline' could motivate an attack on rivals to 'deter internal conflict, encourage group cohesion, and create more control over member' (1991, p 163). While this tilts at the earlier discussion abut the role of proximate fields, this was not, however, supported by evidence in SW9.

The territorial gamble

In the social field of the gang, protecting territory is more than protecting members' homes; it is protecting the embodied reputation of the neighbourhood, something the gang believes it can control or influence. The neighbourhood brand name acts as a reputational moniker against which gang members' own street capital is ultimately measured: a diminished neighbourhood reputation diminishes the street capital of the individual, while a tough reputation is built on a tough neighbourhood, i.e. a diminished reputation for the neighbourhood dilutes or diminishes the street capital of the individual. A tough reputation is built on a tough neighbourhood.

Neighbourhood reputations, like those of individuals, are, however, subject to fluctuations. Rivals have a vested interest in diminishing other neighbourhood reputations in order to elevate and maximise their own street capital. As youngers align their own reputations to that of the gang, and the gang to that of the neighbourhood, any diminution of neighbourhood reputation brings a correlated diminution in street capital for the gang and its members. Any diminishment in street capital or reputation must be quickly reversed.

Violation of gang territory, viewed as a violation of the reputation of the gang corpus, precipitates the collapse of both neighbourhood and gang members' reputations. Young people 'defending their 'hood' or endz must develop strategies to reverse this collapse and maintain stocks of street capital. Several elders/olders participating in the SW9 research reported that this had recently happened in Brixton; according to them, it had lost its 'bullet-proof reputation'. A diminishing reputation makes it easier to denigrate a neighbourhood, and so by association, its populace, specifically its gang-affiliated populace. It becomes easier to desecrate, dishonour and violate a neighbourhood once its moral authority is weakened. An area which once traded on its reputation among those with criminal or gang-affiliations, as indomitable and inviolable. As such it is now considered open to penetration and violation: its moral authority questioned.

The ability to generate reputational deflation increases the effectiveness of group incursion as a tested strategy. An incursion has a threefold benefit – it preserves the reputation of the invading gang, its members and its neighbourhood. The greater the numbers of young people involved in the incursion, the greater the multiplier effect, magnifying humiliation. In Bourdieu's social field casino, it is a sure-fire winning gamble.

Such a gamble has two further advantages. First, it offers an opportunity for individuals to advance or maximise their street capital within the safe environment of group action. Participants are potentially hyped up rather than cautious and wary. Bravado and reckless daring is evident and those who take part claim to enjoy the experience greatly. Second, a group incursion is a gang excursion. This foregrounds gang agency and gang strategy, reaffirming it as dominant to any individual agency. It is thus a bonding experience for participants, offering the rich rewards of boosted street capital, minimised risk, bragging rights, gang affirmation and the creation of joint histories. While such group or joint enterprise is often referred to as 'defending the "hood"', it could perhaps be more accurately described as 'defending the reputation of the "hood" and thus protecting my own street capital'.

Any subsequent decline in neighbourhood reputation affects the host gang and must be arrested as a matter of urgency. Failure to do so will lead to irreparable decline in the neighbourhood rep, mirrored by a decline in the status of its resident gang members. This will mean increased risk of victimisation for all in the hood and will increase the risk of violence. These events also pose a risk to the leader of the youngers, who must quickly orchestrate retaliation lest he experience a challenge to his authority and leadership. Moreover, failure on the part of olders and elders to address repeated incursions and to demonstrably orchestrate retaliation may induce a challenge to the overall leadership and authority of the gang itself. In this way, defending the hood becomes a risk management strategy.

The so-called 'postcode beef'

The gangs in SW9 do not view the local area postcodes, or even the social housing estates as the definitive boundaries of their gang domain or territory. Not least because social housing estates may traverse more than one postcode. The activities of the gangs are also conducted in a social space which is not bounded by postcodes or geographical estate location, a fact that is understood by all gang-affiliated young people:

> 'It's not really about postcodes y' know.' (African Caribbean male younger)

Describing issues of territoriality as postcode wars or 'beefs' is, in many ways, a lazy way of ascribing the spatial dimensions of habitus, social capital and territory. This description also allows for hidden, sub-surface or subterranean motivations to be overlooked or taken for granted.

The 'postcode beef' is sometimes erroneously described as acquisitional 'turf wars'. This is also incorrect, as gangs do not seek occupation or acquisition for gain, of a rival's turf. Many gang-affiliated young people do not view fighting over their own perceived territory as an option, but an obligation. However, their fights are not about expanding physical territory, but about broken relationships; they are related to issues of disrespect and the ritualised humiliation of rivals to gain advantage in the quest for street capital.

In the SW9 research, gang-affiliated young people in SW9 were unanimous in their view that members 'in beef with each other' had previously all been friends, and that the relationship had broken down when one 'dissed' or did something to annoy another, leading to an escalation of conflict.

Beefs tend to result from the demise of interpersonal relationships, and have much in common with the swiftly changing loyalties, divisions and alliances that commonly occur in the school playground. Indeed, as the SW9 research showed many beefs arose at school. If such disputes are linked to gang-affiliated young people, they take on a whole new form and meaning. When the search for distinction occurs in the social field of the gang rather than the playground and is conjoined with aspects of respect, reputation, fluctuation of street capital and access to weapons, the situation can be dangerous.

The term 'postcode beef' has obfuscated the nuances of the multiple interpersonal relationships occurring within the social field of the gang. For example, two young males in separate gangs may be in beef over a previous incident. Should a third gang propose an incursion into the neighbourhood of one of the two in dispute, it is quite possible for the two warring members to unite against the new challengers. This is often the case with extended family or where future business links transcend immediate disagreements. Business links are important, with gangs working collaboratively or separately. Some deals are small, especially those made by youngers, and may involve, one younger asking another for help in return for payment in weed. Other deals are more significant and may involve buying or selling stolen goods.

A beef may result from a soured business deal, for example, when someone refuses to pay for a pair of trainers stolen to order because they are the wrong brand, or when one cousin skims money off a deal involving another cousin. Where honour is at stake, the beef may continue for as long as the warring parties come into contact with each other – for months or even years. Over time, all new and existing members will hear about it. It filters down through the ranks, and becomes embedded in the gang consciousness. Opportunities to resolve the beef dwindles as the warring members avoid each other and the beef endures. Historical narratives become gang mythology, giving olders enduring opportunities to recount their own beefs, or their heroic role in the dramas of others. Olders use these stories to prime youngers in the art of conflict, perhaps framing them as taunts or challenges, such as "In my day, no one come into our area." Thus it favours their interests to nurse such hostilities. Many such beefs do not get resolved.

Box 8.1: Territorial incursions

An incursion is an orchestrated movement of gang members (anything between three and 50 affiliates) into the territory of a rival gang. Such raids on street capital may be frequent. All gangs are aware that the more frequent and repetitive the raid, the greater the loss of street capital for those 'allowing' the incursion. The 'victims' are perceived as weak and not in control of their endz. In the SW9 research, tensions in the summer of 2010 had been going on for 19 months, with incursions from Lambeth to Southwark, or vice versa, taking place every other day.

Incursions are organised using mobile phones and social networking sites. Members group together on bike or foot before entering a rival estate. Some members may arrive by bus from different directions to enhance the impression of an 'invasion'. The visiting gang maximises marketing opportunities by filming their incursion, which is transmitted within minutes on social networking sites. Filming further enhances the reputation of the visiting gang while diminishing that of its rivals.

Once in rival territory, the 'visiting' gang employs strategies from the expressive repertoire. As they are not in their own endz, the visiting members have a vested interest in causing maximum trouble (more damage, greater violence) for maximum effect, by locating and fighting rivals, stealing and causing criminal damage. Residents may be in danger and may be randomly attacked. Members openly brandish firearms, occasionally resulting in individuals being shot. In 2010, for example, PYG entered an estate in SW9 and fired several rounds of bullets at random into a group of GAS gang members as they hurriedly dispersed. Some incursions involve targeted hunts for key gang individuals, while others involve 'fishing' for strays (i.e. hunting missions).

The large numbers involved in such incursions (on average 15-25 young men) demand a police response, typically three or four police vans as well as officers on horseback or mountain bike. Police entry on to the estate is monitored by the gang. Local agencies may attempt to negotiate a ceasefire by calling the elders of rival gangs to a neutral location. Recently, Lambeth GAS gang and Croydon-based gang, DSN (Don't Say Nuttin'), have undertaken incursions involving extensive and sometimes quite serious fighting in Croydon town centre, while another attack on a gang in Croydon by ABM resulted in approximately 30-40 DSN members coming en masse to Stockwell to challenge the perpetrators and reassert their existence.

Planned incursions are a group exercise, although it may be that only a hard core of the group's members are fully affiliated to the gang. Friends are often requested to 'bulk up' numbers, and may be carefully chosen so as to be largely dispensable if caught. To some onlookers, these incidents it may look like massive school fights.

Territory and social field analysis

Territorial disputes are created and sustained by youngers in the elementary gang tier. Such disputes are central to the creation of the landscape of risk for all those in the social field, including non-gang-affiliated young people. Being spatially defined, it also makes the metaphorical landscape of risk a physical reality. This landscape must be negotiated daily by all actors or players in the social field and each 'playa' needs to learn quickly how to do this.

For many the bounded turf of a rival gang makes manifest the proximate field of their rivals. Chapter Five noted the importance of ensuring field stability and of guarding against a field crisis that might generate uncertainty by pitching challengers against incumbents. In this way, it is likely that territorial incursions are undertaken to generate a shock to the proximate field and thus deliberately provoke a crisis.

The manufacture of territorial disputes has important outcomes:

- It may provoke a crisis for the social field of a rival gang.
- It creates new rules for the game, permitting players to influence the rules of the game (possibly to their advantage).
- It upsets the 'game board', thereby wrong-footing others, permitting individual ascension in the field.
- It creates new players in 'the game', allowing gangs to develop strategies against new rivals. This permits inter-group bonding within the gang. It also gives the impression of temporarily relieving the pressure/shifting focus from peers to new enemies although this is just an illusion.
- It permits youngers to generate street capital quickly.
- It creates opportunities for creating instant 'gang history'. This has two benefits: generating oral narratives that valorise key players, and permitting youngers to quickly acquire the mantle of an older as they advise others how to survive.
- It permits youngers and some gang members to act wildly and to test new elements of the gang repertoire.

As a strategy, territorial disputes are supremely suited to the habitus as it relates to personal knowledge of the built environment. Possessing neighbourhood knowledge generates its own street capital; sharing it, generates yet more, while using it effectively maximises street capital. As a result, the landscape of risk is highly localised to immediate or adjacent social housing estates or even single housing blocks.

Viewed through social field analysis, the term 'postcode beef' is clearly a misnomer. This is demonstrated by a recent exercise undertaken by youth workers from the Brathay Trust who took young people to the top of a Brixton tower block and invited them to point out areas they believed were restricted to them. Several young people from Lambeth noted restrictions even within central Brixton, with comments such as "I can't go past the tube station." Such perceptions were relational to each individual and varied considerably, suggesting that the landscape of risk is individually and relationally determined.

As boundaries are relational, variable and not firmly established, several problems arise within the landscape of risk:

- *Fluctuating tensions and perceptions of 'boundaries'*
  Movements of many young people, not just gang affiliates, within this landscape are determined by current tensions between gangs. Gang members are particularly aware that tensions vary hourly or daily, rising and falling quickly. Communicating these fluctuations takes time; others must then verify this new information. In social field analysis, this amounts to sudden rule changes. Within the social field, 'regularity' may be viewed as 'assumptions which can be overturned' (Martin, 2003, p 33). Each change is the result of a player using strategies to achieve advantage, while disadvantaging others. Such changes affect all, although some will be purposefully 'caught out'.

- *Contested boundaries*
  The boundaries of social fields are themselves areas of conflict. As virtual boundaries, they are unseen, highly variable and dependent on the vagaries of interpersonal relationships. Some central neighbourhood areas, such as parks, high streets and leisure centres, may be designated as either neutral or contested places. Safety in these areas is often depends on the current tensions or active beefs, so that may be safe one week and highly dangerous the next. Access may be negotiated, though the granting of access is a further variable subject to change. These daily or weekly variations place considerable strain on youngers and sometimes on olders, who

may be required to undertake negotiations about allowing access to contested areas.

- *Through routes*
  Territories are often separated by commonly established 'through routes', which themselves become flashpoints. Although gang-affiliated young people are highly knowledgeable of local gang boundaries (SW9 has a unique and iconic identity and gang members will have SW9 printed on their tee-shirts), any imposed court restrictions may prevent them from using key routes and push them into disputed territory. Some members use sat nav to monitor the boundaries of local beefs or imposed court restrictions.

- *The imperative of good communication*
  In this landscape of risk, safety is determined by having current knowledge of tensions and rule changes. Ability to communicate changing circumstances to all concerned is both a field rule and an imperative. For example, if an older is off the estate while negotiating with a rival gang over permission for two of their members to enter the area to visit family, he must instruct his youngers to let the visitors pass. If he forgets to phone his youngers to make this arrangement, the visitors will be attacked. Such occurrences are common and have multiple repercussions. There are also examples of information being purposefully withheld in order to cause harm to an individual.

- *Responding to new rules*
  Gangs constantly make minor adjustments to their affiliations and alliances, as do individuals. For example, the presence of an external renegade in a gang's territory instigates new alliances or helps bind together previously estranged friends. In addition, some smaller gangs may no longer need to function and new alignments may be enacted. The elders will thus shift the pieces on the board, so that when a gang member next returns to his endz, he may find that things have been slightly adjusted. This is both a natural progression of new relationships and power dynamics, as well as a deliberate tactic for change.

Olders seldom become involved in territorial disputes, as this may impinge upon the opportunities provided by easy movement across boroughs and rival territory. Having moved on from 'defending territory', they can focus on making money. The practicalities of unhindered movement easily trump fights about territory. For most olders, territorial issues fade into the past; for others it remains. This view often depends upon how quickly a younger becomes an older, their personal and gang relationships and loyalties.

Olders must adjust to the relative freedom of the higher tiers once they leave behind the more constricted world of the youngers. This new freedom is earned and negotiated rather than simply granted by dint of age of length of time spent in the field. This new reality needs careful testing and assessment over time within the constantly changing dynamics of the social field. Danger and the possibility of attack is ever-present, so olders must remain vigilant, negotiating access via networks where possible. This new social reality may lack clarity and may be confusing for some members. Some gang members in SW9 believed that agencies underestimated the difficulties encountered by olders in renegotiating territory, although those professionals who took part in the research considered territorial issues to be equally dangerous for both olders and youngers:

> 'It's just so serious. Sometimes 'cos of that age group we miss it, we think everything is not that bad, but is bad, it's very bad.' (White female professional charity worker)

This fluctuating landscape of risk, with its temporary truces and negotiated 'hood passes', are further reasons for increased neighbourhood violence. Both intra- and inter-gang disputes create a complex topology where violence is a constant threat. It is this topology that players in the social field must navigate and survive.

Chapter Nine explores this landscape of risk further, and considers how young people become involved in gangs and the factors that influence them.

Learning the risks of the game: life in the landscape of risk

'A friend is one who has the same enemies as you have.'
Abraham Lincoln

This chapter examines in more detail how young people learn the rules of the game, how they join the gang, and the strategies they employ to survive this landscape of risk. I propose that young people must first recognise their social field and identify their position in it, before developing a shared understanding of the stakes and what is happening (Bourdieu and Wacquant, 1992). By so doing, they learn the rules of the game before learning how to play it. In this context I propose that school is the key location where the rules and risks of the game are learnt.

Learning the rules of the game

I have theorised that the social field of the gang, with its imperatives to generate street capital and its vicarious fluctuating nature, creates a landscape of risk for young people. This concept usefully combines Bourdieu's social topography (Bourdieu, 1969) with aspects of my early organising concept of domestic violence and the Duluth Model (see Appendix C). In the same way as women in a household characterised by domestic violence devise survival strategies and techniques, so too do young people in the social field of the gang. This metaphorical landscape of risk is, for many, made manifest in relation to territoriality and the so-called 'postcode beef' (see Chapter Eight).

Risk, usually in the form of victimisation, comes from multiple directions in this social field: from gang affiliates and peers, rival gangs and the police. Interaction with each group may diminish street capital, leading to victimisation and violence – a social norm understood and accepted from an early age. Those in the gang social field are most vulnerable, although non-gang-affiliated young people in SW9 are also at risk, and usually have a basic understanding of the issues of street capital and associated dangers. For some young people, gang affiliation is the best option of mitigating the risks of victimisation.

However, several different narratives have emerged, indicating different push/pull factors for gang affiliation. I examine these in more detail before considering how young people mitigate risk and minimise victimisation.

Early recognition of the social field

Young people living in SW9 develop an early awareness that gangs operate in their communities. They may gain this awareness by witnessing a particular event, or it may be common knowledge within their circle, something they have grown up with. They become aware of criminal activity, the importance of relationships, alliances, allegiances and risks. At some point, opportunities present for closer involvement and several factors determine whether or not they enter the social field of the gang and, if so, how they enter. These factors include, among others, exposure to the normalisation of gangs, learning to play 'the game' at school and family pressure.

Normalisation

Growing up in deprived or contested neighbourhood where urban street gangs are a social norm does not automatically mean all young people affiliate. However, proximity to the gang or exposure to those involved and their activities begins a process of normalisation in which gang life is seen as part of the fabric of the wider community:

> 'It was just part of my environment. Kids hanging around, you just wanna be part of it. Some were older, some younger. At first, I didn't want to get involved. I could see however it became routine for them, stealing phones and robbing handbags. It became quite attractive. I got involved 'cos that's what was happening every night.' (African Caribbean male younger)

This normalisation process includes a growing awareness of the benefits and commodities acquired, accrued or accessed by the gang. While economic capital and access to it eventually dominate their motivations, younger people are initially attracted by other benefits, such as excitement, risk and the range of opportunities which they perceive will be provided by closer affiliation with the gang, i.e. fun, protection, status, respect and generating street capital. The active involvement of family members in the social field increases the effects of normalisation on young people.

Learning how to play the game at school

It is the social field of the wider neighbourhood which ultimately provides the crucible for the emergence of gangs.[1] Within the social field of the wider neighbourhood it is the schools which play a crucial formative role in early development of gangs.

All the young people and professionals in this study claim that schools are central to the understanding and genesis of violent street gangs in SW9, with widespread consensus of the role played by schools, and later by colleges, in allowing gangs to coalesce, recruit and sustain their activities. This occurs primarily through the provision of a communal space where peer groups of all types naturally form, build relationships and break up. At school young people quite naturally align and identify with different peer groups from different neighbourhoods.

The coming together of a peer group that then engages in antisocial behaviour or criminal activity is a well-known and natural occurrence for many young people. The economic disadvantage and social deprivation of SW9 and Lambeth provide the push and pull factors that may lead such peer groups to criminal activity. Where educational and economic opportunities are limited, peer groups may begin to use instrumental strategies to raise economic capital (Pitts, 2008b). The benefits of such activities become increasingly obvious, as do the rules of how to obtain them.

Under these conditions and within the social field of SW9, opportunities exist for young people to establish themselves in the elementary tier, and members view this as a normal and natural progression within their peer group.

Some young people already have network connections and affiliations with local street gangs or criminally active family members, so the normalisation of the street gang in the social field is replicated by the normalisation of the gang within the school, the school being a central component of the local neighbourhood and the habitus of young people. Moreover, Pupil Referral Units, established to provide education for excluded children, are particularly fertile ground for gangs and gang recruitment, making them dangerous spaces for some young people.[2] This is particularly problematic if the gang is criminally active or violent.

Given the complex interactions involved in child development normalisation processes, it can be difficult to distinguish how gangs utilise schools in active 'recruitment'. In this way it is possible to view 'recruitment' as nothing more than the normal process of choosing which friends to 'hang with'. Indeed, Hallsworth (2013) refutes outright any notion of gang recruitment. However professionals and young people who have recently exited gangs conclude that the very fact that the peer group is a gang and the gang is a brand compels the gang to actively 'recruit' members from their peers where levels of trust are highest. Some professionals view this as cold-blooded recruitment from a rich pool of unsuspecting prospects. On the other hand, young people tend to view it as the continuation of a gradual process of coming together or 'getting closer', and believe that this process will, and does, happen regardless of location. The school merely provides an opportunity for regular interaction on a daily basis. Densley believes that gangs are highly selective about who joins them, with trust and proven ability being key deciding factors (Densley, 2013, p 110). In my street capital theory, it is those young people with high street capital who are approached for gang affiliation, while those with lesser reputation or street capital are more likely to be subject to other influences.

Social field analysis suggests that all these views are partly true and partly oversimplified. Schools are spaces where young people form allegiances to build social capital and thus avoid victimisation. Schools also form their own social field where the search for street capital or social capital thrives openly often through bullying. In certain neighbourhoods and under certain conditions, therefore, gang affiliation for reasons of protection becomes the dominant response for many.

For many young people, gang affiliation is not seen as 'recruitment', a term more favoured by professionals, but simply as 'getting involved'. This suggests a more gradual process, seen by many as a normal progression of life in their social field. Young people themselves commonly identify four key elements that determine their involvement in the social field of the gang: normalisation; family; the search for reputation and respect; and school. For many young people, the social field presents opportunities for all of these aspects to convene.

Schools also provide a captive audience for potential marketing of brand names, generating opportunities for individuals or gangs to develop strategies for mutual benefit. In the school environment, fear of victimisation compels many to seek closer affiliation with peer groups or with those in the gang's elementary tier. Fear of isolation or being designated an 'outcast' is a critical consideration for many who actively develop strategies to form closer links to any dominant gang. For many, the decision to get closer to the gang or to affiliate relates directly to their need to mitigate their own current or future victimisation.

Similar strategies for involvement take place in colleges and particularly in Pupil Referral Units, such as Park Academy in West Norwood, SE27. Local professionals and residents believe that particular schools are linked to particular gangs and act as feeders for the gang. Local children may feel pressure to affiliate with the local gang, especially if the gang is dominant within the school setting. Others act on individual agency, having assessed the risk of potential victimisation. Young people may experience pressure from the gang on the estate on which they live as well as at school, leading them to feel that the gang is inescapable.

Family pressure

For many, the family is a major source for push factors into the gang or affiliation to the gang (Vigil, 1988a; Moore, 1991; Decker and Van Winkle, 1996). For many, the family has a major influence over gang affiliation. If family members, particularly siblings, are involved with gangs, young people are more likely to affiliate or become involved in criminal activity. Gang involvement of other family members, especially siblings, is a major risk factor for young people in determining their involvement with, or affiliation to, criminal activity and street gangs (Moore, 1991; Curry and Spergel, 1992). Klein and Maxson (2006, p 147) noted that 'adolescent peer pressure influences exert a strong proximal effect on youth attitudes and behaviour during this life stage'. Vigil (2002, p 2) also notes that 'when street socialization replaces socialization by conventional caretakers' that young people can find strong attachment in street culture belief systems. Medina et al (2013, p 6) concur that having a gang-affiliated sibling is a significant factor for gang membership.[3] While family gang involvement in gangs does not necessarily mean that all family members will affiliate, the proximity of criminal activity and access to criminal networks may well have a negative influence on young people, either pushing or pulling them into gang involvement or affiliation.

Many young people have an older sibling who is affiliated to a gang, and sibling pairs do exist in gangs whether or not the younger member has been actively pressured into joining. The regular involvement of a sibling in gang activity will demystify the gang in the eyes of the youngster; its players, its history and structure become recognisable, allowing the youngster to feel protected and more predisposed to gang involvement. This association is strengthened by witnessing regular interaction between gang and other family members. While some young people may experience mild pressure from family members to join the gang, coercion is seldom required. Joining motivations include witnessing a sibling gain access to and retain rewards; a desire to emulate a sibling's example; and the desire for protection. These normative behaviours mask the risk while accentuating the rewards and opportunities for fun. An older brother may hold the dominant male position in the household, making his views influential and obscuring other options, such as opting out of gang involvement.

Seeing a sibling reap the economic rewards of gang involvement makes this option both attractive and alluring to younger family members. In addition, affiliated siblings provide ready-made access into the gang, negating the need for initiation, providing protection from initial bullying and expediting progression through the lower ranks. Older siblings have established links, alongside access to stolen goods and rewards as yet unobtainable by younger family members, but the youngsters can at least trade on their siblings' street name and street capital, if they are an existing player.

Youngsters do not receive formal invitations to join the gang, and there is no definitive point at which a potential recruit is deemed to be 'ready'. Instead, youngsters are tested over time through a series of simple repetitive approaches, for example, requests to carry information or goods. Nonetheless, it is considered hugely flattering for young people to be invited to 'hang with' the gang at which point, from the gang's perspective the new recruit is a safe bet.

There may be further influence from close family friends and extended family members – cousins and second cousins, for example – a dynamic that increases youngsters' risk of gang affiliation.

> 'My network was very corrupt when I was young, you know, uncles, aunties, cousins, family. They were into drug dealing, robbery, fighting, just general criminal activity.'
> (African Caribbean male independent operator)

This risk may be accentuated by the introduction into the family unit of new boyfriends, fathers or step-brothers with criminal or gang connections. The local network also acts to encourage younger family members to get involved.

Some families are acknowledged as organised criminal 'cartels' in their own right. It is possible for a young person to be both a gang member and a member of the family cartel (an organised crime network or firm established and run by a family). Wider opportunities for economic gain then present themselves via expanded markets and trading potential for both parties, such as the cartel supplying the gang with drugs, setting local prices and controlling distribution. In *Reluctant gangsters*, John Pitts notes that the crack business in one borough he studied was controlled by members or close associates of four families (Pitts, 2008b, p 71). Should the prospective member choose to play both sides, even openly, he will expose himself to several potential risks. He will always need to be explicit who he is operating for at each stage. He may need to absent himself from the antisocial elements of the street gang in order to avoid prosecution, which may lead to his exclusion from the cartel.

Intergenerational involvement occurs when parents or guardians seek to actively involve siblings in pre-established criminal activity (Sutherland, 1947). Evidence from the SW9 research suggests that the PDC (the longest established operating gang in Lambeth) fits this profile. Those members who are criminally active acknowledge that they have this "whole underworld going on that we wanna keep alive, y'know?" (African Caribbean male elder).

Interestingly, this static structure, evolved over time, only seldom fits the reality of SW9 where families tend to be much more fluid; young people may be single mothers or grandparents, siblings may be related through only one parent, step-fathers or new boyfriends are common and uncles widespread and numerous. In this reality, intergenerational pressure need not develop over generations between blood relatives but occurs regularly via evolving domestic relationships. In Lambeth, several entire families well known to the police are linked into criminality, with the young male members particularly being involved in gangs.

Some families in SW9 claim that 'street socialising' is beneficial. This may involve instructing youngsters about the rules of the local street code by exposing them to gang or other criminal activity, something they claim is a 'real education' and will keep young people safe (Anderson, 1999). They attribute recent deaths in the borough to the arrival of families new to Brixton whose children are "not schooled in the ways of the road". These new families are unsure how to 'play' the area, how to adjust and to ask the right questions to get the right information. Consequently, they put themselves in difficult or dangerous situations.

Getting involved in the gang

Recruitment is required to sustain the status quo of the social field, maintaining the privilege of the incumbents. It permits the expansion or consolidation of power and control, of business opportunities and networks. Recruitment is, however, a contentious and misunderstood issue, with gang researchers and professionals working in the field often failing to agree on its dimensions and modus operandi. The term 'recruitment' is itself problematic, creating, for some, expectations of formal membership offers or contracts. Hallsworth and Duffy (2010, p 6) view the term as 'the language of control' and not representative of real life in the gang. Aldridge and Medina (2008) found the concept of membership in relation to the gang social field 'alien' to the young people they interviewed. The young people in their research associated the term with regular subscription dues for sports activities or social club membership, so, given its unsuitability in the context of gang fieldwork, this finding is unsurprising. Aldridge and Medina's findings (2008) further align with American research[4] claiming that joining a gang is akin to joining a school friendship group and that 'only in a minority of instances does anything resembling "recruitment" takes place' (p 17). For Aldridge and Medina joining a gang is achieved through 'developing a different kind of relationship within existing contacts' (2008, p 17). There are also reports of initiation ceremonies in the American literature, although Aldridge and Media find no evidence of this in their research. Why their UK evidence supports one aspect of the American experience but not the other remains unexplained. The minority of instances where they did identify recruitment into gangs also remains undeveloped.

The behavioural mechanisms, choices and influences determining gang affiliation are more complicated than this overview suggests. While it is likely that the UK situation differs from that of the US, both similarities and differences should be fully explored.

The reality is that push/pull factors operate alongside gang strategies and individual agency. Central to this is the imperative for young people to mitigate the risk of victimisation. Some aspects of 'recruitment' are very covert and almost imperceptible, leading to doubts as to their existence, while others are more overt. Recruiting new members seldom relies on one technique.

Factors influencing gang affiliation

The lure of the game

Several centripetal forces operate to bring gangs and young people closer. In the social field of SW9 such elements may prove seductive and irresistible. Here there is an opportunity to escape the mundane reality of life with few prospects of employment and build a new life narrative or street persona. For some, the gang offers excitement, drama and opportunities for distinction.

The charisma and aura of the leader around whom members congregate may also influence gang affiliation. Potential members in the neighbourhood are familiar with the brand name and reputation of the leader prior to affiliation For youngers in particular, this reputation may be elevated, exaggerated or lionised. It is flattering to potential members to know that this person now wants to meet with them and possibly even invite them to join his group. Certain leaders? may also have acquired symbolic capital (the 'degree of accumulated prestige, celebrity ... honour ... knowledge ... and recognition') (Bourdieu, 1993, p 7)

It is hard to underestimate how much young people in general wish to be seen or known to be 'cool'. Within the social field of the gang, this desire is amplified. In terms of street capital, 'cool' is a status to be achieved and earned. The concept is thus interwoven with complexities of reputation, respect and ability to build and retain social capital.

A further seductive narrative widely recognised and highly attractive to young people is one that rebrands and reframes the gang as a street family.

Street family

In the landscape of risk created by this dangerous social field, young people have created the enduring overarching narrative of the street family.[5] In a social field of limited trust where information is critical, one must create useful relationships that, albeit temporary, appear constant. Young people in the gang thus nurture the narrative of a 'fam' (family) or 'band of bros' (band of brothers), grouped together through common background and common purpose – to survive. For many, this is a logical extension of school friendships, neighbourhood acquaintances and propinquity:

> 'I just think it's a group of people that has grown up together and they sort of like, 'cos they have grown up in a way where they've built a defence mechanism where they've had to fight for their own stuff or defend everything they have just in case. So they've got that mentality.' (African female gang consultant)

This narrative of cohesion and shared purpose is compounded through shared experience, longevity and family links. It is also further compounded by shared language or speech and by a shared knowledge that only those within this social field understand what is being said, or what is happening. It is thus highly exclusive and exclusionary. The inability of many young people to leave the social field and their deep immersion within it effectively dictates that 'survivors' will find shared experiences and common ground. Thus the concept of the street family is born:

> 'It's a group of people who have grown up on the estate together. It's just like a family, it's like a family out there – a street family. If anything was to happen to your family, what is your first instinct, to protect your family, innit. So that's what they are, they are family, anything that goes wrong they will protect it.' (African female gang consultant)

Several other benefits are realised through the nomenclature of street family:

• It sounds cool and implies an alternative family structure.
• It implies a common purpose and thus becomes an attractive centripetal force in gang affiliation.
• It is supported and nurtured by olders/elders as a way of group bonding.
• It means that recruitment into the gang often becomes viewed as an invitation to become part of the family.

So powerful and seductive is this narrative 'on road' that many young people reject the term 'gang' and only use the term 'street family' or 'fam', which they believe more accurately conveys their experience. As this term is less pejorative and thus more attractive, it importantly provides a narrative of succour, support and protection:

'It's a group of friends that grew up together. A community. They are part of the community. The young people are a group of friends who protect people who are in the estate in a way. 'Cos there are a lot of people who will come to this estate and will disrespect or try to disrespect anyways, so they try to protect the estate in some sense.' (African female gang consultant)

This narrative permits the community to reframe gang activities into a more acceptable narrative.

This is however all an illusion as the reality is rather different. Far from being a band of brothers, relationships are transitory, trust is a purchasable and rare commodity, and even the closest friendships are ever-changing and negotiable. The conflict and convulsive struggle of the social field determines that each young person is ultimately on their own, left to generate, maintain and monitor their own street capital, often at the expense of others. In many ways, the gang represents a congregation of rivals, masking mutual exploitation for personal gain. To put it another way, it appears that the gang retains the dividing and shifting loyalties of candidates as seen in The Apprentice (BBC TV) in the hot-house environment of the Big Brother House (Channel 4 TV). Add to this teenage hormones and emotions, and it becomes a highly volatile mix. The nature of the social field locks everyone into permanent competition and ensures that all must generate street capital. No-one is immune from street capital deflation, even 'brers' and 'bros'.

The familiarity of this street family narrative with its romantic leanings of nostalgia and hope means it is widely embraced and adopted by young people who genuinely believe it to be true. Even some local youth workers in SW9 give it credibility and repeat it unquestionably. It is primarily, however, a coping strategy to manage risk. Over time, most young people come to realise that the gang does not embody family values, and when trusted friends turn against them, they feel bitterly betrayed. As Densley noted (2013, p 36) 'if the gang is a family ... then it is an abusive one – gang love is very much conditional'. In this illusory world, young people feel bounded by a deeply emotional contract. If this contract is broken, there is a risk of increased violence in the social field, as well an increase in the severity of that violence.

'A lot of people don't trust a lot of people. A lot of things can happen when that trust has gone.' (African female gang consultant)

Some young people recognise and adapt to the reality of rivalry earlier than others, realising that the street family generates increased, as opposed to decreased, risk. One strategy available to them is to manage their own risk more effectively by becoming independent or solo actors in the social field.

In addition to normalisation processes and family pressure, factors influencing gang affiliation include strategies by peers and olders to recruit young people directly into the gang. Once the youngsters enter their sphere of influence, they often have no choice but to affiliate.

Recruitment into the gang may represent a succession strategy on the part of younger members or a conservation strategy (Swartz, 1997) on the part of incumbent olders seeking to maintain their status quo. For newly affiliated members, recruitment often represents a survival strategy, as they recognise that they must have a formal relationship with the gang if they live in the neighbourhood. For some, therefore, affiliation is a strategy for advancing within the social field and a way of navigating the landscape of risk.

Inducements

Young people may be induced to join a gang by the lure of the trappings flaunted by other members – expensive cars, motorbikes and jewellery – or by accepting gifts from them. Young people tend to notice and be impressed by such unobtainable ostentatious exhibits, sometimes at a very young age. As one ex-gang member in SW9 explained:

''Cos you are looking up to certain man and certain man have nice 'tings. And they ain't getting it from doin' right. They getting it from doin' wrong.' (African Caribbean male older)

For many young black men living in impoverished neighbourhoods, prospects and opportunities are limited, something they come to realise early.

Grooming (extenuated gifting)

Although interactions between olders and youngers are rarely viewed as a form of 'grooming' in the classic sense of the term, there are aspects of such behaviour that fit with the ways in which more experienced and established members invest time and energy in youngers to prepare or subtly coerce them to affiliate, as noted by one older in SW9: "What draws people in is there are father figures." It is notable that Hallsworth and Duffy (2010, p 6) view the term 'grooming' as reflective of practitioners' language of control rather than a reality of the social field. Toy (2008), writing from a practitioner's perspective in Southwark, notes that: 'Organisational gangs use social motivational factors to their advantage in the identification, recruitment and grooming of prospective gang members.' This includes family connections, cultural and religious connections and antipathy towards the police.

Grooming in the traditional sense involves aspects of seduction, flattery, attention, enticements and inducements from an older, mature or experienced person to obtain sexual favours from a younger person who is less mature or worldly, or is unwittingly attracted to such moves. Youth work professionals in SW9 recognise such tactics at play. In SW9, olders undertake a type of grooming by identifying vulnerable or needy others and providing them with treats:

> 'My son (aged 11) was approached by the lead guy in GAS gang who said, "Oi, young man, do you want to make a quick bling bling; I'll get you a better bike. You'll have all these girls falling after you; you are just the right age, I can groom you." I said to my son, "Do you know what groom is?"' (West African female resident)

'Forced' affiliation

Professionals in SW9 often refer to the 'forced involvement' of young people in gangs. This loaded expression needs further explanation. Professionals and young people, both gang-affiliated and non-gang-affiliated, disagree about the level of 'force' exerted in such situations. The term implies that individual agency is extinguished; this is highly unlikely. It is more likely that the individual accepts he will be safer in the gang than outside it and adapts his individual strategy accordingly. Evidence suggests that while bullying and intimidation are widely used within the social field, often leading to affiliation, some young people resist coercion, possibly with the support of their families. This supports the view that some young people manage to retain a strong individual strategy or personal agency.

Some young people refer to peer pressure as the main reason for seeking to affiliate, often expressed as 'giving in'. This is often determined by what happens at school, the primary social arena for young people. Others refer to external social pressures that act against them and effectively 'force' them into gang affiliation by closing down other options or opportunities.

Some young people experience 'force' through acts of aggression and violence that translate as being 'told to do something'. In the SW9 research, young people recounted numerous cases of initially declining gang affiliation only to be subjected to constant harassment, 'giving in' only when family members were harassed. Another example of 'forced involvement' is where a young person shows they can be trusted by agreeing to hide stolen goods or weapons on behalf of the gang.

Young people with previous offending histories may already be involved with a gang. Indeed, gangs are more likely to make overtures to young people already inclined towards criminal activity. Personal networks are also of interest. Where local gang involvement is the norm, those outside it may be called to account for their non-involvement. Young people may sometimes be intimidated into joining a gang in order to avoid rumours that they are snitches.

The landscape of risk, however, is unevenly distributed. New arrivals are particularly at risk and may be subjected to threats of 'forced' involvement. Young people with no prior relationship with the gang are also at risk. These two high-risk groups may be targeted to hide weapons, with threats and intimidation ensuring compliance. As bullying escalates, young people often feel forced to choose between acting for the gang (and thus affiliating) or suffering further victimisation. One route offers protection, the other offers constant fear and harassment (Pitts, 2008b). Those with strong family bonds find such overtures easier to ignore or overcome (Hirschi, 1969).[6] Those without such support may have no alternative but to join the gang. Many of the young people in the SW9 research claimed to be too afraid to leave their house because of pressure from the gang to affiliate and their families may also feel threatened. Abuse may also be directed at other family members. The young person will feel responsible for bring this pressure upon the family and thus may affiliate to the gang as a way of relieving this pressure and reducing the risks of his family being victimised. Affiliation is therefore a calculated strategy of risk mitigation.

Risk mitigation

Paradoxically however, affiliation is a risk and a gamble in its own right. The two key narratives of risk mitigation are protection and peer pressure.

Protection

Individuals motivated to join the gang for protection do so to mitigate risks of victimisation. Young people unaffiliated to the gang may face isolation or exclusion by their peers. Those choosing not to affiliate may find themselves shunned and at increased risk of victimisation, although this is not always the case. One young gang member articulated it thus:

> 'If you are not part of it then for young people you are totally ignored, you don't belong to anything. Then you think, God, what can I do to be part of this to get into it. So in many ways they are forced into it. If they haven't got someone behind them to give them a different direction, they feel lost. Isolation is the worst thing that can happen to anyone.' (West African male younger)

Those who are shunned are designated as outcasts and may have to sever contact with their peers, potentially reducing their access to crucial information and further increasing their isolation and potential victimisation. Isolation prevents them from raising their street capital, leaving them in permanent victim status. To mitigate risk, it therefore becomes crucial to remain a 'playa'. One professional suggested that this potential isolation was difficult for mature adults to fully comprehend, and that it was one of many factors taken into account by young people deciding whether or not to join a gang.

Non-affiliated young people in gang-affected neighbourhoods are also at high risk of victimisation. The 'protection' narrative provides many young people with an easy route to affiliate, offering a trade-off or bargain: gang involvement will stop the threats and the violence. However this choice may indeed be fake, i.e. the situation is not always this clear-cut as the social field is possibly even more threatening and dangerous for those in the lower ranks. Those with low self-esteem or limited individual agency may enter the gang via this route; having experienced regular victimisation, they see gang affiliation as an opportunity to be left alone.[7]

> 'They don't force you – but it plays on your mind. If I act more like them, then they'll leave me alone. I know it's a contradiction but it's how it happens.' (West African male younger)

Peer pressure

A further strong motivation for gang affiliation is peer pressure. This acts in two distinct ways, first as a quest for respect. This is a 'pull factor' for young people who want to emulate their peers, including olders, and who are willing participants in affiliation. Emulation of peers brings street capital; surpassing peers brings envy from other members, and kudos and increased street capital.

In the second scenario, giving in to peer pressure by emulating peers is a way of mitigating risk. Here young people begin to fear that they are falling behind and out of step with their peers. They may be the object of ridicule at first but this eventually turns to isolation or victimisation. Young people may conform with their peers against their better judgement, perhaps being threatened or compelled to do so. At the same time, they may see the benefits of following their peers and falling in line. Many see it as an opportunity to increase their street capital, a benefit gained as soon as they affiliate. Peer pressure may be so compulsive, repetitive, overwhelming or coercive that young people feel they have limited choice or no choice other than to conform. For most, conforming is a natural process which they will view as 'keeping their friends'. For others, it is a question of 'giving in' to a group dynamic that only those with substantial individual agency can resist. In the context of the urban street gang, peer pressure is most often associated with engaging in criminal activity.

A central construct of peer pressure is its ability to make people get involved in things they would not otherwise have done. As one young affiliate in SW9 noted:

> 'You are involved in the peer pressure so much every single day, it becomes ... you!' (West African female younger)

Peer pressure puts considerable strain on young people and it is strongly linked to their levels of street capital. A failure to act in ways that meet the peer group social norms may be read as a challenge or as a show of disrespect to the gang. Your reputation will suffer if you fail to fall into line or assuage such pressures as daily requests via social networking sites to engage criminal activity. At the same time young people are surrounded by subliminal messages about limited educational and employment opportunities. If the adults around them reinforce these messages, young people come to believe that they may as well get involved.

Giving in to peer pressure alleviates the pressure on young people. Most young people start with little or no self-respect or peer respect and must acquire these attributes as they develop their personality. As they become increasingly aware of the rising street capital of others, any refusal to join in with group-validated action diminishes their own street capital. This dilemma is only resolved by giving in to peer pressure and salvaging one's street capital. Individual strategy thus merges or aligns with the now foregrounded and thus dominant gang strategy. One gang member expressed the quest for respect as a form of self-gratification:

> 'At first you are pleasing somebody or some people. After a while it becomes self pleasure, 'cos after a while there is no-one left to please, everyone knows what you do.' (West African male younger)

Risk mitigation for experienced gang members

Experienced gang members sometimes leave their original gang to join another gang, especially if they move to a new neighbourhood. An elder who is contemplating admitting a new arrival must consider several issues, not least the individual's network connections, including local and extended family, brand name and level of street capital. Experienced gang members understand that a known brand name confers considerable advantages. New arrivals without a brand name must start again at an age-appropriate rank and develop a rapid strategy to re-establish themselves.

Those seeking to return to the gang are generally young men aged from 19–25 who seek to re-join following time away in fatherhood, employment, college, or incarceration. They seek to rejoin at the mature level by getting involved in high-yield criminal activity, such as cash–in–transit robberies (see Chapter Seven).

Post-gang affiliation

Once in the gang, risks are usually multiplied, and seldom diminished.[8] This fact alone offers a valuable counterpoint to those who seek to join gangs for protection. Setting aside the increased risks from rival gangs,[9] there are two key elements to consider in relation to affiliation: first, demonstrating allegiance to the new gang, and second, building trust. Both are key factors in building street capital and thus advancing in the social field.

Demonstrating allegiance

Some urban street gangs are thought to have developed ritual initiation ceremonies to demonstrate allegiance. These are secretive events that are unknown to professionals. This research found no evidence of such rites of passage occurring in SW9, where demonstrating allegiance to the gang is essentially about building trust and establishing new relationships. Prioritising gang strategies such as hiding weapons or drugs may be advantageous, although many members do so through fear rather than as a positive strategy to advance. Most commonly, allegiance to the gang and the trust of members is earned by running with the gang over time, undertaking activities with members or approved by them.

Building trust

The ability to create, build and sustain trust between new and existing members is of key importance. This is no simple achievement, given the constantly shifting alliances, allegiances and relationships in the landscape of risk. Knowing whom to trust, and then keeping that trust, presents daily challenges. Information remains central to monitoring actions. Building trust brings members closer to the inner circle and provides greater opportunities for respect and financial gain, along with opportunities for increasing street capital.

A younger's trustworthiness is tested and assessed within the group in a number of different ways. Initially this is simply: will you be where you said you would be at a certain time? Will you make yourself available as promised? Will you provide your support as offered? Will you bring the weed as you said you would? Further testing or auditioning will follow, for example, through fighting. Trust is enhanced by keeping silent, sharing proceeds, favouring other members with kickbacks and stolen goods, or appearing as a witness in court. This finding is confirmed by Densley (2013).

Many young people in the SW9 research commented that gangs were not places where people could be trusted; 'friendships' were transitory, and characterised by double-dealing, backstabbing, cheating and set-ups. This suggests that the struggle in the arena of social competition is intense. In some instances, gang members are forced to trade in one friendship for another in order to avoid victimisation: we won't hit you if you give someone up. Indeed, one young gang member was inadvertently caught out as having given someone else up when his mobile phone was stolen by his peers who then accessed his calls.

Playing solitaire: risk mitigation through individualism

Within the social field of the gang, it is still possible to pursue individual strategies by not affiliating and some young people choose this as a way of minimising risk and victimisation. Different types of individualism operate, however, and it is important to differentiate between them.

Some 'independents', also known as floaters, operate between gangs without affiliating to any single group. This strategy requires careful risk management within the social field. Some individuals manage to resist being pulled into the gang structure or having direct affiliation with any specific named brand; they come from the local neighbourhood, know all the actors, share the habitus of the social field, know the codes, the rules and 'the game' – but choose to play solitaire. They keep their personal movements and contact details private. Such individuals have often been involved in instrumental crimes from a young age, and may have come to some agreement with elders to operate independently, i.e. elders have agreed for them to 'float' between gangs. They may also be able to access elders more readily than non-independents should they need to. This is referred to as 'an independent pass':

> 'I sold cannabis, then Class A. It was always a temporary motive. I'd sell a while then go back to weed. I needed to make college happen, but it also passed for university, my savings, my house, my clothes. It wasn't about chains or trainers, but the bigger picture. I needed to do this to get to here. It was never meant to be forever.' (African Caribbean female independent operator)

Their vulnerability to victimisation may be reduced by their isolation from the street family, as rivalries within the gang hierarchy do not apply to them. Conversely, they may be at increased risk of victimisation as all gangs in the neighbourhood treat the soloist with suspicion.

Soloists employ elements of the gang repertoire that best suit their skills and network connections, for example, drug dealing. This becomes their chosen strategy for raising economic capital. As survival is the primary concern for these individuals, the role of soloist or independent may only be adopted for a time-limited period, e.g. until they have made sufficient money, as a result increasing street capital and reputation is often a secondary consideration. However maintaining a rep that indicates you are 'not to be fucked with' will greatly assist your ability to 'float' between gangs (think Omar in The Wire). Increasing street capital and reputation is often secondary to survival. Alongside the survival instinct is an ability to convert network connections into local power and authority. As one independent operator put it:

> 'I've been in a lot of situations. Even when young I saw a lot of things. I was on a mission, though. If I made it, I made it, if I didn't, I didn't. I did a lot of good things. I did some fucked-up shit. I have a good heart. Even though I had money, I didn't trouble people. I had the power to be that middle girl. I had that power. I never told my sister what I did. I would do it all again. I've gone to college, university and supported my sister. She knows I am bad and won't take any shit from anyone. I do believe it was survival. I never got greedy, that's why I survived. I paid my way through uni and put a roof over my head.' (African Caribbean female independent operator)

Once young people become involved in the social field of the gang, life becomes a constant battle to maintain street capital while maintaining or improving field position in the landscape of risk. Young people often refer to this process as 'survival'. Chapter Ten examines in more depth the strategies employed by young people to improve their chances of survival.

Notes

[1] See discussion and footnote in Introduction. Vigil (1993) identifies seven steps frequently involved with gang affiliation. See also Howell (2012, p 229).

[2] Notably the murder of Zac Olumegbon outside Park Campus Pupil Referral Unit in West Norwood in 2010.

[3] Two additional findings in this recent research are worthy of note. Firstly they found that 'pre-existing problems and anti-social behaviour were the strongest predictors of both joining and staying affiliated to gangs'. Secondly

they identified that parents who knew their children's peer group were less likely to have children who joined and remained in a gang (Medina et al, 2013, p 6).

[4] It is common for children to have involvement with many peer groups during school-life and adolescence. Some academics have argued that therefore we should view gang not as 'organisations' with boundaries but as social networks (Fleisher, 2006; Papachristos, 2005).

[5] The concept of gangs as families is a common concept in US gang literature. Vigil (1988a) suggests members join gangs as they do not have their own family or because their own family is dysfunctional. Morales (1992) suggests the street gang can function as a 'surrogate family' within which members find emotional and physical protection, recognition, affection and loyalty. Ruble and Turner (2000) consider street gangs as 'family systems' with structural hierarchies with gang leaders in the role of parents taking decisions for younger members. They argue that viewing the gangs as such helps to explain gang functions, hierarchy, cohesion and internal power organisation.

[6] See also Sampson and Laub (1993) who suggest that social bonds will alter over time and that while young people with weaker social bonds may be pulled into gangs in their teenage years, this will decrease with age as they form stronger social bonds with others outside the gang.

[7] These two similar but slightly different narratives are explored in depth by John Pitts in *Reluctant gangsters* (Pitts, 2008b).

[8] Risks include those associated with drugs and drug dealing (Decker and Van Winkle 1996); use and access to firearms (Decker and Van Winkle, 1996; Decker and Pyrooz, 2011; Thornberry et al, 2003); serious violence (see Decker and Van Winkle, 1996; Decker and Pyrooz 2010; Papachristos 2009; Curry et al 2014). Gang affiliation leads to increased involvement in violence and delinquency alongside increased victimisation (Decker et al 2008; Taylor 2008).

[9] Medina et al (2013, p 4) found that gang membership increases the chances of offending; however they 'did not find evidence that joining a gang makes it much more likely that young people will be fearful of crime, be the subject of violent victimisation, or suffer injury from violent victimisation (as has sometimes been reported)'.

TEN

Surviving in the game

'Doesn't the fight for survival also justify swindle and theft?
In self-defence, anything goes.'
Imelda Marcos

The landscape of risk inherent in the social field of the gang affects young people in different ways and depends on the perceived proximity to danger or on the gangs involved. Members become cognisant of some, but not always all, the dangers. To survive in this social field, members must adapt and learn quickly. To do this, some employ their individual agency or strategise their way to distinction. All, however, must employ and adapt their personal survival strategies in order to avoid victimisation. This chapter examines the key survival strategies identified in the SW9 research.

Maintaining awareness of field position

A decline in street capital, individual reputation or field position is described as 'sliding' or 'falling'. As one member put it, 'Once you have fallen, you can be targeted.' Thus it is important to maintain your reputation and your 'visualness' (i.e. visual presence and visual impact). Falling occurs when, for whatever reason, an individual's street capital takes a downward turn. Other gang members are usually the first to notice it happening. The individual concerned may become aware of the situation through comments or rumours, but are more likely to become target of disrespect, violence or attack. Falling may occur as a result of a single event where an individual 'loses' their stripes – for example, by failing to carry out a request, or reneging on their word – or a cumulative series of events, such as absenteeism, a failure to stand up for oneself, allowing others to show disrespect, or no longer having an appetite for 'the game' or for violence. Members assess views on your recent performance, swapping stories about how you have 'lost it' and that you are *'well off your game'* –thus the perceived slide begins. Minor events and altercations accumulate to push the individual further down. Other members may nurture a vested interest in another's fall and actively seek to expedite this or take advantage of the decline to elevate themselves. This can be both overt and covert, and may include informing on the victim's activities. Sliding is therefore dangerous for a gang member:

> 'I had started to slide down. My reputation got tarnished a little bit. I was on cocaine. I'd lost my way. I was using instead of serving. I'm doing things I'd not normally do. People would be carrying on with me and I'd let them get away with it. So when I got my "little touch", everyone thought, "Well, I want a piece." So they came to get their piece by intimidation and all sorts, robbing my home, burglaries and to just ... know what I mean?' (African Caribbean male elder)

Challengers may develop strategies to precipitate the fall or slide of other members in order to advance themselves. Members who are already in the process of falling may be further disadvantaged by double-dealing rivals informing on them or setting them up as victims of robbery or reprisal. One ex-gang member in SW9 recounted in detail a series of events that occurred when his reputation began to slide, the trigger being a popular belief that he owed money. First his car was scratched, then his house was burgled. When he entered the house, he smelled gas and noticed the knobs on the cooker had been smashed off.

When an individual's street capital begins to decline, it is imperative to take correction action to prevent further victimisation. This often requires a trigger event, usually violent, to demonstrate a return to form. The fall must be arrested quickly and suddenly to recoup reputation and boost street capital, as slow, cumulative increases often pass unnoticed. Some members in this situation develop a strategy around a key event to get them noticed and halt their decline. Other possibly strategise to deliberately over-react to some minor infringement to show they are 'on it'. Others too may orchestrate a large-scale revenge attack or 'spectaculars', or simply issue threats that they are then expected to carry out. As a result, other hitherto uninvolved members, may find themselves a suitable or opportunistic target of another person's attempt to recoup their field position. Those members who are unable to develop survival strategies have to leave the social field openly, or manufacture a suitable exit.

Hyper-vigilance

In the gang social field, young people manage their personal safety and any potential decline in street capital through a state of hyper-vigilance, whereby they remain constantly alert for the next challenge, test or attempt to diminish, or acquire, their street capital. This state of permanent alertness means a readiness to challenge any visual or aural slight usually requiring them to respond quickly and violently to defend their street capital from deflationary pressures. A fast, proactive response enables the individual to control the situation. Any perceived slight or vague threat needs to be identified and challenged. An example of such a slight is the 'visual bump' (Katz, 1988, p 110), whereby someone stares at another person for too long, as if sizing them up for a fight (known as 'screwing' in SW9). This is considered to be bad manners, and is seen as a challenge to both authority and street capital, demanding an immediate response. A failure to respond is tantamount to 'falling', and is seen as an open invitation to victimisation.

In group situations, there is an imperative for members to evidence and display to others they are 'on it' regarding monitoring their personal street capital through hyper-vigilance. This may be perceived as acting out of bravado or 'doing masculinity' (Messerschmitt, 1993). It suggests one is 'battle-ready' (Sampson and Lauriston, 1994) and shows that the group is prepared or 'locked and loaded', 'ready to rumble'. The slightest event may then trigger an incident or be picked up through this hyper-vigilant state. For some, this becomes almost a paranoia which may in turn be exacerbated by smoking high grade skunk on a daily basis or partaking of cocaine.

Some members operate on the basis of 'selective vigilance', for example when an incursion is expected or if they feel their reputation or individual street capital is falling. Group vigilance also plays a role: a 'slight' or perceived 'diss' may be overlooked or ignored by an individual, only to be identified by another vigilant gang member, who is quick to point it out and demand an appropriate response. In these circumstances, the target of the slight or 'diss' feels the need to address the issue and react, lest he be mocked. Any reaction may now be more violent than the situation merits in order to dispel any doubts that he is off-guard and to further demonstrate he remains vigilant. In any case, random, perceived slights are a daily occurrence and must be prevented or addressed immediately.

Threat assessment

In street encounters, it is common for gang members to challenge others in order to quickly determine the level of threat they pose to themselves or to the gang. This proactive, provocative action is known as 'the squeeze'. It begins with a member challenging another person's right to be in a particular 'endz', or postcode area. He will then try to establish the reason for the trespasser's visit – is it to spy, or to visit a girl? If the latter, then which girl? She will then be required to vouch for him. The squeeze provides an opportunity for tactical engagement, risk assessment, information collation and verification, and premise for future action.

Throughout this encounter the way in which the visitor responds is of key importance. If the response is vague, e.g. '*I come from SW2*', then the enquirer knows you are new or not from the area. If your response is more specific and voluntarily includes a local road name for example, then the visitor might be considered local. If the squeeze continues, e.g. '*What part of SW2?*' this is an indication of pending confrontation.

This is a widely recognised filtering or sifting process that is used as a form of linguistic set-up. Had the individual been known in an area, the challenge would be along the lines of "Yo, what's happening? I know you through somebody," in other words the challenge will be less confrontational. These questions quickly allow the enquirer to ascertain how much is known about the visitor, enabling them quickly to assess their connections, street capital, authority and 'permission' to enter the social field. If the visitor is to be invited in, they will have to provide a reference or a name.

The respondent's answers, demeanour and body language determines whether the enquirer allows them to move on. Those who are unsure how to respond, or who are hesitant or untruthful, are deemed suspicious. At this point the questioner makes a 'move' – most likely a sudden, unprovoked stabbing. It is therefore important during this street challenge not to hold out on answers or to be seen to give any attitude. Thus, if you are not believed, are rude or lie, it is possible, and even common, to be stabbed or shanked, in the leg or buttock. This may happen before asking questions to disable the visitor. Subsequent questions asked of the visitor will then be deemed more truthful as the victim now seeks to avoid further injury and is aware they are potentially in danger. These situations are extremely dangerous, even life-threatening, as they may provoke a counter-attack or show or disrespect by the victim, thus paving the way for a more serious violence. There is no way of knowing what the outcome will be in such situations.

Even those with legitimate reasons for entering gang territory, such as former residents visiting family, may be at risk of attack. In one incident in SW9, a young man originally from Angell Town visiting family who still lived in the area, was challenged by GAS gang on entering the estate. His justification for being there was discounted, and he was stabbed several times.

The constant need to remain vigilant leads to numerous confrontations and is partially responsible for the increase in violence in the social field. Practitioners and academics often refer to such incidents as 'respect issues'. This need for constant vigilance is extremely stressful for young people.

Buying protection

To maintain freedom of movement and avoid potential victimisation, including random violence, youngers often move around in small groups and are seldom seen alone. Indeed, young people cite the protection afforded by group movement as their primary reason for gang affiliation (Pitts, 2008b) with the ability to now hang out with a group of friends and achieve a greater freedom of movement:

> 'OMG I can go anywhere, I can do anything now I have joined the gang.' (Latino female younger)

Respondents in the SW9 research gave examples of non-gang-affiliated young people buying protection by paying a 'passport tax' or 'hood pass' to gang members to allow them to move through an area, to access a facility or visit family. Such taxes often took the form of a few pounds in cash, a small bag of weed or the provision of useful information.

Living 'off the hood'

If parents realise that their children are being caught up in gang life, they may attempt to mitigate the risks of further involvement by moving away from the neighbourhood. This does not necessarily mean that the young people will give up their affiliation; many remain loyal despite living away from the estate, or 'hood.' Such affiliations may lessen and change over time.

Other young people affiliate through friends or family to key groups based on distant estates; they may live in West Norwood (SE27), for example, but affiliate to GAS in SW9. This presents logistical problems for local agencies trying to manage young people. Members living off the territory are more at risk of violence arising from fluctuating tensions and sudden rule changes within the social field. As intermittent visitors, they are less well known and recognisable. They may be less well connected and must strive to keep open effective channels of information and communication.

Multiple membership

Young people living 'off the hood' may adopt the survival strategy of 'hedging their bets' and affiliating to two or three different gangs. However, problems may arise if the different gangs separate or start a 'beef'. Individuals with more than one allegiance will then be in the position of having to decide which gang they support.

Switching allegiance

One survival strategy within this landscape of risk is to facilitate the rule change yourself – by switching allegiance and aligning with those challengers who are 'on the rise' as this appears to offer the best bet for future gang or group opportunities. Others may decide to prioritise their own individual survival strategies and thus make any decision to switch allegiance based solely on how they perceive their own individual progress, i.e. they do not really hold any loyalty to one gang and essentially any gang will do as long as they personally advance within it. Some youngers view gang membership as fun and do not fully appreciate the potential dangers they are putting themselves by switching allegiance so readily. As one respondent in the SW9 research put it:

> 'The worst thing is you will see someone in GAS gang today and he'll be with PDC tomorrow then he'll be with OC the next day.' (African Caribbean male Youth Offending Team professional)

As always there are independent actors (floaters) in the social field moving between gangs and conducting their own personal business with each of them. Ability to act in this way reflects a high degree of individual agency and careful strategising:

'I deliberately didn't join up in a gang so that I could walk around free. But then all those other people can't.' (African Caribbean female independent operator)

Temporary allegiance and confederation

A further survival strategy, undertaken by the whole gang, is to shift allegiance or to 'merge' with another gang, a frequent occurrence in SW9 throughout 2011/12, when police reported that gangs in Brixton were coming together in response to incursions from groups in Peckham. During this time the local Loughborough Bois, based at Loughborough Junction, merged with the GAS gang, and members of MZ (the Murder Zone gang, from the Morelands Estate) were seen regularly in Angell Town. The motivation for co-joining appeared to be to protect the GAS gang from multiple rival gangs.

Currently, besides having a history of rivalry with Peckham, the GAS gang has 'beef' with groups from Tulse Hill and also Stockwell (the ABM gang) and is thus 'surrounded'. Recent escalation in tension has been attributed to the GAS gang leader showing disrespect towards rivals on YouTube. One respondent in SW9 described the situation thus:

'Oh it's real. That's real now. Now it's getting even more stupid. 'Cos Brixton was one place and now you've got several estates and lots of young people on these estates can't come from one estate to another. It's getting mad.' (African Caribbean male older)

The police claim that merging is a form of protection. As most evidence points to large gangs breaking up into smaller ones, this counter-movement of merging remains under-researched and unexplained.

Gang 'confederations' have always existed to some extent, with reports of gangs from as far away New Cross (Lewisham) undertaking incursions into SW9 and prompting affiliation with Peckham gangs in order to undertake 'smash-and-grab' raids. Indeed, gang rivalries appear to extend across London and it is not uncommon for one gang member to telephone another to request assistance in an ongoing beef. There have also been examples of gangs outside SW9 gathering together to attack GAS, prompting GAS to create loose affiliations with other gangs in the area. In this way, a dominant gang such as GAS attracts several different smaller gangs who retain their own identity while simultaneously supporting the larger group. Such gang franchising present a different challenge for police. GAS have thus attracted several different smaller gangs who may retain their own identity while supporting GAS.

There are also a range of smaller gangs in SW9, or its immediate proximity, such as TN1 and TBlock in Tulse Hill, Acre Lane Campaign, and Frontline Bangers. In these gangs membership is restricted to those living on the estate. Local tensions and incursions often result in these small spatially localised or nascent gangs joining larger groups. Such constantly evolving situations, which are negotiated with considerable skill by olders and elders, and are often precipitated by a crisis, are difficult for both police and local young people to monitor. How such mergers play out over time is a subject for further research.

Visual presence, visual impact and physicality

Visual look and impressive physicality are further ways of mitigating risk of victimisation acting as a visual signifier that 'you are not to be messed with'. Such attributes also signify a potential ability to defend your reputation (Winlow, 2001). In the gang social field, physical build is important, acting, as 'crude bodily capital' (Wacquant, 1992). Members who are overweight or in poor physical shape will not command the same respect as those who are fit and muscular.

One ex-gang member described himself as a 'Staffie' – short and stocky, i.e. like a Staffordshire bull terrier. This is, for many, the perfect build for street physicality and includes speed, strength, pounce, power, aggression and courage. Such branded attributes are matched with the mentality to win and with stamina.

> 'The build is very important. It's very rare that I would look at a man who's not well-built, who is overweight and unfit and all those things. I'd respect him but he'd have to have some attribute that would back me off. If he doesn't have that he's gonna find it very difficult to get that street credit. 'Cos street credit is based on competitiveness, aggression, athleticism, physicality, the gait – you know it's all part of it. Me, I'm a Staffie – short and stocky. I've got the perfect street build for street physicality 'cos I will have the speed, the strength, the pounce, the power, the aggression, the courage behind it.' (African Caribbean male elder)

One ex-gang member suggested that one reason for the increased use of weapons in some gangs is the slimmer build of new arrivals, which has led to an increased reliance on firearms, although there is no evidence to suggest this is true or that his view widespread.

Code switching

The social field of the gang operates only within its own boundaries, and most adults and residents move around SW9 unhindered or unmolested without having to acknowledge or answer to the gang. According to Anderson (1999), young gang members are able to 'code switch' when they move beyond the gang social field, that is, drop the mannerisms, attitudes, language and behaviour associated with street life and temporarily adopt those of the wider community, including showing deference to adults or those in authority.

Some gang-affiliated individuals with considerable social skill play different social fields effectively, only entering the social field of the gang as required, for example to buy drugs or sell stolen goods, what Vigil calls 'flexible identity' (Conchas and Vigil, 2010, p 58). In this way, many residents, or even parents, remain unaware of the gang or of their child's involvement in it. Gang-affiliated young people may live in one social field (the community) and attend church every Sunday, but still run drugs in the evening or hide guns at home. The parallel world of the gang may be obscured (even from researchers) and can lead residents (and some researchers) to conclude that there is no gang activity in the neighbourhood.

It appears, however, that fewer young people are now either able, or prepared, to switch between codes of behaviour. Professionals working with gang-affiliated young people in SW9 reported gang members using monosyllabic speech and claimed that they no longer showed deference towards adults in a professional setting. This may reflect the habitus of the individual, illustrating how deeply entrenched they are in the gang, or it may be that some members find it too stressful constantly to move from a street to a more deferential persona, and find it safer to remain in the street world where issues of lack of trust and perceived lack of respect are easily compartmentalised and addressed. Some never learn to adjust or adapt to adults, or they lack the social skill required to adjust or code switch. Their way of speaking is, therefore, in uncompromised 'street' language.

Many young people stay fully immersed in 'street' language, mirroring their total immersion in the social field. Gaining and maintaining a 'rep' is so critical for many young people, gang-affiliated or not, that it is almost impossible for them to adapt to other social fields. They may lack the social skills required to do this, or they may just choose not to adapt. They expect and demand respect from adults as they would from peers. Should they fail to be accorded this respect, they fail to give it back. In the gang social field, respect has such overwhelming centrality it cannot easily be set aside or discounted. Interactions with adults in proximate social fields are now frequently 'read' by young people within the context of their gang social field, which they have effectively 'transported' with them. This is not altogether surprising, as it is the rules and context of their own social field that are paramount in determining their survival. It is dangerous for them to drop these rules, even temporarily, while visiting a Youth Offending Team officer or probationer. Over time, many seem no longer willing or able to drop their street persona or temporarily shed the behaviours associated with their social field.

Teachers and professionals unfamiliar with the pressures and imperatives on gang affiliates to avoid victimisation tend not to make the connection between monosyllabic language and the gang social field. They attribute this way of speaking to members' lack of vocabulary, accusing young people of failing to make an effort or refusing to live in the 'real world'. Some professionals view gang-affiliated individuals as having more individual agency and craft suggesting they exaggerate the fears or sensationalise territorial issues as a means to get resources, avoid statutory obligations or to denigrate rivals. Other professionals, however, see many gang-affiliated individuals as having more individual agency or strategy than that, suggesting that while a failure to communicate might be a survival strategy for some, others possibly exaggerate their fears or sensationalise territorial issues as a means to get resources, avoid statutory obligations or denigrate rivals.

Developing dual personas

Agency professionals working with gang-affiliated young people often refer to their two personas: the street persona and the 'real' persona. The street persona shows no fear, is full of bravado and cheek. The 'real' persona, however, may be scared and intimidated, unsurprising when a younger is only 12 or 13 years old. This suggests two separate codes of behaviour.

Early in their gang induction, youngers may meet an older displaying scars from stab wounds, with a reputation for attacking other people with a knife or taking part in notorious robberies. The older may show them how to handle a firearm, and invite them to *'run with us bruv'*. While they may be excited by the prospect, the youngsters are also often conflicted by their 'real' persona. By now, they may be too scared to show their 'real' persona to peers and thus do not refuse the offer to run with the gang. Indeed, youth workers in SW9 have reported young boys crying for their mothers when they are trapped in violent situations or are themselves the victims of stabbings.

By contrast, a youngster's street persona may lead them to instigate a violent incident or carry out a leader's instruction to *'Stab dem yout' dere,'* i.e. stab a rival without hesitation or deliberation. As one member put it:

> 'Because they are just 13 , they don't know any better. They
> don't have no fear.' (West African male younger).

Such control over youngers enables olders to develop reputation by proxy.

The development of a dual persona appears to enable young people to compartmentalise their experiences 'on road' and rationalise their violent behaviour.

Risks associated with territory

The fluctuating landscape of risk within the gang social field, with its temporary truces and negotiated 'hood passes', are further reasons for neighbourhood violence. Both intra- and inter-gang disputes create a complex topology, with violence being a constant threat. Players in the social field must navigate and survive this topography. Two key survival techniques are to avoid 'slippin'' and restrict one's movements.

Avoiding 'slippin''

The term 'slippin'' (which means being in the wrong place at the wrong time, and is derived from taking a chance and 'slippin' down a back alley') largely relates to individuals being caught entering or encroaching on another gang's territory, or turf. Being spotted results in pursuit, challenge and confrontation, with the trespasser attempting to return to their group or 'endz'. Slippin' is more serious when it involves groups. If the trespasser is quick to return to his group, his fellow gang members will be there to retaliate against his pursuers. Such incidents happen frequently on public transport or on routes through rival territory, e.g. During the SW9 research, one popular local boy (aged 15) was isolated on a through route in rival territory. He was confronted by the rival gang and shot in the leg, although he survived and his family were rehoused outside the area.

Young people fearing victimisation may be too frightened to leave their estate after a 'mix-up' with someone from another area. Fear of traversing another area has a significant impact on their lives, severely restricting movement. Youth and probation workers in SW9 cite it as a major reason for young people failing to attend meetings. Indeed, in one such episode, a gang member arriving for a Youth Offending Team appointment was spotted by a rival who later turned up with a car full of rival gang members to confront him.

Restricting movement

Many young people, including non-gang-affiliates living in the neighbourhood, restrict their movements to mitigate risks of victimisation. This can have a major impact on their lives. It means they must adopt survival strategies such as seeking permission from olders to pass through an area. It is up to the older to decide whether or not they have the credibility to be allowed to do so. One older noted the use of a commonly heard phrase to grant permission: *"I allow you."* Youngers will understand the full conditional meaning behind this phrase.

Others stay indoors as much as possible, or only move around the estate with family or friends, or in protective clothing. Some young people have even been known to wear bullet-proof vests.

'I know here in SW9 there are certain individuals who can hardly get off the Angell Town estate. There is one guy we know of in Angell Town estate who wears a bullet proof vest almost permanently. Although it's a relatively small area some people just can't go across it 'cos of fear of reprisals or conflict. The world they inhabit can be very small. They tell us they could get attacked. So some people would rather go to Harpenden House, Norbury [probation office] than come here. Like in LA, there are streets they just can't enter. I have clients who have similar issues. One of my 18-year-olds stays on his estate all the time 'cos he is afraid of coming up here. Others would be afraid to go outside the borough. The Intel [intelligence held by statutory authorities] confirms some of this.' (Professional)

Some choose not to traverse certain locations and carefully monitor timings as they traverse neighbourhoods or catch public transport. Some change their appearance and dress differently to avoid being victimised. Those most at risk are those considered to be 'waste man' (dispensable, unconnected, useless), those with 'little names' (i.e. no reputation to speak of) or those who have appeared on social networking sites as they are easily recognisable. Public transport, 'chicken shops' and take-away outlets are dangerous hotspots for many.

Self-restricted movement may extend to an unwillingness to leave the borough, a particular problem for students in Lambeth attending college in other parts of London. Wider family members may help 'squash' any beef and make such transitions easier, but those failing to mitigate the risks of victimisation often fall victim to rival gangs, sometimes unwittingly. The risks are greatly heightened for new arrivals, but also extend to non-gang-affiliated young people moving through territory claimed by, or associated with, certain gangs.

Fear of victimisation prevents young people from attending job interviews, new schools, colleges, youth offending services, youth clubs and probation services:

> 'They won't talk but just say, "Can't go Peckham, man, can't go Peckham."' (African Caribbean male ex-older)

Statutory services professionals report some young people suddenly become sullen or withdrawn when told to attend offices or locations in areas they realise are deemed 'out of bounds' for them.

Risks at the boundary of the social field

The social field is bounded by the point at which its influence ends. Bourdieu notes that field boundaries are themselves objects of struggle and argues against positivist approaches that attempt to delineate precise boundaries, instead referring to boundaries that are more 'relational' (Swartz, 1997, p 121).

However, the question of the social field boundary merits further research, as it posits many interesting questions relating to how it might be recognised. For example, the social activities of a resident who chooses a different route out of the estate because gang members are blocking a stairwell are effectively moderated by the social field of the gang. While many people in SW9 live their lives without influence from gangs, police acknowledge that local communities are generally cognisant of their activities. Taking forward Bourdieu's argument of 'relational' boundaries, it is an individual's relationship with the gang over time that determines their own personal boundaries. It is likely that for both individuals and for communities these boundaries vary and remain in a state of constant flux.

State agencies risk further blurring these boundaries by crossing into the social field of the gang from their proximate social fields. This has the effect of impinging on critical aspects of gang life: respect, reputation, territory and street capital. In the recent past, such interloping was excused by gang members as simply the legislative powers of the statutory authorities to; stop and search, arrest, detain, imprison and license. However through such activities, these agencies now play an unwitting role in the social field by creating opportunities for gang members to generate street capital. Or possibly by creating a mini-crisis in the social field which then alters the status quo. Either way, entering the gangs' social field is viewed by gang members as a 'legal violation' and a major disrespect which must be challenged and met head on. Moreover entering an estate to undertake a stop and search operation might inadvertently place the young people at risk. This can occur when those gang members who are subject to a stop and search are seen talking to police. This later brings suspicion of them being an informer.

As they interact with gang members in their social field, agencies unwittingly provide opportunities for young people to challenge them and by so doing raise their street capital. Thus gang members pursue strategies of talking back, 'giving cheek', making threats and failing to attend appointments, or, more seriously, physical assault, intimidation, getting arrested or lying in court. All of these strategies provide opportunities for increasing street capital, which is maximised if such behaviour is 'performed' in front of other gang members who report back to others about how their peers have held their own and how funny it was to watch. To some researchers, this is 'doing masculinity' (Messerschmidt, 1993).

Strategies enacted at the boundary of the social field include the intimidation of professionals. Not all agency workers entering the gang social field become targets, with fluctuations in tension and rule changes within the field determining the nature and level of interaction between gangs and professionals. Police are particularly at risk when they enter the gang social field, however, with incursions seen as shows of 'disrespect', undermining respect and 'rep'. This often leads to confrontations as members retaliate, physically or verbally, to maintain their street capital.

Ethnicity

Ethnicity generates its own risks within the landscape of risk. The ethnicity of gang affiliation is a direct reflection of the ethnicity of the local neighbourhood or estate.[1] SW9 (essentially Brixton and Stockwell in the borough of Lambeth) are long-established residential locations for black African Caribbean populations. The *State of the borough report 2012* (Lambeth First, 2012) cites Brixton as the most populated area of the borough and describes it as the heart of Lambeth's black community. Lambeth itself hosts the third largest proportion of black Caribbean people in London, at 9.8%, with Stockwell described as ethnically and socially mixed.

The Lambeth wards in SW9 are listed among the 10% most deprived wards in the UK. African Caribbean and black African populations are disproportionately represented in these neighbourhoods (Lambeth First, 2012). It follows that most gangs members in SW9 are young men of black African and black Caribbean origin. The black African population (largely West African), at 11.5%, has recently overtaken the black Caribbean population of Lambeth, which stands at 9.8% (Lambeth First, 2011). In addition, there are a few white British and white Portuguese gang members. While this reflects the borough population as a whole, some wards and estates have higher concentrations of different ethnicities, although specific data are hard to obtain. Many estates are known to house both long-term residents and new arrivals.

New arrivals (notably asylum seekers immigrant families and those being rehoused in the borough) in the social field experience heightened difficulties and dangers. The distribution of capital in the social field is unequal, and odds are usually stacked against them. Their field position is low, placing them at high risk of victimisation. Within this landscape, accessing information about the social field and the community is critical. This involves overcoming language difficulties if arrivals do not speak the dominant tongue; becoming familiar with a bewildering range of individuals, including which ones to avoid; and learning and interpreting the rules of the 'road' and the localised street language and idioms. Although new arrivals help each other by exchanging information, there is considerable pressure on them to acquire knowledge quickly. Some manage to immerse themselves in the social field, while others are unable to cope, and withdraw from it entirely.

Because new arrivals have few connections – known as 'network poverty' (6, 1997) – they are unsure of how to 'play' the area. They must take care to maintain the rule of no grassing while asking the right questions to get the right information. They may unwittingly put themselves at risk by, for example, being unaware that a gang operates in their local pub and stolen goods are sold there. As one gang member put it:

> 'Connections and knowledge re the information supplier is the key – "Can I milk this situation for my own ends and advantage?" is always being asked. Who I know might protect me or get me out of trouble, so I need to know who I need to know. As I am coming up, I need to know who is who. If I call an older he can then intervene and "squash" any trouble for me.' (African Caribbean male older)

It is not easy to determine the role of ethnicity in the levels of violence experienced in this social field. There does however appear to be a lower threshold in this social field as regards the dosage of violence meted out as part of the Sanctions Repertoire. There is a need for further research in this area.

While no single ethnic group dominates all gangs in SW9, white members are in a minority. In Brixton, for example, there may only be two or three white individuals in a gang of 30 to 50 members. From their own internal reviews of offending patterns and arrests, the police in SW9 claim that certain activities are associated with ethnicity:

> 'You can have black British, black African, black Jamaican and they will all be in the same gang and will all have distinct responsibilities.' (White male police officer)

This finding was not corroborated by the current research, however, and further evidence is needed to examine the extent of ethnic specialisation in certain strategic actions or types of offending. However, this research found that at least one gang in SW9 operates along these lines, with several respondents indicating that Jamaicans mainly deal with cannabis and drug dealing while Africans take care of the violence. Black British gang members are allegedly involved in both.[2]

Any such patterns may fluctuate according to the characteristics of the gang, such as the ethnic composition of gang members, offending history and family connections. High forms of particularised trust among groups of members sharing cultural or ethnic origins may also provide an explanation. Toy (2009, p 35) notes that 'some gangs use cultural connectivity as part of the recruitment process' and cites as examples the DFA gang in Southwark (primarily Nigerian) and the Woolwich Boys in Greenwich (Somalian).

I would suggest it is unlikely that these examples are evidence of gangs established simply on the basis of shared ethnicity. It is more likely they are new arrivals to the area, experience network poverty and thus seeking group cohesion and shared protection.

Notes

[1] This finding was also affirmed by Aldridge et al (2008).

[2] See Grund and Densley (2012).

ELEVEN

Creating the house advantage: the role of information

'There are two rules for success:
1. Never tell everything you know.'
Roger H. Lincoln

For all strategic actors in the gang social field, information is a critical daily necessity. For incumbents, quality, timely information provides what might be termed 'house advantage'.

Information, specifically the flow and use of information, its exchange and transmission as a commodity, affects all actors in the social field:

> 'To operate, you have to know what is what.' (African male older)

Information exchange is crucially linked to the other fundamental field component: trust. Both Putnam (2000) and Coleman (1994) identify trust as a key component of social capital and Fukuyama sees trust as a basic source of social capital (Fukuyama, 1995, p 26). Field (2008, p 71) citing Dasgupta (2000, p 333) views trust as an attribute of groups and institutions that is often based on reputations, themselves mediated by third parties. This is a certainty within the social field of the gang. For Fukuyama, if members have a wide radius of trust, any externalities arising from this are more likely to be 'positive and benign'. Conversely, a narrow radius of trust signifies potentially 'negative externalities' (Fukuyama, 2001, pp 8-10). This appears to apply to the social field of the gang, where trust is in short supply. Densley (2013) identifies problems of risk and vulnerability associated with generating trust and suggests that any doubts a gang may have about the trustworthiness of new recruits is addressed in part through the use of symbols. In this regard, he uses a novel application of signalling theory as a way of reinterpreting street codes and street reputation. In the social field of the gang, trust is tested daily, via relationships and instincts, but most importantly through sending and receiving information.

Community engagement

In the social field of SW9, the dealing and trading of information is a central tenet of enormous importance. Described as the first direct benefit of social capital, such trading facilitates access to broader sources of information while providing new opportunities to improve data quality, relevance and timeliness (Adler and Kwon, 2002, p 29). In so doing, it offers a method of community engagement and social control. For elders, information equates to 'informational capital' (Bourdieu and Wacquant, 1992, p 19). This extends to knowing the community, what it fears, wants, needs or is prepared to do. It also extends to knowing criminal offending histories as well as the social norms of permissible actions and sanctions. To know all this is to know the social field. Key holders of information become 'community operatives',[1] providing a valuable social service to the community or the gang through the network. This role is sought after and accentuates the importance of social skill. It is a role largely held by females. Access to the network equates to power:

> 'Your group will tell you who is in the gang so you can then recognise them. You must find out which gang controls which space or area, who deals drugs, where to go and not go.' (New immigrant Latino male younger)

Those unconnected to the network, ex-communicated, exiled or not yet linked in, are thus severely disadvantaged. Such poor connectivity is described as 'network poverty' by Perri 6 (1997).

As information is shared vertically (between ranks) and horizontally (between peers) and with proximate fields (wider family and community), the ability to trade in information becomes both a form of community engagement and an opportunity for developing social capital. Social skills are thus brought to the fore.

For elders and incumbents having and holding this knowledge confers both social skill and the authority to have it collated, sifted, sorted and overseen: this brings power and opportunities for control. Those with this authority may contribute to, or even be, the community voice. It confers the power to correct misunderstandings, arrange things, mend or break reputations; to become the conduit or siphon through which knowledge and information must pass; to develop a broad reach across different communities or a 'deep reach' into silent and hidden communities; to contact prisoners; and to act as 'virtual manager' of their business. In the gang social field where innumerable people have criminal interests or affiliations, both past and present, the importance of this knowledge is amplified. In enables those who possess it to operate at the interface of legal and illegal activity, and this is a powerful place to be. Supreme authority is ultimately held by the gang leader and his inner circle, providing them with a house advantage; as one gang member in SW9 put it, "They got the dirt on y'all and know what's goin' down."

Brixton and its environs have a long association with criminal cartel families (Sanders, 2005). In such circumstances, intergenerational transference of information and knowledge is common (Sutherland, 1947). This may simply take the form of schooling youngsters in street life, or it may go further, inducting young people into the workings of myriads of local criminal contacts. Any young person coming from or linked to cartel families has a head start, an advantage and an easy passage into the gang. Successful operation in this social field requires knowledge of local history. Failure to know or how to use information results in 'blind moves', i.e. taking the wrong course of action due to the fact you did not have access to the full or correct information.

How is information used?

Beyond the obvious value of 'knowledge is power', information allows gang members to employ individual or gang strategies to increase their street capital. Beyond its obvious value as a signifier of power, information acquisition enables gang members to increase their street capital through a variety of gang or individual strategies. Three principal strategies are evident:

Appraisal and monitoring

Information is required by gang members at all levels, but is particularly valued by those in the higher ranks or mature tiers, as it enables them to appraise the skills, ability and capacities of other members. Knowledge of rivals, key individuals in proximate social fields, statutory agencies and authorities (particularly the police and criminal justice system) is also important.

Before accepting new affiliates, peers and olders assess their qualities and attributes, and the potential benefits they may bring the gang, considering such questions as what information they can provide, who they know, what their offending history and criminal tendencies are, and whether or not they are trustworthy. Leaders request feedback on their capabilities, performance and propensity for using violence, to then appraise his skills. If the informal appraisal is positive, their skills will now be considered more desirable by the gang. Such informational reconnaissance helps 'narrow the field' of recruits (Densley, 2013).

Neighbourhood intelligence is required daily by all members of the gang in order to monitor business in the social field, but also in the wider community and among network connections. This involves accessing details of all the latest incidents and business activities, including which individual relationships have newly formed or broken down, and the movements of good and services.

To fine tune their knowledge and monitor developments, gang affiliates and those on its periphery undertake constant tension monitoring to assess levels of threat, to manage risk and self-regulate their own movements. In a highly localised, fluctuating environment largely influenced by external factors, there is a need for constant updates.

Marketing (giving out information)

The second principal strategy for acquiring information is proactively to advertise or market individual or gang brands. This is either done internally through informal conversations with other members, or more publicly, through social networking sites.

Internal marketing provides information to existing members, including advice on social norms, how to act, and what is and is not permissible. Gang history (and mythology) is shared/divulged by peers and olders. Such mechanisms set boundaries and establish a shared sense of belonging. It is also important for existing gang members to learn the boundaries of the social field so they can develop advancement strategies accordingly.

External marketing is aimed at those outside the gang, ensuring that the group sends out the correct messages about itself and presents the right image. This differentiates the gang from rivals, clarifying roles, leadership and history, and establishing a brand identity. It signifies operational procedures and sets the expectations of members. It clarifies how sanctions are employed and how members may access economic capital. This information is shared informally in peer groups, sifted and absorbed by prospective members. It allows outsiders to differentiate the unique superior qualities of a gang. The right messages will attract new joiners.

Trading and exchange

The third strategy involves using information as a tradable commodity in the social field and beyond. Possession of information builds reputation and provides the holder with a tradable asset. In the social field of the gang, this equates to a formidable local currency or social capital that elevates street capital and reputation. Those in this elevated position are assumed to have strong internal links to the network and trusted knowledge of the social field; those who recognise that certain information is valuable, and demonstrate a working knowledge of the social field, are therefore deemed to be useful, smart, important and trustworthy. In contested arenas and disadvantaged communities where collective efficacy is low, transmitting information is one way (along with fencing stolen goods) of building trust.

Gang members at all tiers trade information. Female gang members appear to excel in this social skill, and it is often their sole function to trade information. Information transactions involve one actor collating intelligence or information then sourcing another actor to whom information is transmitted. This recipient may be known or the agent may just choose to divulge it. Either way, it constitutes a strategic action, as the informant retains the objective of, for example, seeking favour, building trust, enhancing their profile or increasing their proximity to the gang. It constitutes a play for increased social capital, which is traded reciprocally for information. The greater the value, authenticity and uniqueness of the information, the greater the transactional cost. Such strategic action naturally indicates the alignment of one individual or group with another and this builds trust and increases the potential for further information exchange. As gang networks are dense, close-knit and highly localised and all members know one another, it is important to keep connections and information sources fresh. (Gee, 2002)

All social fields trade information. However, in the context of the social field of the gang, trading and transmitting information affects the social field in unique ways. Under the code of the street (Anderson, 1999), grassing may lead to wider reverberations (Evans et al, 1996; Yates, 2006) or 'negative externalities (Fukuyama, 2001, pp 8-10)) in the field. In the contested arena of the gang, the transmission of information involves strategic action with explicit implications and possible consequences for several actors. It may, for example:

- raise or quell tensions;
- be more significant to some individuals than others;

- have wide repercussions among the group;
- have unforeseen and uncontrollable consequences;
- affect a wide range of agents, increasing potential outcomes;
- be misread by a number of 'interested parties';
- place individuals in danger.

Information transmission may be conscious or unconscious ('dry snitching'), or done over time in order to 'bank' knowledge that can be traded at a later date. Gangs seek new recruits to access their connections and networks and then build on their affiliations. Affiliations afford protection and reduce risks, plugging young people into a wider network.

> 'It's all people who are in trouble: people are being looked for. Basically people are either in or out of the gang – a lot of that goes on. You become persona non grata very quickly and the word goes around both within the gang and outside it. Information comes from abroad as well with links to the Caribbean and Africa.' (White male resident)

Information is graded by quality and importance. Poor-quality information is passed to youngers; as they often trade in rumour and gossip, the quality of their information is questionable. More credible information is passed to members in the next tier, who trade in higher-quality information or intelligence. If the information is deemed to be accurate, it is passed to elders. Members transmitting high-grade intelligence are rewarded in kind and allocated street capital.

The network

The network is a social grouping of connections and relationships, and comprises the gang itself, its affiliates, families and those in the wider neighbourhood.

A network, alongside social norms and sanctions, forms one of the triumvirate components of social capital (Halpern, 2005, p 10). Importantly, such networks build trust as 'networks of community engagement foster sturdy norms of reciprocity' (Putnam, 2000, p 20). In SW9, such networks are both 'high density' (where all the members know each other) and 'high closure' (comprising mainly intra-community as opposed to inter-community links) (Halpern, 2005, p 10).

A successful street gang has a network of sources providing it with information. This network is not restricted to gang members, but stretches deep into the community to include lovers; immediate and extended family; school, college or work colleagues; and church and social connections (Putnam, 2000, p 21). Of course such networks may benefit those within the network but have negative effects for those external to it (Putnam, 2000, p 21). In disadvantaged communities, networks support each other through altruism and an obligation to overcome disadvantage (Stack, 1974). Generally acknowledged, this fact helps move information (and stolen goods) around the community, reinforcing network durability and internalisation.

> 'Gangs spread it around amongst each other. Olders will be approached – they have links, networks, connections, families. Some knock-off shops and market stalls will take the goods. Sometimes it gets stolen to order. They can be traded in barber shops etc. Offers are made to get people things which are then stolen or passed over when received.' (African Caribbean male older).

A 'durable network' (Bourdieu, 1980, p 2; 1986, p 248) represents a substantial form of social capital that can be accessed and utilised. Bridging networks improve links to external assets and improve information transmission (Puttnam, 2000, p 22).

Family, or extended family, is linked into the network alongside acquaintances, connections, friends and lovers, providing the hidden backdrop and wallpaper to the neighbourhood. It is both extensive and all encompassing. Many local people are both well connected and long established in the community, with connections strengthened through church attendance or prison. The network works for you and against you at all times, acting as commentator, judge and arbiter of behaviour. It also operates as a strong communication channel, similar to an underground network of fibre optic cables, reaching deep into the community. Like the Hometree in Avatar,[2] it is the communal repository of all past and current knowledge. Like the HomeTree, it is accessible, but not all have the full set of social skills to use it or to interrogate it effectively. This information network is well known, well used and sits above and separate to the smaller, more internalised, gang network. Information is fed into the network and retrieved daily from the network. As broadband varies in bandwidth, so do the interconnecting virtual cables of the network. Hearsay operates as the thinnest and least respected virtual cable. Family communications, in particular those between blood relatives, operate at the widest and most respect bandwidth. Links to professionals are also highly prized.

The network also plays a part in social control, with the dominant views and behaviours of the network acting as a form of social restraint on individual behaviours. This can work both ways; for example, youngsters may come under pressure from family members not to affiliate to a gang. It may also assist those seeking to leave the gang. In gang terms, the network underscores and strengthens the direction given by older siblings. Directions can even come via network links from members in prison:

> 'My nephew got stabbed. I've got other nephews in jail too. I got a call from a prison before I heard it from the family. That's the network.' (African Caribbean male Youth Offending Team officer)

The network may at times allow individuals to be absent from the gang, for example, if a young person displays a key talent that could be a passport out of the neighbourhood to a better life. The gang network is used to access intelligence and information for the purposes of appraisal, monitoring, marketing and trading. The wider community network provides details of family ties, relationships, addresses, business links, schooling and so forth. Both gang affiliates and peripheral members provide details of criminal activities – who is dealing, where the stash is hidden, what is transmitted upline (up to the higher tiers of the gang). Two key requirements exist: the need for constant updating, and sifting or grading information.

To stay abreast of recent developments, maintain reputation and reduce risk, young people network constantly, often sounding people out to build a picture of activity, separating fact from fiction. While the subject matter is of interest to all, members understand that information management is a challenge they will never be on top of:

> 'It's all about your crew; about what's happening in Peckham; about your cousins in Gas gang, business deals. It's everyday changing. It's impossible to keep on top of it. Otherwise the shootings won't be happening, the robbings wouldn't be happening. You will never be on top, never, never, never.' (African Caribbean male older)

Actors in the network include all those in the social field of the gang, as well as peripheral members and those in the wider community who have some involvement with the gang. Within the social field network, two key groups are worthy of closer attention: girls and young women, and new arrivals (often immigrants). The role of women relates to the gendered roles within the social field and that of new arrivals relates to issues of ethnicity.

As we saw in Chapter Five, the strategic use of social skill is crucial to being an effective information trader. It is thus a role favoured and actively sought by women, who often have highly developed social skills. One key role is to manage the links with other strategic action fields proximate to the gang, with successful individuals becoming a valuable resource for gang elders and incumbents. Good management may help keep a crisis at bay by giving early warning of any problems. Thus a gang social field that is well connected is better able to weather a crisis should one arise. It may also be in the gang's interest to monitor the number of people with access to proximate fields, e.g. residents working as council staff.

Strategic action using information

All strategic actors in this social field trade/exchange information. Transmitting information is a form of strategic action (see Table 11.1).

The challenges of trading information

Transmitting information across the social field presents many challenges/potential difficulties. A failure to implement strategic actions to address these issues may lead to serious consequences for the trader, as illustrated in Table 11.2.

Social skill may also be exercised by information traders knowing who to approach first, who will forward messages furthest or quickest, who will add drama, emotion or embellishment.

Social networking sites

Over the past five years in SW9, visual strategies such as videos disseminated via social networking sites have taken over from graffiti and tagging walls as a way of building reputation and marketing brand. Youngers who once used tagging as an expressive repertoire strategy now use Facebook, Bebo and other social networking sites to create a virtual identity, raise their profile, create hype around their brand name, and socialise in the unpoliced world of the internet. Older gang members, however, tend not to use this medium.

Table 11.1: Strategies for gaining and using information

Strategy	Comment
Disinformation and misinformation	A member strategises to increase their own street capital by embellishing details. Involves members exaggerating their involvement in events to increase their own street capital. They may circulate alternative versions of events – either among peers in their own gang or among rivals – perhaps distancing themselves from any involvement or supplying false details.
Double-dealing (being 'snakey')	Involves passing on information despite being asked not to do so.
Dry snitching	Involves trading information by mistake, or trading information without taking account of the implications this may have for others. Older gang members may use this strategy to their own advantage by getting youngers to pass on information unwittingly.
Planning sanctions	Involves acquiring information to gain a tactical advantage when planning a sanction such as a robbery. Some sanctions may be planned gradually following weeks or months of information retrieval.
Using girls as information traders	Involves girls collecting mobile phones dropped during altercations in order to prevent rivals from accessing critical information for monitoring personal safety, or to cut a member off from his vital information networks. Girls may also de-crypt the phone to access vital personal details and then report back on network connections and inter-personal relationships
Independent operators	Involves independent operators risk assessing their situation and choosing not to share ortrade information in order to preserve their own safety

In this social field, things move quickly, with information traded in a variety of different locations and a variety of different ways. Virtual communication is aided by new technological developments. Facebook provides a forum for multiple users to message one another, while Face Time and Skype enable real-time video conversations, providing users with an powerful outlet to dramatise raw emotion.

Approaches are made hourly to young people and accepted by phone. In this fast-moving world, new alliances are made, and new boundaries drawn, with information further communicated by phone. Social networking sites act a constant messengers, keeping young people abreast of information without which they are at risk of victimisation.

Chapter Twelve examines further how girls and young women use their social skill to trade information, and considers in particular the gendered nature of the social field.

Table 11.2: The challenges of trading information

Challenge	Comment
Confidentiality	Breaking confidentiality, for example, passing on personal information or contact details of former friends – puts members at risk of victimisation.
False bravado	Young people may provoke/challenge rivals by phone, as in this example given by one ex-younger in the SW9 research: "I done it bruv, you know I done it. So come on bruv, come on we'll sort it out. I'm waiting." This (often false) bravado increases street capital as well as compromising safety.
Erosion of trust	Swapping information can easily erode trust between gang members or between gang members and wider network connections, threatening personal safety in a way that would not happen in other social fields.
Verification of connections	Members need to be able to establish their credentials if caught in rival territory. An inability to provide information or answer questions in a satisfactory way increases the risk of attack.
Credibility	The importance and veracity of information is assessed according to the source. Information from high-ranking gang members is more credible than that from youngers.

Notes

[1] Fligstein and McAdam (2012, p 77) identify information collection and sharing as one of the functions of what they call internal governance units.

[2] Avatar is a movie directed by James Cameron and released by Twentieth Century Fox in 2009.

TWELVE

Playing the queen: gender in the gang

The social field of the gang is highly gendered, replicating the gendered social construction of the wider community. Bourdieu (1984) views gender as a stratifying feature of the social field, secondary to economic, cultural, social and symbolic capital. In all social fields where capital is unevenly distributed, the male/female binary is a form of domination evident in all social hierarchies (Swartz, 1997, p 156). Thus the hierarchical power relations of the social field dictate that capital allocation is weighted towards men, compounded by the fact that male and female roles and social aspirations are determined by the habitus and the social norms operating within the field.

As a 'structured arena of conflict' (Bourdieu and Wacquant, 1992), the social field is also defined by the internal struggle for power and dominance. This internalised hierarchical structure replicates opportunities for patriarchy, male privilege and male violence. Indeed, male violence dominates as a key strategy for advancement. In this way, the hierarchy favours males over females. As a result, the gang repertoire – including tried and tested opportunities for generating street capital – is largely gendered in favour of men, and physical violence is more highly prized than social skill. This, in turn, means that women tend to occupy subordinate roles in the social field of the gang.

Instead girls and young women simply operate and strategise differently within the social field to locate positions of power and influence which provide opportunities for them to manufacture their own street capital and thus advance.

In a social field relatively well stocked with interpersonal and family connections, there are opportunities for those with social skill to increase both their social and street capital. Social skill is thus a capital asset for women in particular. Before exploring this in more depth, we look at how other academics have traditionally viewed the role of girls and young women in the gang.

Traditional gang research perspectives on girls and young women

The roles played by girls (females aged under 16) and young women (females aged 16 and over) within a gang have received scant academic focus in the UK.1 Male-dominated criminological research has frequently overlooked such roles, a fact compounded by the variant definitions used to define the term 'gang'. The gang agenda has been characterised as overwhelmingly male (Batchelor, 2009, p 401), focused on narrowly defined criminal roles involving men but largely ignoring women unless their roles are overtly criminal. Thus a persuasive gender imbalance pervades even contemporary academic studies on gangs.

Traditionally, in both US and UK gang studies, girls and young women are framed only in relation to male members (Campbell, 1990, p 166), viewed variously as 'stereotypes' (Hallsworth and Young, 2010), 'bad girls' (Campbell, 1984) and gender traitors acting as either tomboys or sluts (Chesney-Lind, 1997). Hallsworth and Young (2010) identified a gendered narrative in early gang studies that suggested that men joined gangs for excitement and transcendent action while women joined because they needed protection, money and love, a characterisation they describe as the 'deficit model', depicting women as 'sad and needy' (Hallsworth and Young, 2010, p 86). Batchelor (2009), however, found that girls also responded to the thrill of offending.

Other contemporary gang studies offer a 'more nuanced portrayal' (Miller, J., 2001, p 16), identifying increased victimisation of females who join gangs alongside the more affirmative benefits of empowerment, refuge and resistance (Campbell, 1990; Moore, 1991; Joe and Chesney-Lind, 1995; Joe-Laidler and Hunt, 2001; Miller, J., 2001).

In a more recent study by The Children's Commissioner (Beckett et al, 2013) identified a range of different roles for young women in gangs, each of which brought different levels of risk including exposure to sexual and physical violence. These roles include:

- Gangster girls – young women adopting a masculine presentation with in gangs;
- Female family members of gang-affiliated young men;
- Girlfriends (wifeys);
- Young women who have children with gang-involved males (baby-mothers); and
- Young women in casual sexual relationships (links).

They noted that these categories were not mutually exclusive and that any protection offered or assumed with such roles is 'precarious and can be easily withdrawn'. Risks can be assumed to be internal to the gang but also external through association with the gang. Moreover they noted that 'the roles that different young women can attain, and the degree to which they can retain these, are generally determined by young men' (Beckett et al 2013, p 34). Interestingly they identified that 'the role of "gangster girl" was the only one in which young women's status was constructed without explicit reference to their association with a gang-involved young man' (Beckett et al 2013, p 34).

Reported levels of gang membership also vary, depending on the research methodology employed in the gang study. Self-reported studies suggest that male/female gang membership is almost equal (Batchelor, 2009), while qualitative studies suggest that gangs are largely dominated by men (Esbensen et al, 1999). A recent study in 2011 for the Office of the Children's Commissioner for England identified an estimated 12,500 girls and young women have a close involvement with gangs, (Pearce and Pitts, 2011, p 19). Southgate (2011) reported that girls, 'frequently "drifted" into or became implicated in gang activity, rather than "joining" gangs per se' (p 21).

Reports indicate that there are high levels of offending among gang-affiliated young people (both female and male) across all categories (Bennett and Holloway, 2004; Smith and Bradshaw, 2005; Sharp et al, 2006). As violence by girls and young women in gang settings is normalised, participants acknowledge a high threshold of tolerance of violence (Batchelor, 2005, 2009), with violence often framed as self-defence or preventative (Batchelor, 2005, p 369).

Young (2009) argues that women may group together (creating associations largely based on experience of shared trauma) and that this does not fit our perception of gangs. Joe and Chesney-Lind (1995) and Miller, J. (2001) recognise the significance of peer groups for validating identity and providing support.

It is within this somewhat unsatisfactory research context then that the roles played by girls and young women in a gang are generally characterised as 'secondary' (Aldridge and Medina, 2007, p 7); 'ancillary' (Pitts, 2007b, p 40); 'background' (Kintrea et al, 2008, p 25); and 'auxiliary or associate' (Densley, 2013, p 79).

Batchelor (2009, p 408), however, offers an alternative, suggesting that girls' violence illustrates risk taking and 'demonstrates the positive contribution violent behaviour can have in terms of their sense of self and self-efficacy'. Seeking to distance herself from the dominant discourses of the female victim, Batchelor implores researchers not to settle for simplistic gendered accounts of those involved and argues cogently for researchers not to view women as merely passive victims but as 'agentic social actors' (Batchelor, 2009, p 409).

Social field analysis

Most gang research appears to have misinterpreted the role of girls and young women in the gang. Social field analysis, however, offers us the opportunity to reconceptualise this gendered account, offering an alternative perspective that acknowledges the agentic female strategic actor, struggling to generate and retain her own street capital in this social field. Let us now consider how this new perspective offers a fresh insight.

The ubiquity of street masculinity

We know that the hierarchical structure of the social field privileges males with their strategic action based on violence. In the gang's social field this context of male violence or 'street masculinity' (Mullins, 2006) is normalised.

Undoubtedly, the gang acts as a location for 'doing masculinity' (Messerschmidt, 1993) as other opportunities are blocked off (Taylor Gibbs and Merighi, cited in Newburn and Stanko, 1994). Messerschmidt (1993) argues that masculinity is not performed, but rather has to be made, and that criminality is one means of production. It is, therefore, a type of structured action (Messerschmidt, 2000). The gang provides a social arena for men to demonstrate 'manly' qualities, albeit what Connell describes as 'subordinated masculinity' (Connell, cited in Mullins, 2006). The imperative to generate street capital for men is further underpinned by concepts of fragile masculinity and the normative values of the social field.

How masculinity is made depends on one's social field. In the gang social field, there are few opportunities to develop a plausible gendered self other than crime and violence. Traditional working-class opportunities of paid employment (hegemonic masculinity) are largely unavailable (Pitts, 2008b; Winlow, 2001) to young black men in this social field. Sartre (1963, p 95) calls this 'subjective impoverishment'. Barker (2005) contends that this creates such pressure on actors in the social field that they are prepared to face potential injury or fatality to achieve their goal of constructing a plausible gendered self. In addition, the habitus determines what structured actions are effective for 'doing masculinity'. These opportunities abound in a social field where the rules are set by men.

Sartre (1963) argues that gangs are cognisant of a future where hegemonic masculinity is denied them and thus street life becomes a 'field of possibilities' through which gender can be accomplished and the bounds of race and class can similarly be transcended. For example, 'robbery provides a public ceremony of domination and humiliation of others' (Messerschmidt, 1993, p 107). Katz (1988, p 225) refers to this public masculinity as the preserve of 'hardmen' – the equivalent of 'badman' in SW9. Messerschmidt acknowledges that under some circumstances criminal activity becomes a resource for enacting 'street masculinity' (Mullins, 2006). Street masculinity is embodied in the militaristic concept of gang 'solja'. This then becomes the defining epithet for male gang involvement. It is within this gendered social context that girls and young women must struggle.

Entering the game

To play, one must first enter the game. The gender imbalance within the social field leaves girls and young women in capital deficit from the outset. As they quickly learn, to survive in the social field they must struggle for status and distinction in the same way as young men (Cobbina et al, 2010), building street capital via reputation. Opportunities to achieve this are more limited for them than for boys and young men, further confirming and compounding the gendered relationships within the social field (Firmen, 2010).

Street capital in the social field validates patriarchal attributes such as physicality and a propensity towards violence, and gang repertoire strategies are strongly gender-biased towards males. Girls and young women must therefore find their own way to become 'playas'. They may do this by creating new field positions in the hierarchy and strategically positioning themselves within the field to maximise their advantage. Thus they generate street capital using strategic actions that favour social skills rather than violence.

Those females most likely to advance in this social field are those who can quickly recognise their structured position within a highly gendered field. A special few identify opportunities to use their social skill in playing the game. Skilled actors have a better understanding of the complexities of the social field, its ambiguities, nuances, networks, allegiances and uncertainties. This gives them greater insight into what is possible and achievable and what is not. Socially skilled actors are more adept at framing stories (Goffman, 1974) aimed at inducing cooperation, which can be used to target action against opponents (Goffman, 1959; Bourdieu, 1977; Coleman, 1986; DiMaggio, 1988; Fligstein, 1996). It may be the case that partial immersion in the gang social field assists socially skilled young women to more clearly identify those angles and benefits that will give them the edge. Knowing how and when to use social skill is a social skill in itself.

Recognition of field position means recognition of one's vulnerability. Once this has been acknowledged, girls move quickly to mitigate the risks through enacting strategies of risk management, such as agreeing offers of 'protection' from the gang. This 'protection' may be real, inferred or assumed. It may allow them to move around the neighbourhood unmolested. Crucially, it may allow for greater safety at school and college, at least to begin with. Girls may also self-impose restrictions or sanctions in order to minimise risks. This is thought to be a short-term and worthwhile strategy.

Female gang affiliates report that an early objective on entering the game is to develop strategies to achieve peer 'recognition', which suggests that girls are engaged in a fierce competitive struggle with their female peers as well as being in competition with boys. Finding it harder to build street capital, girls may develop strategies to identify both the advantages and disadvantages of situations and make adjustments accordingly (Cobbina et al, 2010).

Some girls and young women achieve rapid street recognition through gang association, the benefits of which are quickly identified and embraced, for example, piggybacking on brand names to accelerate their street capital. Others develop early sexual strategies, a dangerous trajectory discussed in more detail later in the chapter.

One of the key strategies enabling females to enter the game early is to demonstrate knowledge of the game. This may be proven through personal contacts, and also through 'minding one's place' and learning the rules, such as 'not grassing'. Those who demonstrate such knowledge gain the trust of other gang members and improve their status.

The gendered differentiation of roles is acknowledged by both males and females in the social field of the gang. One respondent in the SW9 research noted that the boys "run in a pack and take care of business" while the girls "do their own thing but they are behind the boys" (African Caribbean male elder). Male respondents often stated that gang girls largely sat alongside the boys as a group and only a few were actively located within the gang itself, such a position tending to be privileged and uncommon. Those with the appropriate social skills may exploit this gendered differentiation of roles (Campbell,

1984; Miller, J., 2001; Cobbina, 2010; Firmen, 2010) in order to gain a number of clear advantages. Girls may act as conduits or perform specific tasks. They may be distanced from gang violence, allowing them to operate their own sub-social field of respect and reputation along gendered lines. They may be called on to access the network or to address confrontations with other girls. They are the fixers, the mixers and the public relations agents of the gang, all roles that require social skill.

The importance of social skills

Social skill is essentially an individual competency. The way it is used is largely determined by an individual's position in the field hierarchy, the opportunities available to them, and their ability to mobilise and motivate others, and provide meaning and clarity of purpose. These are all strategies available to socially skilled actors in the pursuit of street capital, be they male or female.

In the social field of the gang, it becomes clear to them early on that girls and young women are unlikely to ever be leaders. While some women achieve equal status with male peers in the gang, they are more likely to occupy subordinate roles. In the gendered social field, girls and young women may be permanent fixtures but are frequently viewed as neither incumbents nor challengers. This perceptional oversight provides them with a parallel social space whereby they can strategically employ social skill to generate street capital and seek advancement and distinction. Indeed, the gendered field acknowledges this role and permits this set of actions. Boys commonly describe girls as being 'in the game, but not in it to win it'. While socially skilled males are often marked out early for positions of leadership, socially skilled females are often considered to be 'manipulative'.

Boys will largely leave this function of social skill to girls, viewing it as 'girls' business', but socially skilled boys and young men will recognise its importance and centrality to the field. In this way, girls and young women become an important element in gang operations, working for the gang, part of the gang, but seldom 'running' with the gang. This association of social skills with the role of women mirrors wider social structures and is thus widely accepted as normal. Girls themselves quickly realise that they must excel in their role as they have few other routes by which to generate and maintain street capital and survive the landscape of risk.

It is through the use of social skill that girls and young women seek to generate street capital. This provides them with a more equal chance in the game, as this is one aspect that they play well. Playing the game in this way means that the roles and strategic actions of girls and young women are almost universally misread, misunderstood and mis-characterised by men in the social field, and importantly also by academics, studying the social field, the mis-characterisation of their function as simply 'background' or 'auxiliary'.

The extent to which girls employ social skills, and their ability to employ them successfully, depends on their individual agency. Girls may use their social skill to acquire street capital, build reputation, secure partners, obtain goods and services, and move up in social rank. As with boys, levels of agency vary; some girls are active, intuitive and self-determined, while others are fragile, vulnerable and nascent.

Some girls choose not to completely enter the gang's social field, only its periphery, adjusting their proximity accordingly. Due to the specific role played by girls, e.g. transmitting information, it is also possible that some girls become unwittingly intertwined with a gang or at least fail to fully comprehend the level of their own involvement.

While some agencies report a rise in girls' involvement in gangs, it is difficult to assess the true situation, as their involvement tends to be less visible than that of male members. They operate both at the core and the periphery, connecting the gang to the wider community network, and are involved with members at all levels. While their strategic actions are often perceived stereotypically as being 'back-office', or low-level functions, they actually perform a critical set of functions, sustaining the social field while maintaining or enhancing their own field position and street capital. Sometimes acting under duress and sometimes under independent or individual agency, they are at once girlfriends, baby-mothers, intermediaries, players and spectators at 'the game'.

The social skills spectrum

The various roles played by girls and young women in the violent street gang depend on age, status and agency, with each role representing a strategic action to advance status and street capital. Strategies employed will thus vary depending on these variables, in addition to proximity to the gang and to the tier of the gang with whom they are involved. The roles employed demonstrate varying degrees of social skill (see Figure 12.1). At one end of the social skills spectrum lies the employment of violence, associated in this social field with few social skills. At the opposite end of the spectrum are sophisticated roles requiring and denoting a high level of trust and social skill, such

Figure 12.1: Social skills spectrum

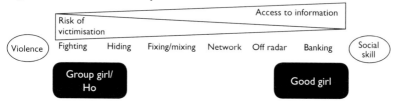

as banking and money laundering. Along the spectrum is a range of activities or roles that denote varying degrees of social skill.

Those employing actions at the violence end of the spectrum tend to have fewer social skills, and may be new to the gang, young, or inexperienced and yet to fully comprehend the many nuances of playing the game.

The more experienced or socially skilled tend to avoid violence, generating street capital by positioning themselves as invaluable conduits of information, using their ability to avoid detection or suspicion. Such clever deployment of social skill increases their trustworthiness and gives them access to privileged information. Unlike those at the lower end of the spectrum, where trust and information are in short supply and actors are vulnerable, girls at this end are able to minimise the risk of victimisation.

Sitting alongside the social skill spectrum are the sexual narratives that indicate vertical field positions. The ability of girls and young women to deploy social skills is of paramount importance in their sub-field. The way in which they display their ability – their demeanour and deportment – are also important, as these are the qualities that differentiate 'good girls' from 'bad girls' ('hos' and 'bitches'). More of this shortly, but first let us consider the strategic actions available in the spectrum of social skills.

Reputation (or street capital) management

Monitoring personal street capital is as important for girls as it is for boys. In addition, a key role for girls is to use their social skills to manage the reputation and street capital of their lovers. Through personal validations, testimonials, endorsements and tributes, girls and young women can influence the rise or fall of a man's street capital. Girls add a reputational caveat behind certain male gang members. Such reputation enhancement is used boost brand names in the same way that logos confer recognition, but through verbal caveats that often act as warnings – e.g. "My Man lives there – but be careful cos he will ..."

Goffman (1959, 1974) tells us that dominant social actors have high self-esteem while dominated actors (girls and young women) must employ coping strategies to address stigmatisation. Here girls and young women seek to bond in peer groups, which often have a life outside the gang, to provide mutual support and thus avoid stigma and loss of street capital. Here issues of reputation are critical, as a damaged reputation represents more than just a loss of street capital – it is prima facia evidence of lack of social skill. Street capital must be regained quickly or the social trajectory is all too familiar. When street capital deflation occurs for boys, it is often recoverable via extreme violence. For young women and girls, loss of street capital deflation is often linked to sexual reputation, which is seldom recoverable once they have been characterised as a 'ho' (slut). In such circumstances, violence may be used to redeem street capital of another sort.

Violence

In the social field of the violent street gang, there are always options for girls to advance their status and street capital through physical violence, although this indicates/confirms a lack of social skill. In SW9, assaults and fights between girls in school playgrounds are common, but they are not usually related to gang rivalries.

Research indicates that physical violence is becoming more frequent between girls in the social field of the gang (Cobbina et al, 2010). There are several possible reasons for this, all of which require further research:

- repertoire strategies are becoming 'gender neutral';
- girls and young women are more restricted in their current strategies and seek to move beyond them;
- social skills strategies are available to fewer women;
- the use of violence to underpin social skill is becoming more widespread;
- more women are entering the social field without social skills (at the violence end of the spectrum).

Some girls do develop a reputation for using violence and this may become a way of generating significant street capital, thereby elevating status. Most girls and young women use violence strategically to defend reputation, which is carefully monitored. Even those considered to be socially skilled may need to use violence at certain times to have an impact.

Hiding

Hiding drugs or weapons gains the trust and respect of the gang. Girls tend to be the main players here, as it is widely accepted that they are less likely to be suspected or stopped by the police. Socially skilled actors become adept at performing this strategic action. If they are caught by the police they are social skilled enough to claim they were forced into hiding the goods – which may of course also be true. Those who act through individual agency are motivated by expectations of deferred favours. Girls who take on the role of hiding drugs or weapons are often linked to the gang through close family.

Some girls and young women view hiding goods as a way of getting closer to the gang or to an individual with whom they are romantically linked, being accepted by the gang or even entering the gang, with a promise of deferred benefits; others are bullied or coerced into the role, often because they are in a relationship with their aggressor and are afraid of being assaulted if they refuse. Many are employing strategic action to raise their profile as a player. Hiding weapons brings acknowledgment and recognition, closer proximity to the gang and a reputation for being trustworthy. This sense of individual agency may, however, be an illusion. While those new to the gang may view a request to hide a weapon as a thrilling opportunity for closer affiliation, it is more likely to be engineered by the gang as a test of social skill. Interestingly, independent operators are just as likely to achieve respect by refusing to hide weapons or drugs for gang members.

Fixing and mixing

Another way to demonstrate social skill is to 'fix' spectators for forthcoming fights. This involves facilitating attendance by texting details of the event to friends, passing on messages and 'hyping' the 'fixture', with the aim of creating an en-masse spectacle. Such is the normative nature of these events and the pack mentality that accompanies them that the assembled group, often still in their school uniforms, usually pay scant attention to the presence of CCTV or other capable guardians. In SW9, several street fights have occurred outside the Youth Offending Team offices and Brixton police station. At such large-scale disturbances, girls associate with boys, hyping up the situation and generating considerable excitement. When things 'kick off', they pick up items such as phones and jewellery dropped or torn off in the fight, and later 'clean' the area of evidence, often claiming to have been part of the gang, playing an active part in the event. For them, centrality to the action brings increased street capital. Stolen mobile phones are used to access contacts, messages and key information.

Girls and young women also play key roles in obtaining and distributing stolen goods to the network. This strategic action increases their gang and network connections. Sourcing and placement of goods may be linked to female shoplifting groups. These activities generate detailed information about the criminal activities of key families and individuals. Orders for stolen goods may be taken by girls and items sourced by boys. Social skill are enhanced by an ability to match products, steal to order and fulfil requests quickly.

Monitoring activity

Girls and young women use their social skills to act as 'touchstones' responsible for monitoring activity, especially reputations – who is being talked about, and why. This is a passive activity, where girls act as listeners. More proactive roles include operating sanctions by proxy, for example spreading rumour and gossip, and then monitoring the effects. Girls and young women may act as the eyes and ears of the gang, picking up information and intelligence – who is moving around, where they are going, who has been seen where. Girls often change their appearance so they can move between estates and neighbourhoods without being recognised, gleaning intelligence from locations such as beauty parlours and nail shops.

Socially skilled women may be trusted to broker deals and act as sounding boards for elders. They may be required to verify vital personal information, alibis or situations, validate incidents or gain access to key people across rival gangs.

Staying off radar

Socially skilled young women maintain a low profile or go 'unseen'. This permits unrestricted movement within the social field and across postcode areas. It allows them to maintain a degree of distance from the core of the gang and the social field. This makes it easier to stay safe and avoid victimisation, as they can claim to have had no, or limited, involvement in violent gang activities. This frees women up to take part in peripheral activities such as hiding weapons, drugs and money, to the advantage of male and female gang members alike.

This advantage is then maximised by both males and females as the females are used to hide weapons, drugs and money, which generates trust and builds street capital, and also permits demonstration of social skill.

Laundering and banking

A high level of trust and social skill is evident in the strategic action of banking (holding money or drugs) and laundering (transferring money). An older may use his girlfriend's credit card to pay for items such as car insurance or car hire. Some girlfriends may even exploit their own credit rating to hire vehicles for men in their own name. Girls and young women may or may not facilitate such actions willingly, but either way, they are accepted as a consequence of the affirmative sanctions repertoire, or of being in a relationship with a gang member. Socially skilled girls and young women position themselves as reliable facilitators of such actions.

Influencing sanctions

Social skill plays a key part in influencing the actions of others, be it strategic action or the employment of sanctions. Mead (1934) suggests that social skills are used to induce cooperation. Girls and young women are central to reputational (street capital) deflations through the sanction of gossip. Their proximity and centrality to the gang network permits them to operate highly effectively and manipulate the network using gossip and rumour to influence sanctions.

Not all gossip and rumour will carry the same effective value in the social field. It can be made more effective by techniques of framing the discourse to advantage the aggrieved party (who may or may not be the source). Those trading and exchanging the information (rumour or gossip) can be placed in a powerful position to use their social skill to frame the desired outcome (Goffman, 1974). This might be achieved by framing the storey in existential terms with questions of value, trust, membership and victimisation, e.g. Why me? What have I ever done? What am I getting out of this deal? How would you feel if this happened to you? Skilled social actors have a strong sense of what can be achieved in these situations and will utilise their skill to redefine events and suggest alternative courses of action.

One example of gaining advantage by using social skills to frame the discourse to your personal advantage is the use of set-ups or honey traps. Set-ups or honey traps are one example of how girls and young women use their social skills to advance their field position, with an unwitting ex-lover or friend as the victim:

> 'Girls will set you up. They will sleep with you and then go through your pockets. They will phone guys who will be waiting for you when you leave the flat. That's how people run up this information, they will get girls in. Boys are clowns when it comes to girls.' (African Caribbean male older)

Samantha Joseph famously employed this strategy in the 'honey-trap' murder of Shakilus Townsend in London in 2009.[2] It should however also be acknowledged that men often recognise these social skills held by women. There are also examples where women in domestic violence relationships have been manipulated or compelled by men to utilise their social skills to the advantage of the male, e.g. to instigate a set-up or honey-trap. In such scenarios the woman may be employing a risk avoidance strategy and may act under duress to avoid becoming a victim of male violence herself. Here the use of social skill becomes a survival strategy.

Boys believe girls are careless with information, seeking to impress others with personal titbits and often dry-snitch. They are also used to set-up boys for attack by rivals.

Controlling the network

Social skill for females in this social field is primarily defined by connectivity to the network (see Chapter Eleven). Here girls and young women can efficiently demonstrate their multiple contacts and, by effectively operating and maintaining the network, play the central role in ensuring the network functions effectively and extensively. This includes maintaining connectivity to the network for those in custody. Connectivity is everything: it provides news, knowledge, personal facts, histories, biographical checks, sexual histories, family histories and fast verification.

Network access is effectively controlled by girls and young women. The network extends beyond the gang to the wider community, the world of work, and family and overseas relations. Part of women's role as controllers of the network is to maintain field relations with proximate fields – fields that are linked but not geographically connected.[3] Though external, these linked fields can affect decisions and outcomes in the gang; for example, the death or imprisonment of a relative or friend are usually mediated via women thus enhancing their role and their status. The timing of the delivery of information is also an acquired social skill.

Some young men in the study expressed a general distrust of young women because of their powerful position and their ability to mediate with proximate fields, along with their ability to access the network and control information.

Trading information

The social skills needed to operate and maintain network connectivity and control within the social field effectively positions girls as Information Traders collating and distributing information, transmitting messages, ultimatums, rumour and local community knowledge. This strategic role is seldom formalised but raises their profile placing them in a pivotal position within the gang and between gangs. Their ability to play both sides of rival gangs gives them a further privileged role, accessing and holding (or withholding) information otherwise impossible to obtain. Issues of trust and veracity are central to trading, with social skill determining that higher quality information is traded for a higher price. Information obtained by putting themselves at risk comes with a high bargaining price, providing the trader with increased purchase within the gang.

Information traders maintain regular contact with gang affiliates and the wider community network. Early receipt of information provides additional advantage, and some build a reputation around being the first to know about something or having the most truthful account. Others gain a reputation for not telling tales. Having widespread, accessible contacts demonstrates formidable links to the network – valuable social capital in its own right. Such network connectivity represents a form of street capital that may be achieved without violence, one that is both tradable and widely recognised. In a field crisis, for example, after a fatal stabbing when men generally lay low to avoid police attention these women become critical in updating gang members on police activity, current investigation developments, arrests, who is in hiding, etc.

Girls often alert gangs to imminent incursions, passing on information from girlfriends on other estates. This allows the targeted gang to 'group up' or hide weapons nearby. Such tip-offs often result in rivals having to change their plans.

Exposure to risk

When viewed holistically within the social field, the role of girls and young women becomes more significant. As network controllers, they are key arbiters of reputation. Using a metaphor from the world of tabloid newspapers, they can make or break reputations, giving them influence over fluctuations in street capital. In the gang social field, this makes them 'playas'. Over time, they may even become powerful 'playas'. Girls and young women have created a pivotal role that, albeit not always immediately evident, elevates them from the traditionally gendered perspective of secondary players, or, more accurately, enables them to operate differently within the gendered social field of the gang.

Such roles make females strategic players, but this role also generates challenges. Firstly men understand their strategic importance as reputation-makers leading boys to be very wary around girls: 'Rule of the road – never trust a girl!' This places girls and young women in potentially dangerous situations in the social field.

Men are keenly aware of the social power available to girls and young women through the strategic use of social skills, so they seek to control this power and regulate it through the use of sanctions, and by trying to 'manage' the girls' reputations. In addition, the process of advancement within the social field can be as equally brutalising for women as it is for men. This dynamic is perhaps best illustrated by considering women's exposure to risk.

In the social field of the gang, girls and young women are at risk by dint of their gender, their relationships with the gang, the violent norms of the social field and the roles and strategies they employ. They are equally subject to the sanctions repertoire by men who seek to control their 'movements and mouth'. Sanctions include punishments for both minor and major infringements of gang rules, for failing in business transactions and for a range of other misdemeanours. For example, one recent incident in SW9 involved a gang girl being raped as a punishment to the boyfriend for not paying his drug debts. She may also be expected to bail him out of debt and may be at further risk if she fails.

Casual violence and gendered male violence is ever present. Male gang members may order their own girlfriends to administer sanctions by proxy, for example, telling them to attack another girl when they see her, e.g. *'when you see this girl* – *'Punch her up!'* although this would only be seen as low-level violence. The level of violence used is determined by how serious a player the victim is. As one respondent put it: "She might get mashed up but it's not that people want to kill her" (West African female older). Girls and young women are often collateral casualties in events where drug dealers have had their premises raided by another gang. In such circumstances, the victim may be pistol-whipped or assaulted.

In one recent incident in SW9 gang members seriously injured a member's girlfriend when she visited his house, as revenge for his refusing to leave the house and confront them. For some gang members, and for some transgressions, girlfriends are 'fair game' and easy targets for sanctions. It is a huge insult to a member to have his sister or girlfriend become the target of a sanction; this is seen as a challenge to his reputation, respect and male dignity.

Indiscriminate violence and 'slappings' occur by way of men 'controlling' a girl's strategic actions, or 'keeping her in line'. Such assaults are considered to be justified by unwitting infringements of gang codes or rules, or by a failure to perform a task. In one incident, a young girl was beaten up outside school because she owed £1,000 to a gang member. Exposure to sanctions or violence[4] is clearly a downside to any association with a gang. Young female gang members may be unaware that they are putting themselves at risk, or they may consider it a risk worth taking.

Sanctions sometimes involve sexual violence or rape.[5] Most female gang members believe this only happens to 'slags' (in other words, not to them), indicating that victims lack social skill. Rape and sexual violence towards girls and young women is, according to the SW9 study respondents, both overstated by the media and underreported by victims.[6] Female respondents in the SW9 research considered rape to be a reality, while some male gang members thought it was an urban myth. Agency workers and professionals acknowledged that rape and sexual violence occurs within the gang social field in SW9; however some local police officers denied this while other officers claimed incidents were underreported.[7] The concept that girls and young women might be subject to gang-related rape and sexual assault as part of the sanction repertoire is rejected by Hallsworth (2013). Group rape was generally acknowledged to occur on occasion, and images of group rape have been found on gang members' mobile phones, but this is not peculiar to Lambeth. On the whole, young male gang members distanced themselves from group rape, saying it had nothing to do with gangs. As one young African older stated: '*If that's going on its separate. That's not cool. You don't get stripes for that.*'

Overall, two separate narratives from male gang members were evident in the SW9 study: that sexual violence and rape is used as a sanction, and that most 'rapes' are in fact not rapes but consensual sexual relations, but girls who hang out with gang members misrecognise signs and gang norms and thus claim it as 'rape'.[8]

Those most at risk of sexual violence are girls with limited self-esteem or low levels of individual agency or social skill. They are more likely to be coerced, intimidated or forced into situations where sexual violence may be used as a sanction. They may be new to the gang and unskilled in reading warning signs and potentially dangerous situations. Indeed, agencies reported some quite young children involved in sexual activity. A failure to mitigate risk is viewed by some as indicative of poor social skill. As lack of social skill becomes increasingly perceptible to others, the risk of victimisation increases. A girl with poor social skill is thought to have a 'loose mouth', to be someone who cannot be trusted. This combination of poor social skill, untrustworthiness and inability to manage or mitigate risk exposes her failure to play the game. This increases her vulnerability even further, and she finds herself 'sliding'. Denounced as untrustworthy, she is restricted or denied access to information, shunned by both boys and girls.[9] This has the effect of cutting her off from the network and all lines of effective and valuable information. She is now 'information poor' and very vulnerable. Lacking in social skill, she is thought to be 'morally loose', with only viable route left to her – using her body and sexual talents. She is branded a 'ho' by the boys and a 'slut' by the girls. This compounds her exclusion and vastly reduces her street capital to the point where she operates in a kind of internal exile – shunned by both genders, a 'card of no value in the game'. Such double exclusion seals her fate. She will be used and abused by both genders. Young men will view her as a group girl/ho. She may drift into prostitution and drug use. Her body will becomes a tradable commodity, available on demand.

Gendered narratives

The influence of social skill in the social field of the gang cannot be underestimated. It confirms girls' field position and determines their roles and strategic actions. Its most visible impact is in conferring what Schalet and colleagues (2003) call the 'discourse of sexual respectability'. Anderson (1999) refers to something similar in his discussion of 'decency'. This discourse seeks to differentiate between 'good girls' and 'bad girls'. However when this is reframed in the context of the social field we see the utility of the social skills spectrum as a device to illustrate the perspectives articulated in the SW9 study.

The social skills spectrum (Figure 12.1) shows that girls and young women with limited social skills are denied access to information and trust, which inhibits their network connectivity. This pushes them further to the opposite end of the spectrum, where fewer strategic action opportunities present themselves and they are refused opportunities to build street capital through information trading. In this way, the spectrum operates as a vertical hierarchy (or slippery slope), with 'good girls' (those with high levels of social skill) at the top, and 'hos' ('sluts', with no or very limited social skills) at the bottom.

In this SW9 study the female narrative on girls and their relationship to the gang differed noticeably from that provided by males. Female respondents identified three distinct types of girls each of whom had varying degrees of affiliation with the gang and who each performed different roles:

- Tomboys – who sought to emulate the boys and fight;
- spectators and facilitators – who hung back and watched from the sidelines but who occasionally made things happen;
- elder's girlfriends – who were exclusive to elders, unapproachable and often lived 'off the hood', in another part of town.

In general female respondents referred to girls and their relationship with the gang as being either 'good girls' or 'skets' (sluts).

Let us now examine these narratives within the framework of the social skills spectrum.

At one end (the top) are good girls, who are socially skilled and well connected. Respondents described them as attending 'good' schools, living in respectable areas and generally not seen on the estate, or if they are seen, they pass unnoticed. They are not 'street girls' or 'on road'. Their parents may have no idea that they are involved with a gang or even know the gang. Such girls are considered safe, i.e. trustworthy, and have no criminal record. As one white female professional put it, "They can walk in and out without anyone realising. Those are the ones watch."

At the lower end of the spectrum, only two key strategies are available: violence (largely fighting or robbery) or pursuing sexual strategies. Some females strategise that a sexual relationships with a dominant male will raise their profile. Some strategise to become pregnant to maintain that access and maximise street capital.[10] They seldom realise that if they initiate the sexual strategy, it will fundamentally alter how they are perceived by the gang.

Other sexual strategies include developing a hyper-sexualised physicality. By evidencing a hyper-sexualised form (as visualised through manicured hair and nails, clothing, dancing and feminised physique) girls and young women seek to maximise their street capital in the same way as a young man who amplifies his muscular physique. By enhancing their physical attributes, females attempt to raise their profile for selection and prove that they are 'playas'. Some use physical enhancements to show that they are good girls, looked after and cared for, and that they possess a high degree of social skill. Good girls wear real designer labels while bad girls will wear fakes. Here abstract notions of social skill are externalised to advertise field position and rank, and are recognisable by all.

All participants in the SW9 research were quick to identify that those girls who used violence as a strategic action were more visible and hung out with the boys more regularly. They were said to be 'street girls'.

Some girls with considerable individual agency who hang out with the gang believe they can count on the support of male members, but this is not always the case. If they live 'decently' (Anderson, 1999), they are unlikely to get involved in anything requiring gang support. This strategy therefore indicates a lack of understanding and a consequent lack of social skill.

Strategies used to earn respect may therefore differ, depending on levels of independent agency. Girls are under more pressure than boys to act out gender-determined roles, such as being 'respectable'. They are also highly aware that they are at risk of losing street capital if their reputations are undermined.

Misreading your hand

To use the metaphor of the casino and the game, it is possible to misread your hand in the social field of the gang. In this world if situations or values are mis-read or misunderstood and your decisions or actions are ill-informed then essentially your bets are lost. Such wrong moves can cost you dearly in the game.

Men claim that most girls affiliating with the gang know the outcomes they seek and follow their own individual agency or strategy. They also accept that roles for girls within the gang are limited. For many girls, it is the point and method of entry into the gang that seals their social fate. It was an often heard comment in the SW9 study that all boys understand that if you are an 'exclusive partner', it is recognised that you would not go into a gang by 'using sex' as strategic action.

A girl regularly having sex with gang members is considered 'available'. She may believe that she is employing agency and strategising using free choice but men believe she has mis-read the group dynamics and social norms, perceiving her to be freely available as most boys already have their own girlfriend or 'personal girl'. Personal girls are not assaulted. These other girls are thus assumed to be 'group girls'.

Perception of the girl's role is effectively gendered with two different perspectives now playing out:- She believes any sexual encounter is strictly between her and her 'boyfriend'. Conversely he perceives her as a 'group girl', not his personal girlfriend, so he believes he is justified in having sex with her and then inviting his friends to do so. Male gang members felt girls needed to have a better understanding of this particular scenario believing that girls often mis-read the group dynamics and access the gang for the wrong reasons: i.e. that girls mistakenly believe they will gain status, respect and profile through sexual encounters. Such poor choices confirm her lack of social skill and limited street capital. The boys believe she lacks individual agency which makes her appear weak, emotionally vulnerable or romantically deluded. Some male gang members suggest such girls have 'domestic issues' or low esteem and *'don't wish to attach to anyone'*. These perceived qualities place her at risk of increased and repeat victimisation. Her strategy of trying to link into a gang male to associate with his power and authority is not validated by the boys.

How she is now treated depends upon how she fits in within her female peer group. If she has few female friends and no active social group then it is likely she will try to affiliate to a group of boys. This way she will try to acquire street capital through association with them. Having gained regular access to the gang, she will then try to access the higher tiers. This strategy is doomed to fail.

The boys assume the girl is approaching the gang in this way because no Leader will seek her out for her charms. Through such assessments she is identified as 'street' and not 'decent' (Anderson 1999). Boys have concluded that 'decent' girls would not act this way, thus confirming her subordinate status as a potential 'group girl' (a 'Ho' or a 'Jezzy') and ensuring she is 'passed around'. During this time she is increasingly mistrusted and isolated as boys keep information from her to mitigate their own risks. Initially she may not be fully aware she is being passed around until later, nor may she be aware of how she is viewed and labelled. This process is well understood by the boys. Girls with low self esteem or limited social skills or experience are particularly vulnerable to being played in this way. In such circumstances sexual violence is a possible or likely outcome. Now an 'internal outcast' she will be victimised and liable to group rape.

Another scenario recounted by male gang members in the SW9 research was of girls seeking access to the top tier by offering a leader sexual favours. This may or may not lead to a relationship. The most likely outcome is that he will tire of her, or she will fall pregnant. Either way she is dropped and relegated down the ranks as he moves on to another girl. Her reputation declines and she is now viewed as a 'group girl'. She tries to reclaim her status and connections by sleeping with the second-ranking male, but this strategy is also doomed to failure. As she moves down the ranks, she may become aware that she is 'falling'. But such is her strong affiliation with this group, she would probably prefer to put up with it than to withdraw. There may still be some advantage to her to put up with the situation. Overall, her reputation is likely to suffer, and she risks being shunned by other girls and labelled a 'slut'.

There may be an alternative outcome, depending upon the girl's behaviour and how she carries herself within the gang. If she has become a 'bad girl', using violence to increase her street capital, her reputation need not suffer, although even if she does succeed in reaching the alpha male, there is no guarantee of his protection, and she could still fall down the ranks at any time. Girls with strong local connections will not necessarily have to 'use' sex to approach a gang, but those just starting out 'on road' with little understanding of the group dynamic are vulnerable to mistakes, e.g. getting attached to a group for the wrong reasons or to one other person without realising they view her as a group girl.

Chapter Thirteen discusses how reputation management in the gang is used to determine the fate of members of both genders, alongside other penalties and rewards in the sanctions repertoire. This critical repertoire is represented as a wheel of fortune, where actors keep spinning but not necessarily winning.

Notes

[1] For an in-depth account of the role of girls in gangs, see Batchelor (2009).

[2] 'How lovestruck boy was lured to his death', Chris Summers, BBC News, 4 September 2009.

[3] Fligstein and McAdam (2012) posit that if two fields share direct social relations, they are related to one another through routine interaction.

[4] For a detailed account of gender-based violence in gangs, see Firmin (2009, 2010, 2011).

[5] For a detailed account into sexual violence, see Beckett et al (2012, 2013).

[6] Beckett et al (2013, p 43) found that only 1 in 12 of their 264 interview respondents thought that young people would wish to report or even discuss sexual violence. Reasons for not doing so included judgement by others, fear of retaliation and a lack of faith in the ability of services to protect them.

[7] Launching a report by the Centre for Social Justice on the sexual violence towards girls and young women (Centre for Social Justice, 2014) Deputy policy Director, Edward Boyd noted that their research had 'a parallel world where rape is used as a weapon' and where gang involved young women lead 'desperate lives' which takes a toll on the girls education, families, friends and communities (BBC news 23/04/2014, www.bbc.co.uk/news/uk-26698890).

[8] A recent qualitative study of gang-associated sexual violence towards young people by University of Bedfordshire identified high levels of sexual violence and exploitation within the gang environment. Motivations for sexual violence included peer pressure; demonstration of status or power; inter-gang conflict; an attempt to gain status or respect. In addition many of the behaviours were not understood to be sexual violence or conceptualised as such (Beckett et al 2013, p 29).

[9] Miller, J. (1991) argues that women in gangs find ways to manage the tensions between their feminine gender role and their assumed gang role, (requiring toughness) by taking on male attributes of aggression or violence or by denigrating other women.

[10] Thomson, (2000, p 425) argues that young women gain respect and authority from motherhood, although such respect is short-lived in the social field of the gang.

THIRTEEN

The wheel of fortune: the sanctions repertoire

In any social field, it is firmly in the interests of leaders (incumbents) to maintain social order and thus retain their privileged field position. In addition, a set of internal rules must apply to the social field that govern strategic action and are understood by all. These rules are enforced via the sanctions repertoire, which permits street capital to be instantly adjusted, inflated or deflated. The sanctions repertoire is a set of recognisable strategic actions, tried, tested and governed by the habitus. It acts as the key mechanism by which those in the social field of the gang reinforce social norms and maintain social order.

Incumbents use the sanctions repertoire both formally and informally to manage street capital and thereby maintain social norms and social order (Luzetti, cited in Halpern, 2005). While some sanctions are indirect and subtle, the gang social field provides latitude for sanctions to be both overt and severe: more so than in other social fields where reputation and street capital are less important. Sanctions also operate as a mechanism for making numerous minor adjustments to interpersonal relationships. In this way, sanctions are used by incumbents to maintain their field position and control challengers through expressing and reasserting power dynamics and rank.

Sanctions are however used by all members of the social field as strategic actions and mechanisms to achieve slight advantage as they jostle for a new and improved field position. In this way a quick verbal putdown or punch provides a strategic action of advancement. Conversely, and just as importantly, sanctions may be used to block or curtail the strategic action of others.

In the social field of the gang it is incumbents who are most skilled and adept at using the sanctions repertoire. Skilfully employed sanctions can be used to regulate street capital of challengers, e.g. by allocating a severe beating for getting it wrong; or oriented to build trust and respect, e.g. praise for jobs well done from an elder to a younger. In such ways, employing a component of the sanctions repertoire will affect either a rise or a fall in a person's stock of street capital. Thus it becomes the accepted field rules for maintaining social order within the social field.

As discussed in Chapter Three, the 'settlement' of the social field includes a shared understanding of the rules governing the social field (Fligstein and McAdam, 2012, p 88), including which tactics are legitimate and permissible in the field. Different interpretive frames operate within this field, however (Goffman, 1974; Fligstein and McAdam, 2012), which means that it is possible for a sanction to be interpreted differently depending on the field position.

Affirmative sanctions

In the gang social field, gifts, rewards and praise represent positive or affirmative strategies to bind the recipient to the giver (Halpern, 2005). Promotion is another form of positive affirmative sanction. Again this can be viewed differently by each member, depending on their field position, i.e. it will be a positive affirmation of one member while quite possibly a rebuke to another who is not promoted.

Favours and gifts

Favours and gifts are used within the social field to build trust and demonstrate reciprocity (Putnam, 2000, pp 20-1, 134-48). They help members to bond with other, or they help generate links to those outside the social field, such as family or the wider network. They are a means of reward, and may be granted in public or in private. Public anointing, i.e. a public show of reward and favour will help maximise street capital. Gang members seeking street capital must build trust and develop mutual obligations.

> 'I would suggest that what happens is they'll buy food for you ... it's almost like a Robin Hood thing, so that if you are really stuck, they will buy you food, they'll look after the family a little bit. They'll look after the little ones, there is a sense of community in looking after each other, but then you have to pay back, don't you – you keep your mouth shut.' (Professional)

Favours may be specific (one deed undertaken in exchange for another) or generalised (no immediate return favour identified, but an expectation of future reciprocity – a favour 'called in') (Putnam, 2000, pp 20-1). In this social field, the former is more common. Bourdieu (1977) observes that the giving of gifts within the social field is ultimately done for strategic benefit and investment.

Negative sanctions

The range of negative sanctions is wider than that for affirmative sanctions, which, in the social field of the gang, appears to be rather limited. Negative sanctions range from spreading rumours, though bullying and intimidation, to abduction, rape and murder.

Before addressing these physically explicit sanctions in more detail I want quickly to consider two non-explicit psychological sanctions. These are sanctions which are used negatively to deliberately control other members but may not include any physical action, nonetheless they operate as a useful controlling mechanism. The two controlling sanctions are Fear of Sanctions (retribution) and the use of religion or faith belief.

Psychological sanctions – fear of retribution

The fear of any impending sanction, particularly of physical retribution, can be a powerful psychological tool in the social field of the gang. As such it is used knowingly by those seeking to employ the sanction (usually incumbent olders and elders) not only to generate fear in the target of the sanction, but as a wider mechanism to influence and control the behaviour of others, (usually youngers). Sanctions may be widely advertised in advance by olders and elders. This brings additional pressure on the target, (especially if a bounty is offered for him) but it also utilises the wider gang members effectively as repeat transmitters of the coming event. Here proxy marketing will go into overdrive as members will vouch for the ability and determination of the coming assailant to effectively carry out the proposed sanction.

Fear of sanction depends on context, making it difficult to generalise about such situations, but suffice to say that it mainly affects youngers, new arrivals and solitary entrants with no older siblings or family in the gang, who have few network connections and a poor understanding of the game. Such members are network poor and are yet to understand the rules of the game.

Notwithstanding this, many gang members display, or at least claim to have, a fear of sanctions to some extent, although the SW9 research indicates that it is less of an issue than it once was. It is more likely, however, that fears are not openly expressed, lest street capital be compromised and humiliation invited – the much-vaunted 'badman' image is incompatible with displaying fear. In this social field, street sanctions are swift, sudden and very violent, and as a member you must 'dish it out and take it'.

The reputational pressures within the social field dictate that it is important not to show fear. Some members have a low recognition of potential or future consequences and cannot foresee future consequences Thus in an altercation they may challenge an opponent to bring their back-up. *'Bring your bruva, I ain't feared.'* Such a challenge may later be regretted.

Fear of sanction is strongly linked with bullying and expectations of violence, with new affiliates being at particular risk of victimisation by peers and olders unless they demonstrate strategies from the expressive repertoire, such as fighting, stealing and committing criminal damage. Failure to undertake such actions may result in summary sanctions involving physical violence and casual punishment, which, if carried out in public view, further diminish the victim's street capital. This demonstrates that:

- olders largely employ or control sanctions;
- sanctions reinforce both social norms and social order in the field;
- anyone with a diminished reputation can regain their street capital through swiftly imposed sanctions on others;
- public admonishment increases victims' humiliation and diminishes their street capital (albeit they will later develop strategies to regain it).

Clearly some young people choose not to join a gang. Some young people fear the sanction of their current social field (community, family and police) more than the sanction of the gang, and choose not to affiliate. Other potential members may fear the sanction of exclusion and rejection if they fail to join. Fear of gang sanctions may put pressure on young people to get involved in illegal activities against their will. In one recent such example, during a police investigation of gang members, a hitherto unknown associate of the gang begged to be arrested, only later to confess that he had been coerced into committing robberies and had been reluctant to get involved.

Other members hide their fear of sanctions by strategising to use others as their proxy, e.g. using youngers to deliver drugs to an area where he himself expects to be attacked. If youngers refuse to do so, they themselves will be subject to a sanction of violence from the older. Thus the fear of sanction is transmitted to others while being reduced for the older in a process of downward risk transference.

A gang member may well expect retribution but not necessarily fear it, especially in planned altercations with rival gangs, where precautions can be taken to mitigate risk by calling on the back-up of other members ('grouping up') and carrying weapons.

In the SW9 research, olders and elders reported a recent change in gang members' perception of field values, with many claiming to be unaffected by the fear of retribution. As one older put it, *"They just have no fear, they carry no fear."* For youngers the fear element is now just considered part of the game, a natural feature of their way of life. Such views contribute to a general bleak outlook on life for youngers. A younger may have returned a stolen chain at the behest of an elder ten years ago, but not nowadays. The basic rules of the social field may be the same, but the way in which young people interpret them has changed. The new frequency of life and death scenarios now facing young people have altered perceptions and parameters. There is no guarantee of a younger carrying out the wishes of an elder, so while the threat of retribution exists, both the severity of the sanction and the fear of it have diminished.

> 'It's not like that anymore. It doesn't work like that no more. You've got to have that rep, know what I mean. You've gotta have a rep. So people would say, "Oh, he used to be the hardest man in town and he still runs things neatly, give it back to him." That's the only fear of retribution, otherwise they will have no fear.' (African Caribbean professional, ex-elder)

Psychological sanctions: use of religion or faith belief

A further psychological feature of the sanctions repertoire is the use of faith, belief or religion to control, sanction or influence behaviour. Associating faith with an inducement to act in a certain way is a powerful incentive for any believer. Using religion or faith can be done subtly or overtly.

Religion and faith belief can be used as affirmative enticements for gang recruitment. For example, a gang may present itself as an Islamic group in order to entice Muslims to join it. Religion and faith belief may however also be used by the gang as a way of controlling or coercing members. In the period 2001 to 2005, Lambeth police also reported cases of olders instructing gang members to attend and make monetary contributions to mosques, with reports of members being coerced into joining the gang and styling themselves as Muslims under threat of physical retribution.

Media stories appeared about 'the Muslim Boys', a term Pritchard (2008) claims to have been coined by the police, and the gang (allegedly an offshoot of the PDC) achieved national notoriety.

Pritchard concedes that during this time 'the vast majority of PDC had adopted Islam as their religion' (2008, p 232).

The original Muslim Boy members are now known to be operating within gangs under different names. From 2003 to 2009, there was a spate of young black African Caribbean men in Lambeth converting to Islam, and the original Muslim Boy members are now known to be operating within gangs under different names. Local anecdote suggests that this trend for conversion started in Brixton prison. It is thought that gang members' conversions to Islam peaked around 2006/7, although the practice is now less common and some young people report such conversions are now openly mocked.

There is no evidence to suggest that religious views are in any way a cause of gang violence. The majority of gang members are from Christian families and it is not uncommon for them to attend church on Sunday with their families. A small minority are fundamentalist evangelicals.

Youth workers in SW9 report some young people showing an interest in voodoo (or West African 'vodun'), which has an established presence in several African churches in south London. However, young people are very secretive about it and there is no research around this subject. Some young people talk of gang members being connected to priests who have the power to 'collect souls'. Myths abound among impressionable young people. Some have been heard to refer to Santeria (a belief system that merges the Yoruba religion with Roman Catholicism and native beliefs, and is popular in Cuba). Knowledge of voodoo may be used to enhance a young person's reputation. One African Caribbean youngster in SW9 has enhanced his reputation for being 'crazy' or 'loco' through his knowledge of black magic. He is also known to be extremely violent. In another case, a young person stabbed nine times attributed his fast recovery to witchcraft.

Rumour

A common sanction within the sanctions repertoire is rumour or gossip. In most social fields, this acts as a mild sanction, questioning competence, sincerity, veracity, loyalty, commitment or ability. In the gang, it is a calculated strategic action aimed at raising an individual's street capital and diminishing that of a rival.

> 'Rumours and gossip are central to the way things work now. They play out on mobile phones, and social

networking sites. A large percentage of communication at street level concerns rumour and gossip.' (West African male professional)

Rumours circulate in the social field of the gang much as they do in a Premier league football team – who is in, who is out, who has problems with the coach or their fitness, who is off their game, who has been dropped and who is transferring. One could equally apply the analogy of the stock market, where rumours, even unfounded ones, can damage a business's reputation.

In the gang social field, hourly information updates have great significance and centrality in the lives of young people. There is an imperative to obtain information and get involved – if only by forwarding the news on to others. This shows you are a network 'playa'. Moreover, young people use this information to gauge their own safety and that of family and friends; to ascertain whether gang activity is likely to affect them; and to assess risks and plan future group, gang or individual strategies. It is important to be in the loop and not left out. Young people may send or receive 300 texts or more a day. It is possible to find out what someone has said about you 30 seconds after they have said it. Many struggle with such information overload:

'So many things have been put into your head you can't remember it all. So your head is running marathons.' (West African female older)

As strategic functions, rumour and gossip are easy to employ. Information can be transmitted instantly from multiple sources, and actors often have a vested interest in embellishing the news to make it sound more exciting. As one member in the SW9 research put it, "You are not going to tell anyone a rubbish story – you want it to be exciting." Some actors use rumour and gossip as a means of building street capital. Table 13.1 shows various ways in which this can be done.

Information trails may also be potentially dangerous. In one incident in 2010, a Brixton younger had his phone stolen. The phone retained a conversation between the Brixton younger and a Peckham younger in which the Brixton younger agreed to set up one of his own gang members. The details of this conversation circulated the network 'like wildfire', with potentially dangerous consequences for the Brixton younger, although he was protected by his reputation for being crazy.

While rumour/gossip are pernicious in all communities, in the social field of the gang it is particularly dangerous. This fact is amplified

Table 13.1: Variables used in strategies involving rumour and gossip

Variable	Impact	Example
Hype and exaggeration	Those involved enjoy the hype and the knowledge that someone is talking about them. It validates them as players.	"Something can be very minor, like something really stupid. But it gathers momentum and gets exaggerated – 'Someone got stabbed', etc – but really it was just a scratch." (Professional)
Reach	In networks with a high degree of 'closure', everybody knows everybody. Mention any name in the community or beyond and there is invariably someone linked to them via the network. This can be claustrophobic and difficult to escape from.	The social field extends into prison, so that even gang members or network connections in custody are kept informed about events outside, and can influence strategy.
Distortion, inflation and extension	Rumours and gossip may be deliberately distorted; elements of the narrative may be deliberately inflated and the rumour may be kept going and extended. All of this can contribute to tensions between gangs. Once information is associated with rumour and gossip, truth becomes elusive. In fact, accurate or truthful accounts may then be discounted as fake. There are only a few actors with sufficient seniority to challenge such accounts. Some members may elect to report stories to the authorities even though they are aware it is a rumour or simply malicious gossip.	Information is often passed on second, third and fourth hand, getting more distorted, glamorised and exaggerated with each retelling. The possibility of conflict is exaggerated, so that members arm themselves in the belief that any resultant clashes will involve weapons. Street names, not real names, are used, e.g. *'Sneaky stabbed someone or Deaky has been stabbed or Man F has got a weapon.'*
Speed and immediacy	Information is transmitted among members in seconds, circulating within the whole network in hours. There is little room for reflection, so the content is highly charged. Recipients feel 'closer' to incidents unfolding now than to past incidents. Immediacy is of key importance; past incidents become less relevant, while current events demand an instant response, which is often ill considered, emotional and a trigger for violence.	Ubiquitous mobile phones and blackberries ensure a ready market for transmitting and receiving information. Broadcasting ability is a high status factor of street capital. Second rate telephony is ridiculed and mocked, compelling individuals to upgrade handsets, service providers and rates. Social networking sites are now also available on mobile phones allowing constant access and the ability to upload images from anywhere at any time.

(continued)

Table 13.1 (continued)

Variable	Impact	Example
Involvement	Elders need to know what information is circulating. The route by which information is fed to them helps determine its veracity and importance.	Members using rumour and gossip as a strategy may actively seek the involvement of higher ranking members or they may wish to keep information from them as long as possible. Some gangs may operate a clear rule that all information is passed upline. However if the rumour or gossip is about the older, members may bypass them and go to the elder if they can – possibly using the wider network to do this for them. Here the speed of this action may wrong-foot the older who can be challenged by elder and looks foolish if he is unaware of the rumour. Certain wider network contacts will be highly influential as opinion formers in any communications – if they can be successfully reached.

by the advent of social networking sites where recorded images and conversations are played again in perpetuity. Visual images are deemed authentic by viewers but they are seldom contextualised, further adding to rumour. Visual content can become highly prized as both credible and verifiable. This content is spread across the network immediately, increasing emotional proximity to the event and for many, establishing its 'realness' (see Table 13.1).

These types of communication are not presented as rumour or gossip, but are deemed to be truthful accounts. This makes them all the more important and believable, particularly in the context of the social field of the gang, where members are aware of the power of this form of sanction. The veracity and credibility of the communicators is assessed continually by others and if they are deemed trustworthy then the posting is deemed credible. Young people use the transmitted information to assess risk, especially where there is a perceived threat. Young people may use their social skills to develop strategies that best determine how and when to use this sanction.

The use of rumour and gossip achieves several objectives. In the gang social field, habitus allows actors to employ actions/behaviours they believe will distinguish them from their peers and bring advancement. Actors use rumour and gossip to influence views/opinions about others and thus diminish their rivals' street capital. The use of rumour is therefore more of a negative than a positive sanction, particularly as others can be influenced or manipulated to support the outcome which is advantageous to the person setting the rumour.

Field position is important as rumour and gossip circulate the social field. Highly ranked members are particularly influential, and any information they transmit or receive acquires additional credibility. Their transmissions are also considered to be more truthful than communications from youngers. Thus as a story unfolds members rush to influence these higher ranked members as they are in a position to:

- Confirm one specific version as 'the truth'
- Support or add credence to a particular version
- Arbitrate over conflicting versions
- Request further corroboration from other sources
- Invite the target of the rumour to give an account of himself

Importantly they are in a position to decide upon any outcome. Information guarantees action, whether the strategy for action is to do nothing or to initiate a confrontation:

> 'Yes, [rumour/gossip] it's very influential. It can do a lot for you or a lot against you. And you need it. You need it. Actually, the more the better, 'cos the more rumours about you, the more gossip, it's easier for your name to spread. So less chance that you're gonna get fronted up. But also, you have [to] watch what it is. So, for example, if it's a negative rumour, someone said they robbed you, then you gotta have a quick reaction on that as soon as you can.' (African Caribbean male younger)

At its most powerful – for example, branding a member as an informer – rumour may even result in a fatality. One elder in the SW9 research noted that 20 years ago any member accused of being an informer might have produced a copy of a police statement to prove his innocence, but that such proof would carry little weight nowadays as the informer could easily fake such a document.

Circulating false rumours may infact be a deliberate strategy to establish a premise that then allows the instigator to challenge to a rival, i.e. instigate or provoke a fight. This device is also used on SNSs towards other gangs.

Gossip and rumour may act as verbal advertising, an affirmative sanction for marketing and publicising members or their gang. Individuals may start rumours in order to build their own reputation, or enhance their brand name or street capital. As one professional in SW9 noted:

> 'I keep thinking of the analogy of a football team and football, you get your rumours, your gossips all the time that will your enhance your teams reputation, who's in, who's out, problems with the coach, who is not on his game, etc.' (White male police officer)

Others use rumour to enhance their reputation for violence. As one research participant noted:

> 'There's so many fake people out there. He'll tell his badman version of events. It'll make you be approved.' (African Caribbean male older)

Gangs may also strategise to use rumour and gossip as a group activity to denigrate rivals online as part of a propaganda war with rivals where they will actively attempt to character assassinate rival individuals or gangs. This gives gangs a sense of control over their rivals' future movements.

One recent incident in SW9, arising from an online post about a male gang member being stabbed and killed, generated a violent clash between two rival gangs, while the named individual was in fact unharmed and at home. A similar incident in Birmingham a few years ago triggered riots in Handsworth. If tensions exist, gossip or rumour may exacerbate the situation leading to rapid retaliation. As one gang member in SW9 said:

> 'Negative rumours where someone said that you were robbed will have to be dealt with promptly. This is to address those above or below me who are looking for weakness.' (African Caribbean male younger)

Rapid, uncontrolled transmission of information via mobile phone and social networking sites may lead to 'viral contagion', causing minor arguments to escalate into huge events. In one incident in

2001, news of a rumoured fight between two individuals on Streatham Common was widely transmitted, leading to more than 300 young people turning up to spectate. Girls, as information traders, are often central to these 'texting storms'.

All young people in the social field actively transmit information; they are all linked in to the network and act as information producers, consumers and amplifiers. Girls and young women often utilise their social skill to play a central role in transmitting information of all kinds, including rumour and gossip (see Chapter Twelve). Describing how girls react to rumour and gossip, one female younger in the SW9 research noted, "I think they see it as everyday life now." Young children (and girls) with limited options to build street capital may be pulled unwittingly into acting as information traders, as they are less familiar with the boundaries of the social field.

Exclusion

Given the centrality and importance of information in the gang social field, any decoupling or exclusion from the network or internal exile may be a dangerous sanction. Such sanctions are often short-lived and many gang members taking part in the SW9 study feared being excluded or set adrift from the gang. They all acknowledged that this would seriously increase their risk of victimisation and loss of street capital, at which point they become easy targets for multiple rumours as to why they are now disconnected from the network. Disconnection from the network increases a member's chances of missing rumours, making them susceptible to random attack. Their trustworthiness is also compromised and they may never regain the trust of the gang.

Bullying and Intimidation

Social order is maintained by bullying and intimidation. These strategies are employed often and at all tiers and are frequently used to supplement the sanctions repertoires. They may be used as a strategy to advance/diminish street capital, often employed by the protagonist to demonstrate superior status/rank in the social field. Often based on structural field ranking (with olders bullying youngers), this strategic action serves several functions:

- it is used as a short-term strategy to recoup diminished street capital and recover 'lost face';
- it builds reputation;

- it may be used as a gang strategy to enhance the gang brand, for example by intimidating local residents;
- it may be directed at individuals in proximate fields, such as local shopkeepers;
- it may be used as a long-term strategy, played out over several months or even years;
- it may be used to exert control and pressure over subordinates and bring individuals into line.

Under the sanctions repertoire, bullying and intimidation become a strategy of rebuke and punishment. This is often where the protagonist perceives an infringement of social norms that diminishes reputations, expectations or trust. It may be in the form of a mild, almost imperceptible slight, or a series of wayward misdemeanours that anticipate a loss of personal or gang street capital. To maintain social order, such actions must be checked and reversed by employing a sanction.

Actors in the gang social field are constantly adjusting their own field position, jockeying for advantage. This leads to constant low-level contention and fluctuations in street capital. Bullying, intimidation and casual violence are employed continually in this field dynamic, to the extent that it becomes normalised.

In the sanctions repertoire, bullying and intimidation are at the milder, more lenient end of the spectrum. If such intimidation is used over an extended period, it becomes harassment, stripping the victim of any remaining street capital and creating a dangerous downward trajectory ('sliding'), leading to random victimisation from others.

This strategy is used so frequently because it is uniquely effective in the gang social field. It works, and all members of the social field know it works. It may be spontaneous or planned; conjoined to other components or a portent of worse to come. It is a reminder, a cue, a signal and a signifier. It is determined by the habitus and bounded by the code of the street, tapping into the key social norms of the social field, such as threats, physical violence, silence, street justice, challenge and retort. It allows for cruel and inventive testing of repertoire variables to the extent whereby the subjugation of the victim becomes the ultimate objective long after the initial punishment is served or the lost street capital regained. The variables employed here alter over time and account for voguish behaviours; for example, stabbing a rival in the leg was a favoured means of assault until the death of Damilola Taylor.

On 27 November 2000, ten-year-old West African, Damilola Taylor from Southwark, London, was found dying in stairwell of a large social housing project having been earlier confronted by gang –affiliated boys in Peckham. After several arrests and a lengthy trial several young men were cleared of his murder. Four years after this first trial, two young gang-affiliated brothers, were convicted of his manslaughter after stabbing him in the thigh with a broken beer bottle and hitting a major artery from which he bled to death.

Stabbing in the buttocks is now more common. Olders may employ this sanction by proxy through youngers, for example, getting boys on bikes to ride constantly past the home of a potential new recruit while mocking him. Home Invasion (i.e. rushing doors and steaming inside to cause terror in a household is another favoured tactic. Sometimes the intimidation ends with the presentation of a request, 'favour', gift or inducement that cannot be refused. This strategy is effective as it is not spatially bound or time-specific. It may also be undertaken virtually or beyond the boundaries of the social field.

What makes this strategy both effective and frightening is not just the inventiveness of the perpetrators, it is also the knowledge that within the social field home invasion or violence to family members can occur with impunity – a reality that is widely acknowledged.

The strategy is also used to intimidate those who witness or report crimes, or appear in court to testify against gang members. It is easy to identify witnesses or informants, especially during court testimonies. In one incident, an Old Bailey trial in March 2011 collapsed when key witnesses failed to attend having been warned off by gang members. This 'cracked trial' shows how much influence the gang has in the social field. It also shows how some members are so deeply embedded in the social field they fear the consequences of sanctions, retaliation and exclusion from the network far more than the court authorities. Bullock and Tilley (2008) identified similar findings.

All players in the social field recognise that bullying and intimidation is frequently a precursor to the predominant sanction of physical violence.

Set-ups/honey traps

Another example of a strategic negative sanction is the targeted set-up or honey trap. As one African Caribbean male younger in the SW9 research said (echoing the views of many others), "Revenge is sweet, it's better than sex or money for some people." The planning of such a strategy, which usually involves targeting an individual for a robbery or revenge attack, takes considerable social skill. The set-up or honey trap usually exploits a girl's relationship with a male gang member, the target of the sanction. In a typical example, he is texted and invited to meet with her at a specified location. On arrival, or en route, he is ambushed by peers from his own gang or by rival gang members. The severity of incidents varies, from fighting to stabbing and even murder, as in the Croydon 'honey-trap case' in which 15-year-old Samantha Joseph lured her 17-year-old boyfriend to a quiet street where he was beaten and stabbed to death by five rivals. Such events may be motivated by a breakdown in relationships, shifting allegiances, revenge, forced pressure and bullying of girls, and by individuals or groups acting strategically to diminish someone's street capital.

Set-ups place all girls (not just those directly involved in incidents) in a potentially dangerous situation, both at the time and as a general rule over time. These activities are referred to regularly as a 'huge problem' by male gang members, and also by agency workers and professionals. In many of these scenarios it is worth noting that the social skills of the girls are used and manipulated by men for their own ends. Girls use their social skills to liaise between rivals in disputes, and once they align themselves with a particular party, they place themselves in great danger from both sides. There are also reports of girls setting each other up to become the victims of humiliation, sexual violence or rape. Such strategies enable the instigator to dominate her rival and diminish (or even permanently destroy) her street capital, while enhancing her own reputation. If this risky strategic action can be pulled off, it will elevate the planner/organiser to the position of key 'playa', adroit at the use of social skill.

Threats and violence to family

It is widely acknowledged by the SW9 study respondents that threats to family are only undertaken in very serious situations. However the knowledge that this strategic action might occur is a powerful controlling mechanism for maintaining social order. The fact it occurs at all in the social field represents a recent rule change. Respondents in the SW9 research also identified this as a change in the social norms of SW9 gangs and there was general consensus that this strategy was becoming more commonplace.

Several respondents reported that the level of respect traditionally shown towards mothers, fathers and grandmothers in the neighbourhood – the 'traditional old heads', according to Anderson (1999) – had declined significantly over the past five years. The targeting of families as a strategic action from the sanctions repertoire was once rarely employed, and then only by olders, but it is now increasingly used by youngers through frustration or to maximise their street capital. While such tactics are apparently not unknown in the garrison communities of Kingston, Jamaica, Aldridge and colleagues (2009) in their work in Manchester found that parents commonly reported 'stories of harassment, threats and actual violence'.

Nowadays if the situation is deemed serious enough, parents or siblings will be targeted. Gang members using this strategy send a powerful message to the subject of the sanction; their ability to access his family demonstrates their power, knowledge and intent. The family sees it as a message to take control and help sort out the situation, for example, by paying a debt.

Targeting family may also be seen as a means of challenging a rival, for example when a gang member is unable to locate a rival with whom he is in dispute. One respondent described how such a challenge might be perceived:

> 'Come and find me, bruv. I can't get you, so I got her. But I'll get you as well. I'll get you but I can't see you. But I saw your sister so I mashed her up.' (African Caribbean male younger)

In the absence of the key target, male family members of the same age – for example, brothers and cousins – are most at risk, followed by female family members of the same age. Mothers are the targets of the last resort and grandmothers are considered to be out of bounds. It is often beneficial for the key target to make himself available for retaliation to protect his family. Sanctions targeted towards the family may be relatively lenient, such as daubing the family home with graffiti, although a serious matter such as debt default will invoke more serious retribution.

Youngers being pressed to affiliate may receive threats of violence to his family. Young people believe such threats are real and gang history examples are cited for emphasis. Youngers know that gang members are aware their domestic arrangements and are capable of executing threats. In addition to this any failure to then respond favourably to gang overtures may result in further threats to family members.

Threats may also be passed to a mother if their son is in jail. At other times gang members will appear in front of the family home, threatening: '*When your son comes out we gonna fuck him up.*' This scenario was reported as commonplace by police.

The new rule changes in the social field which assumes family members as legitimate targets has also led to increased severity of the sanctions employed to now include assault or serious violence as in the recent fatal shooting of a young mother in front of her two-year-old daughter in north London. Elders in the SW9 research believed that such drastic action would only be sanctioned at the top level to protect a leader from a police informant. This change in social norms is mirrored by a widespread acknowledgement that those seeking revenge will stop at nothing to achieve their aim.

Home invasion

A recent escalation of strategic action is the home invasion. This involves a group of young men forcing their way into a home and ransacking it. Home invasion occurs in a variety of different forms depending on the individual involved at the premises and the strategic goal of the perpetrators. Some invasions can be researched and planned over time while others are more spontaneous. For example, at the expressive level they might be undertaken by younger boys to intimidate a gang member who is falling or to pressure a prospective member into joining – in this way the reach of the gang is demonstrated by them forcibly rushing up the stairs into the individual's bedroom to attack. Such events are extremely frightening and may occur when other members of the family are present.

At the instrumental level home invasion might involve a calculated strategy to take out and rob a local drug dealer by forcible entry into the house, ransacking it and locating the drugs stash – either the product or the cash. Such events are violent but also risky for all involved. Severe pressure can be put on the dealer to reveal his stash. It was suggested that they are easier to undertake than a cash in-transit robbery. Victims are also unlikely to report such incidents to the police. As explained by one respondent;

> 'A home invasion would be more of an aggressive nature,
> so targeting maybe a drug dealer or something like that. He
> would get roughed up in the process, of course. I've seen

some foul stuff, man, I've seen people being tied to radiators and stuff, and put on full blast. You know you can't really hold out for too much longer. And there are there other things I don't really want to go into as I don't want to be associated with that. There are horrible things that happen but that depends upon the nature of the individual. So if you are a hard person that doesn't really want to give up what you've got then it might take a little bit longer, but usually the people they are targeting are, like, soft people, 'cos you don't want to run into a place where people have an AK47 in the house.

'When you are doing the research you have to check it out. Some people do like to go to cook houses and stuff like that, but personally you don't really want to go a place that is unpredictable, you know – how many people are going to be in the house, what kind of weaponry have they got, you know, machine guns? So if you go steaming into some big drug dealer's house and there are ten people in the living room and they've got, like, macs [machine guns] in the living room and they, like, start firing shots at you, well ... Mostly it would be, like, drug dealers but of a softer nature.' (African Caribbean male independent operator)

Abduction

A further significant rule change is the acceptability of abduction as a component of the sanctions repertoire. Since 2009 it has become more common to abduct young people from their homes or estate. This represents a significant escalation in violence and is reminiscent of the techniques used by groups in war-torn countries or by more established gangsters. Threats of abduction are commonplace and taken seriously. This strategy has increased in its frequency and violence and is now well established in the social field. Interestingly, Sandberg and Pederson (2011, p 138) in their study of ethnic minority drug dealers identified that 'habitus formed in an actual war zone can be an advantage'.

As with other elements of the sanctions repertoire, abduction represents an opportunity to reclaim lost reputation and street capital. Usually employed as a group strategy, it requires careful planning, with members using violence or social skill to trap their victim.

It is usually undertaken to address more serious issues related to economic capital, e.g. theft of drug money. Young people are held in the boot of cars or at an address until the debt, usually money, is provided. Alternatively house keys may be demanded so a flat can be searched or ransacked.

If the case involves an outstanding debt, the gang may hold the victim until his family delivers the money or he can atone in some other way, by revealing the whereabouts of a drug stash, for example. Such incidents usually involve violence and are seldom reported. This sanction is attractive to those seeking to destroy the victim's street capital. Abductions may be filmed and the videos shown to other gang members or the victim's friends and family, or kept for future shaming.

Playing an ace: the use of firearms

The SW9 research revealed that firearms are actively sought and used by members in all tiers of the gang and also in each of the three repertoires: expressive, instrumental and sanctions. This has contributed significantly to increased violence in the social field. Firearms often appear in the videos shared between gang members on social networking sites, indicating that they are becoming more prolific and available. The way they are used depends on field position; youngers, for example, largely use them via the expressive repertoire to market their image and raise their street capital.

Hallsworth and Silverstone (2009, pp 366, 371) argue that 'Gun-use "on road" is much less instrumental and planned and far more erratic and situational.' However they further contradict themselves by suggesting that gun violence is instrumental and central to drug retailing, which includes 'a "business logic" to punish those stealing from you'. Neither position accurately describes how and why firearms are used in the gang. Bullock and Tilley (2002) found firearm use 'partly symbolic and partly instrumental'. Marshall and colleagues (2005, p 19) noted that 'gang members committed more crime than non-gang members, [and] are more likely to deal drugs, [and] carry weapons'.

While the use of firearms has traditionally been associated with olders protecting assets (drug stashes) and conducting business (drug deals and robberies), respondents in the SW9 research reported a dramatic increase in the use of weapons by youngers as a sanction in the sanctions repertoire.[1]

This dramatic change in local circumstances remains unexplained by Hallsworth and Silverstone (2009). Meanwhile, Hallsworth and

---

Duffy (2010, p 11) argue that while access to reactivated guns (i.e. a decommissioned gun that has been brought back into use) is possible 'it is unlikely that gang members will know how to use these nor have knowledge of their origin'. The SW9 research, however, contradicted this finding.

While guns are available to youngers, their use is regulated by olders and depends on the younger's trustworthiness. As guns are usually 'pooled' they are harder to trace, and may be used on several occasions. Obtaining a gun is not taken lightly. Members have to justify their reasons for wanting one. In the sanctions repertoire, the use of firearms is only deemed justifiable in serious cases of loss of street capital where members believe the issue is worth of what they refer to as 'personal attention'.

Gang members in the SW9 study advised that accessing a gun requires 'planning', 'effort' and 'contacts'. However this somewhat sober account of gun acquisition discounts the high emotions usually circulating within the gang. In one incident suggestive of such high emotions, recounted during the SW9 research, several olders from Stockwell Park, intent on revenge for assault on a gang member, loaded a car with MAC-10 pistols and cruised the estate to locate the assailants. Police tracked the car and give chase, whereby the guns were dumped. In other cases the gun might be used in a cold and calculating fashion.

Young people, including girls, may be intimidated, even at gunpoint, into hiding firearms for gang members, especially if they are unknown to the police ('clean skins'). Others store firearms to acquire trust, respect, money or security from the gang. Holding a weapon, however, confers ownership, and losing it incurs physical assault.

Gang members who suspect the police of intercepting their mobile phones use code words, often girls' names, for guns to avoid raising suspicion. 'Tenesha' may indicate a TEC-9, and 'Barbara' a Baretta, for example.

Ammunition is usually kept separately, as it is often more difficult to obtain than the guns themselves. In SW9, shotguns are currently the weapon of choice, as ammunition is relatively easy to buy from farm equipment suppliers. Olders make the purchases, often parting with several hundred pounds for a gun. Purchases may be funded by the whole gang, and guns may also be rented, for around £200. If a gun is used to shoot someone, the gang must ditch it or sell it on. If it used to threaten or steal but is not discharged, it must be returned to a member in the higher tier.

Any 'hit' sanctioned by an elder is assigned to a trusted member of the gang, who is often retained in this capacity. Most gangs have their regular 'hitters', who are not normally very visible in the neighbourhood, although they are not always the ones to carry out the hit.

The sanctions repertoire acts like a wheel of fortune, generating both opportunities and fear in the social field. The final chapter of this book concludes by identifying the cumulative impact on young people of life in the social field of the gang, arguing that the constant battle for survival engenders enormous stress. I underscore the utility of the social field/street capital theory by identifying its policy relevance. Finally, I return to the metaphor of the casino to answer the question of how and why violence in SW9 has increased.

Note

[1] Sanders (2005), who undertook his research in Lambeth, found that none of his sample of 31 young people had used a gun or knew anyone who had one. Curiously he also reported rising levels of violence following a Lambeth gun amnesty in 1997. The reasons for this are unexplained.

FOURTEEN

The street casino

'*The world is a gambling table so arranged that all who enter the casino must play and all must lose more or less heavily in the long run, though they win occasionally by the way.*'
Samuel Butler

This concluding chapter considers the value of social field analysis, my application of it to the street gang and my overarching theoretical proposition of street capital. In so doing, it explores further the utility of this framework and the policy implications of the findings. Finally, we return to the metaphor of the casino to answer the question of why violence has increased in SW9.

What is new here?

Throughout this book, I have shown how social field analysis, and its methodological application to gang research, provides not only a critical platform permitting in-depth analysis of gang dynamics and behaviours, but also a theorising perspective allowing identification of new changes in the gang's social field. This valuable methodology becomes a generative perspective offering the following advantages:

- the social field and its players can be viewed holistically;
- inter- and intra-gang relationships are exposed;
- general theories of behaviour may be generated;
- underlying structures may be identified, such as the binding concepts of *doxa* and *illusio*.

I propose that social field analysis is therefore a useful diagnostic for investigating the gang domain and its internal dynamics. It facilitates deeper exploration of many assumptions commonly misrecognised or even erroneously made about gangs, for example, that they have 'messy structures' (Aldridge et al, 2008); that they are disorganised, messy and rhyzomatic (Hallsworth and Silverstone, 2009); that they are an obsessive media invention, moral panic or myth (Hallsworth and Young, 2008; Hallsworth and Duffy, 2010); that they are not organised

(Hallsworth, 2013); that no recruitment takes place (Aldridge and Medina, 2008; Hallsworth, 2013); that gang activity is driven solely by drugs and minor disrespect (Toy, 2008); that there are 'gang set spaces' (Ralphs et al, 2009); that guns are mostly used within illegal drugs markets (Hallsworth and Silverstone, 2009); and that those involved are 'psychologically unpredictable' (Hallsworth and Silverstone, 2009). My findings are a powerful counterpoint to such views.

My approach further contests some contemporary beliefs that merely discussing gangs reinforces labelling theory (Aldridge et al, 2008: Ralphs et al, 2009) or defines the researcher as a 'control agent' of an 'emergent gang industry' (Hallsworth and Young, 2008; Hallsworth, 2011). In contrast, I argue that my perspective is firmly grounded in the reality and experience of the social field.

Notwithstanding the ethnographic methodology applied here, several clear narratives emerged from the extensive subsequent analysis of vast quantities of data from the social field, each of which illuminated key findings such as gender differentiation of roles, intra- and inter-gang relationships and the relational interface (or boundary) of the social field.

I further argue that field analysis permits structural mapping of the gang as a hierarchical arena of struggle over different types of capital, power and privilege, while simultaneously highlighting the opportunities and constraints that interface with the habitus.

Importantly social field theory provides the defining goal for all actors operating in the field – *distinction*. Having advanced to distinction, players in the social field can achieve what they have always wanted – a way out of the social field.

A central contribution to this book is that of relating Bourdieu's theoretical debates on capital accumulation to the reality of life 'on the Road', in the social field of the gang. Arising from my analysis of this social field is my identification of the economic mechanism by which actors can identify, measure and comprehend their advancement towards distinction. From here I develop the concept of street capital, which I then use as my overarching theoretical proposition.

Like other forms of capital, street capital may be acquired, traded and exchanged, although its currency functions exclusively within the boundaries of the social field. I contend that this concept is formative in understanding the internal dynamics of the social field, as street capital operates as the *premium* capital. Actors struggle to acquire street capital as an asset, working hard to acquire and maintain it. I have argued that this equates to Bourdieu's concept of the social field as a casino, except that here actors have to stay in 'the game' and keep playing.

I propose therefore that 'life on road', or in the social field of a violent street gang, operates as a form of street casino, where Bourdieusian principles of social field, distinction and habitus dictate strategic action and are geared towards the generation of street capital that, once accumulated and over time, may be cashed in. It is a world of winners and losers, where everyone in the field must play, where rules change and incumbents strive to maintain their privilege. It is a world where players are encouraged to continue playing even though the returns are meagre. It is a world where players believe they will be able to stop their risky behaviour while still engaging in it (the gambler's conceit), and where players believe they must continue to play because their bad luck must end some time (the gambler's fallacy). Mostly they play because it is the only game in town and for many, the only game they know.

Survival in the street casino

The street casino is a dangerous place for young people. It presents an internal world of risk that has a significant impact on all young people in the social field, regardless of gang affiliation; they may, for example, expose themselves to violence as a result of 'slippin'', be forced to restrict their movements around the neighbourhood, or unwittingly enter the social field (or its periphery) physically or through social networking sites. Any young person traversing gang-associated territory is automatically assumed to be connected to the gang's social field, an assumption made primarily by young people but also by the police. It is paradoxical that the risk factor paradigm so geared towards identifying the dangers of gang affiliation so manifestly fails to assess the full range of risks to which young people are exposed post-affiliation. The landscape of risk thus remains uncharted.

Survival in this landscape means making daily risk assessments and adjustments to minimise and mitigate potential victimisation (a heightened challenge for new arrivals), being hyper-vigilant and carrying weapons.

To survive, young people in the gang – even on its periphery – must stay in the moment, mentally embedded in the social field. Stepping out of this arena becomes too complex to consider; they are too involved, there is too much information to sift. They have no downtime, no breathing space and no-one to talk to or to confide in. They increasingly inhabit an exclusive world.

Survival means managing enormous daily stress; there is constant pressure not to be victimised; to know what is going on; to obtain information; to recognise shifting alliances; to know whether it is safe to leave the classroom or the estate; to set aside education in favour of getting through the next few days. While some claim to enjoy 'the game', others use the gang as a collective experience or shared perspective that supports them in managing their stress.

Adult apathy, lack of any early interventions, continuing estrangement from authority and total immersion in a social field that adults do not understand all act as centripetal forces, pushing young people towards the gang. As adolescents, they seek support to address their lack of status and social capital, their fears and humiliations, their desire for distinction and celebrity, and their lack of power. Mostly they want support to find a way out of poverty. If the gang provides this, it seems attractive.

Young people instinctively realise that their lives are predestined by their habitus and their social field. They realise that this may mean a life cut short. This inarguable fact leads some to fatalistic resignation, others to devote their existence to the short-lived 'game'. As Bourdieu reminds us, their social fate is all but assured by the 'role demands' and cumulative actions required by them as they operate within the social field of the gang.

Adults and parents largely fail to understand or recognise this social field; the media misrepresents it, and academics frequently mis-recognise it or ignore it, as it does not fit their chosen paradigm on gangs. The result for gang-affiliated young people is twofold:

- adhesion to the gang;
- fatalism.

Beyond theory to a practical legacy

In reviewing the key findings arising from this social field analysis, it is important not to do so in isolation, but to consider the policy relevance, policy implications and practical utility of the findings. Such a process inevitably throws up new questions and avenues for further research.

This study redefines the lens through which we view gangs, allowing us to move forward from the old binaries of whether or not gangs exist, and whether or not they are organised. As such, it permits us to advance beyond the evident constrictions of the risk factor paradigm and labelling and moral panic theorists. It also closes the chapter on those in denial of the existence of gangs and their impact on young people.

Social field analysis offers a useful interpretive framework and a new way of looking at gangs, allowing dramatic insight into an exclusive world. It permits us to understand that for many young people in certain areas of multiple deprivation, gang affiliation is part of their life trajectory; they become compelled to get involved as there is no plausible alternative. This book highlights the nuances of affiliation, leading to an improved understanding of the complex and dangerous world of the gang. It brings into focus the stresses and tensions of what it is like to be involved in the game, to know nothing else but the game and to accept completely and without challenge that the game is everything. This study clarifies how and why young people are increasingly entangled in this social field and how it is difficult, if not impossible, to desist from this life. We see how gang life affects not just those at the centre, but also those in its sphere of influence, with centripetal magnetism making it difficult to pull away.

Perhaps most importantly it lifts the veil on the glue that binds much of gang life together, the doxa or shared value of the game, and the illusio – the belief or acceptance that the game is worth playing. These principles dictate the logic of the social field, but this approach generates further intriguing research questions. Does the logic have equal effect on all players? If such logic can be identified, can it be challenged, adapted or overcome? Does it offer opportunities for agency intervention?

Altering and improving the social conditions of those in deprived neighbourhoods by investment in education, communities and social infrastructure, and by providing opportunities that increase inclusion and reduce gaps in inequality will take time and political will. While we wait for politicians to marshal the political will to address such problems, we can at least begin to address the gang agenda by tackling the logic of the social field. By demonstrating the gang social field logic as illogical, we can demonstrate that there are alternatives, that players are not bound by their social fate. Ultimately we must demonstrate to the young people caught within the gang that the stakes are too high and that this is not a game worth playing.

My concept of street capital developed and expounded within the context of the search for distinction, provides confirmation of a comprehensive unifying theory of gang involvement – that the social field of the gang and its imperative to generate street capital are inexorably intertwined. While offering a concept of localised political economy, it also offers effective explanations for issues of respect and reputation that are all-encompassing and the source of much violence.

By expanding on the concept of street capital and how it is generated, manufactured, maximised, maintained and monitored, it is possible to provide a reinterpretation of postcode Beefs, group stabbings and territorial invasions.

Importantly, as with all social fields, a clear vertical structure is identifiable in the gang. It becomes evident that all field positions are interrelated and a change in one position alters the boundaries and positions of all other players. We can now see that field position is not determined by age, as once thought, but by the unequal distribution of capital, with subordinate players, including new arrivals, yet to master the rules of the game. Agencies and youth workers may now be able to identify the field position of a young person and interpret their subsequent role and the expectations placed on them. This is of critical importance for new arrivals, who are at greatest risk. Local authorities and local agencies must address the vulnerability experienced by new arrivals into the field, notably new immigrants, as their network poverty increases risk of victimisation. Here lie challenges for housing allocations, social landlords and schools.

We can also see how the field hierarchy has evolved in SW9 since 2005 when only two tiers were identifiable, permitting us to be more alert to the continued evolution of the field and how it changes over time.

The maintenance of social order in the field is worthy of further research, not least the proposition that social order might be adjustable or calibrated by incumbents depending on their perceived level of field control. Again, further intrigues await future researchers. At what points are sanctions introduced? Are they introduced more frequently if the social order of the field is under threat of fracturing? Are there periods of leniency?

The concept of fracturing of gangs is a useful one, raising new questions about the triggers for such events, which may differ considerably across different gangs. A key area for social policy and policy enforcement is how they can influence gang fracturing. Perhaps an even more pertinent question is should they be trying to fracture gangs? How does this fit with youth offending services' early warning systems and enforcement agencies' tension monitoring systems? Do such crisis moments in the life of a gang provide opportunities for outreach services? If convulsive moments can be more easily identified, can the 'innovative actions' of youthful challengers be more easily anticipated and interrupted?

The boundaries of the social field posed challenges for Bourdieu, and these challenges persist. What are the impacts on the gang of proximate fields, such as police, local authority and schools)? What adjustments are made by field players to accommodate or tolerate them? What power and influence do they exert and to what effect? Is their influence equal across all gang tiers or limited to key groups/ individuals?

While it is no surprise to find that the gang social field is highly gendered, my work offers a fresh perspective on the role of girls and young women within the social field. I suggest that they manufacture their street capital in different ways, for example, through managing information networks. Here the concept of social skill is valuable in illustrating how it determines different social trajectories for females. I suggest that those without social skill soon find themselves excluded from information networks and 'untrusted' – a process leading to a downward spiral of sexual exploitation, abuse and increased victimisation. I also offer two distinctly gendered narratives on the social fate of girls and young women entering the social field of the gang. Again it is hoped such narratives will find a useful place in the work of practitioners, trainers, outreach workers, mentors and policy advisers.

The concept of strategic action identified in this work dictates that action is strategically employed as a way of surviving in the social field, of negotiating its logic, risks, threats, boredom, blocked opportunities, deprivation and its fatalistic trajectory. The proposition is therefore clearly established in this work that in London SW9, gangs are perhaps the most effective and productive way for young people to obtain economic capital, and that generally no other plausible alternative exists. Players *must* strategise to raise their status and reputation and to expand their networks and thus rise through the hierarchy.

The application of Bourdieu's succession strategies permits us to view the internal dynamics of the gang more keenly, thus revealing when people are acting out conservation, succession or subversion strategies. For example, it is often younger gang affiliates with little to gain from the dominant groups who initiate or pursue subversion strategies leading to fracturing, while conservation strategies ensure that new 'blood' is recruited at lower levels through family or peers. Until alternative opportunities, logics and social fates are offered, available and accessible, it is likely that these survival strategies will endure.

The concept of strategic action, which is central to this theoretical perspective, also has utility in furthering explanations as to what is/

is not gang-related activity. Actions by individual or duos can now be better understood as operating within the social field of the gang.

The rules of the social field, or house rules, as suggested by the casino metaphor, provide a useful opportunity to better understand the life-world of young people. This explanation clarifies for the practitioner how the social field operates. When linked to the habitus, which governs actions in the field, we can better understand how the social field determines which actions are credible and likely to bring benefits or advancement. In this way, joining a gang might be viewed as a rational choice.

This study also shows the practicalities of the impact of information technology and the centrality of ubiquitous information on those in the field. Key to this important finding is the role played by girls and young women in securing, trading and exchanging information, and managing this process.

The insights offered here of power and dominance operating in the social field will again be of use practitioners, social workers and school teachers. As members struggle for distinction in this social field, they must dominate their rivals and extinguish their street capital. Reputations are diminished through such calculated strategies. Where this aspect of the game endures over time, it becomes a strategic encounter for power and dominance, as illustrated in SW9, where the once-inviolate Brixton reputation has suffered as a result of rivals' strategic attacks.

The social order and field hierarchy illuminate numerous exploitative relationships based on age (between olders and youngers) and gender. It further illuminates the inventive range of narratives used by gang-affiliated young people to make sense of their world, to manufacture myths, to create meaning, to reinterpret their actions and to console their losses. These can now be seen as fake, illusory and distracting as the reality suggests that the social field is violent place where trust and love are scare commodities.

A further key contribution of this work is the identification of the gang repertoire as a series of tried and tested strategies available to players in the social field. This finding counters the 'cafeteria-style offending' theory of Klein and Maxson (2006) and Aldridge and colleagues (2008). Further research is needed into this explanatory concept, not least the proposition of testing and auditioning. While both concepts provide opportunities for agency intervention, further questions arise over selection for auditioning, positive sanctions of encouragement, duration of testing and role differentiation within gangs.

Policy implications

A recent publication by HM Chief Inspector of Prisons, HM Chief Inspector of Probation and HM Chief Inspector of Constabulary (2010) makes some key observations about UK gangs. It notes that gangs and their impact remain widely contested; that interventions are usually focused on enforcement and not on prevention or victims; that community initiatives are mostly for over-18s; that gang-related safeguarding concerns are poorly understood; and that practice guidance, training and joint partnership working is insufficient, with national and local initiatives uncoordinated.

My research is intended to address some of these criticisms, and to help rebalance issues of insufficient prevention and age-biased service provision. I aim to offer an improved understanding of the specifics of gang operations, actions and behaviours in neighbourhoods, thereby providing a practical legacy to benefit practitioners. Specifically, I hope to have an impact on the following policy areas.

Developing a neighbourhood typology of gang activities and behaviours

The gang repertoire provides a typology of neighbourhood gang activities and behaviours that can be logged and mapped over time. Local variations can be added to determine the local bespoke nature of strategies and variables. By analysing gang repertoires, partners will expand knowledge of the local gang context, permitting local verification and categorisation of gang behaviours, identification of activity patterns and local gang evolution, development of early warning or tension monitoring systems and police intelligence systems, and opportunities for prevention or community intervention.

Safeguarding and victim-centred approach

This study reveals the constant daily pressures of survival in the gang, as well as widespread victimisation and its various ugly manifestations. Agencies need to focus on identifying and mapping the landscape of risk that young people must navigate daily, identifying and supporting ways to mitigate risks and minimise victimisation.

It is intended that this new perspective will generate a more empathetic understanding of how we view young people's involvement in gangs, improving knowledge of how and why gangs emerge, operate, endure and thrive. It should also focus attention on the role played by society in creating the conditions for gangs to take hold.

Importantly, the research shows that gang affiliates are not aberrant 'others' but part of the community. I suggest that success in addressing gangs will come from adopting a victim–centred approach based on prevention, where both people and communities are considered as victims.

Adoption of a child-safeguarding model will help identify the stresses and mental health issues arising from living in constant fear, thereby improving targeted support and emphasising prevention alongside enforcement.

This study demonstrates that the support requirements for young people will be complex. The insights offered here will assist in the creation of further assessment tools to measure the cumulative victimisation of young people in gang settings and help to identify how and when agencies should intervene.

By generating a more holistic and detailed review of the young person's specific experiences within the context of the social field, its logic and rules (how/when incidents happen, their frequency and their interrelational circumstances and outcomes), improved targeted support packages can be made available.

Wider partnership role for schools

The centrality of schools to the local gang agenda must be recognised more clearly. Too often schools operate independently of other local agencies and isolate themselves within the community. Schools can be wary of negative media reports or Ofsted inspections. Some deny any role in the local gang agenda while struggling to manage high rates of exclusion or truancy. Critical data is not widely shared and academic research staff are often denied access to staff and students. This study indicates that schools are key actors in this agenda. Consequently, they must play a far greater role in integrated partnership working and also in academic research than they currently do.

Improved interventions and risk assessments for young people

This research provides Lambeth practitioners with an improved understanding of how gangs function in London SW9, and, it is hoped, will lead to improvements in the quality and efficacy of multi-agency interventions for young people. For example, recognising that certain activities, behaviours and exploitative relationships are age- or gender-specific, and understanding the techniques used by gangs to influence, cajole and control young people into gang affiliation will assist early identification of gang recruitment in schools. Insights into the critical importance of IT to gang activity will help practitioners to identify appropriate (possibly 'real-time') intervention programmes, while the different narratives and gendered roles identified in the research will assist in developing bespoke interventions for women. Finally, the research provides opportunities for practitioners to more accurately identify and assess activities or behaviours that pose most risk to young people or to communities.

In this way, police and community interventions, along with practice guidance, training and partnership working, can be refocused on those aged under 18 years. This work should be aimed at:

- profiling local gangs, gang fracturing and evolution;
- better identifying gang-involved young people – better understanding of relationships/proximity to the gang;
- identifying gang grooming and recruitment in schools;
- highlighting routes into gangs and improved early intervention;
- addressing sexual exploitation within gangs;
- identifying and monitoring the use of social networking sites.

Insight into community interventions

Social field analysis illustrates the interconnectivity of the community and the gang social field. It is hoped that this fresh perspective will move away from the risk factor paradigm that often views the community and family as potential malignant influences in gang affiliation, towards one where the family and the community are also victims, experiencing unforeseen and unexpected impacts and outcomes.

By identifying and detailing exactly how local neighbourhoods experience gang behaviour, it is possible to identify opportunities for building community resilience and capacity building. Community interventions can be developed. In this way, practitioners will gain new perspectives on how/why behaviours and activities occur, leading to early recognition of risks, improved coordination of interventions and proactive action planning. Further research will help map the landscape of risk within which young people, communities and practitioners have to operate.

Partnership coordination

My research identifies that gang activities, behaviours and actions are perceived and thus recorded (or not recorded) differently and separately by local agencies. Data sharing exists, but is often nascent or its efficacy is curtailed by the practicalities of coordinating multi-layered partnerships with different definitions and working cultures. This silo approach by practitioners means no single agency has an accurate or full picture of the gang at any stage, and crucial data remains uncollated. Some agencies fail to agree on the existence and impact of the gang. This complex partnership response to gangs prevents an accurate or holistic picture of the gang from developing, which in turn inhibits effective partnership coordination. Adopting a more holistic social field perspective will help refocus partnership working. It is hoped that the insights offered here will direct agencies to alter, amend and improve data-collection methods. Improved data sharing across agencies must be a prime objective, leading to improved analysis at regional and local levels. This in turn will lead to improved targeted commissioning of services.

Gang research

It is anticipated that this book will lead researchers and practitioners to adopt gang social field analysis more widely, leading to further insights and providing answer to as yet unknown questions.

Before we ask new questions, however, let us return to the question that I posed at the beginning of the book: how do we explain the increase in gang related violence in SW9? The final part of this chapter unlocks the answer to this question and clarifies the metaphor of the street casino.

The street casino

Life in the violent street gang can be compared to a casino. The street casino represents the social field of the gang in its totality. It works as a metaphor as it not only echoes Bourdieu's original conception of life, but it represents the uncertainty of all players in the field. It is instantly recognisable as begetting both winners and losers. The street casino never closes. It is persuasive and permissive. It is seductive, addictive and adhesive. It operates its own centripetal force, pulling in new players all the time and spitting out those who have lost everything. It permits players to advance to higher levels at new tiers. It offers endless opportunities for winning that seldom become reality. It offers the promise of a new future, of easy money, new friends, girls, glamour and glitz, but in reality it exerts endless pressure to play with few winnings. It imposes sanctions on those who infringe the rules. It thrives on heightened emotional content with constant diversions to keep players playing, but the house always wins. Players come and go but the game stays the same. It is regenerative. New players are seduced, coerced and expected to play in the street casino – it constitutes their social fate. New rules are introduced that catch out new arrivals while long-standing players know how the game works. It works to their benefit. It a dangerous place of secret players, group players, individual players, spies, informers, double-dealers, thieves, cheats, snakes, outcasts, 'hos', pimps, sharks, bystanders, wannabes, 'wifeys', incumbents and challengers.

They play because they must.

They want to win, and win big.

They dream of cashing in and leaving the street casino.

There are several characteristics and properties of the street casino that explain the increase in gang violence in SW9.

Regenerative, dynamic, evolving

The social field is constantly changing – the game stays the same, but the players change. Recruitment occurs in schools, colleges and through family and peer networks. Dynamic change means challenges. The old certainties and social norms have disappeared. Brixton, once considered inviolable, has lost its 'reputation'. Some believe that the pace of change is accelerating and is further complicated by the arrival of new immigrants in SW9. In reality, the reasons behind this dynamic change are more complex and relate in part to the evolution of the urban street gang. In 2005, Sanders found no evidence of young people using guns, or of gang hierarchies, colours or other signs of 'ganging'. Now, as all these elements have been found to exist, it is evident there has been a significant evolution of gangs in Lambeth since then.

Relational boundaries

While the social field of the gang does have boundaries, these are relational, and neither visible nor well understood. They are also dynamic and in constant flux, as intra- and inter-gang relationships alter, start and end. The social field boundary is thus a dangerous place, exposing young people to the risk of violence. For example:

- non-gang-affiliated residents continually interact with members on the gang periphery;
- there is a widening acceptance among many young people of the logic, validity and characteristics of the social field and social norms of the gang (suggesting embeddedness);
- non-gang-affiliated young and wannabes flirt with gang symbolism and manners;
- social networking sites offer opportunities for gang members to enhance their virtual reputations, meaning that physical territorial boundaries may in the future hold less significance;
- wannabe gang affiliates are easily caught up in peripheral or boundary issues, putting them at considerable risk;
- the social field is increasingly portable into other fields.

External pressures: increased tensions

A number of external issues (including the increased use of police informants, court appearances involving multiple offenders charged with 'joint enterprise' and the legacy of unsolved murders) have recently increased tensions within the social field, leading to increased violence. Each issue creates a situation of diluted trust, suspicion, recrimination, revenge and intimidation.

More players in the game: increased social competition

The gang social field now has more, and younger, players (tinnies) in the game, thereby extending the social field. This means more people both in the social field, and on its periphery. As a result, the social arena is more crowded, more contested and more dynamic. There are more ways of being victimised, more ways to advance, more opportunities to diminish a rival's street capital, more variables with which to develop strategies, more repertoire components to test, and more inventive ways (online, for example) to provoke and mock rivals.

In this more dynamic and contested field, there is a greater need to stand out from the crowd, to fast-track strategies, to boost stalled reputations and gain advantage over others. Distinction in the field becomes more difficult. This engenders more competition and greater risk taking, including employing random or extreme acts of violence that earn mega-street capital.

Increased social competition plays out in a variety of important ways:

- greater imperative to build and maintain street capital;
- increased tension across the field;
- decline of respect towards olders and adults on the social field periphery as young people challenge those in dominant positions who appear to be hindering their advancement
- greater opportunity for adhesion and entanglement with the gang for those on its periphery;
- the fraying of the social norms, which translates into more trigger incidents and a lowering of the benchmark regarding what is acceptable;
- increased violence.

New arrivals/new players

New arrivals within the field have few contacts and limited information and thus experience 'network poverty'. SW9 has recently witnessed an influx of immigrants from different countries, noticeably from West Africa. Some may have played the game before, but most do not yet know the rules of the game, and are at increased risk of gang affiliation and victimisation as a result of inadvertent shows of disrespect towards affiliated members or unwitting trespass on gang turf ('slippin'').

Compulsion to play: the imperative to build street capital

Increasingly young people feel they have no choice but to enter the street casino. Once they have entered the street casino, players are compelled to play. For many, playing now becomes a compulsion. Street capital, once obtained, must be protected and maintained. In an increasingly crowded social arena, distinction becomes more elusive. Street capital deflation is more likely to occur with more players in the field. The pressure to maintain 'rep' leads to 'loco' (crazy) behaviour, hyper-vigilance and numerous small-scale but increasingly vicious reprisals. Those who seek rapid advancement and have nothing to lose take bigger risks and use greater violence, which in turn puts them at greater risk of victimisation. The dangers are magnified by the pressure to avoid deflation of both individual and gang reputation. Some respond to this by taking greater risks, developing a reputation for being reckless or 'out of control'. Others develop a fatalistic 'live for today' attitude as they manage downward their expectations of survival in the social field. In these circumstances, it is not uncommon for dangerous and reckless incidents to occur where boys as young as 13 are attacked by groups of up to 20 young people rushing at them with knives. The imperative to build street capital suggests an 'anything goes' attitude. This has left many ex-gang members in their mid-twenties feeling out of touch with fast-moving developments.

Being seen to play: incursions and group violence

It is increasingly important for young people in the street casino of SW9 to be seen to be players. Maximising street capital through group violence and group incursions is a central factor in the increase in levels of violence in SW9. Incursions into rival neighbourhoods are the supreme platform for generating street capital, providing a test bed for the gang Repertoire and allowing gangs to engage in violence that is more permissive and extreme. With multiple actors involved, each wishing to generate street capital, such events are hard to control. Incursions are viewed as a violation; they inflame emotions and invoke swift responses, often raising the stakes and resulting in tit-for-tat violence.

Playing for longer: an extended field

As other plausible alternatives, e.g. employment and further education, are increasingly unavailable to young people in disadvantaged neighbourhoods, the logic of affiliating to gangs becomes stronger and more convincing. The longer this situation prevails, the more young people enter the social field, and the longer they stay. Thus the social field is extended at either end of the age spectrum. Roles are found for tinnies (aged 11 to 13) who employ the gang repertoire at an earlier age. By age 14/15, a young person may have been in the social field for three or four years and new tinnies look up to him. At the lower end of this extended spectrum, youngers are compelled to employ the instrumental repertoire at an earlier age. At the same time, those in the higher age range stay in the gang longer as alternative career opportunities dwindle. Thus fewer gang-affiliated young people appear to mature out of crime. This extended social field of criminal opportunity offers numerous possibilities for trying and testing new strategies. Young people may therefore grow deeper into crime rather than out of it.

Increased immersion in the game: embeddedness

Embeddedness works at two levels: players become increasingly embedded within the gang and the gang increasingly embedded within the neighbourhood.

Relationships between young people and the gang appear to be solidifying. Beyond fun and money, the street casino offers young people something more profound than simple transient pleasures. It has become a complex social field where many become immersed in concepts of personal status, respect, reputation, street capital, future aspirations, interpersonal relationships and networking. The street casino offers continued membership while the age profile of members extends at both ends of the spectrum. This is compounded by difficulties experienced by those seeking to leave the gang. Members are more likely to switch to being part-time members or negotiate reduced involvement than to leave the gang completely.

Getting stuck in the game: increased adhesion to the gang

The street casino is not only dangerous, but also seductive and highly adhesive. The gang's strong gravitational pull makes it increasingly difficult for people to leave. For many, the gang is not something through which they pass, but somewhere they get stuck. The tiered structure facilitates this by offering an increasingly established route for young people as they advance in the social field. Each tier offers a complement of opportunities and trajectories, fitted to age bands, skill sets and dispositions. For those entering this all-encompassing social field aged 11, this may well be the only world they know, and can survive in, by age 25. Moreover, this embeddedness reinforces the authority of the gang as the principal agent of social control in their neighbourhood. This ensures that gangs are increasingly embedded in the neighbourhoods of SW9.

Several features of the social field act as a potential adhesive, keeping members in the gang:

- in the social field of SW9, there is no plausible alternative to affiliation;

- by age 19/20, many young men have no experience of anything but gang life;
- peers and friends remain in the gang;
- part-time affiliation is possible;
- becoming older means less trouble, less hassle, fewer fights but more money;
- all network connections can be retained;
- stronger links to prisoners are possible;
- there is a constant need to fund the rising costs of an increasing and preferably highly visible social life;
- the need to self-restrict neighbourhood movements decreases with age, allowing increased social mobility;
- affiliation provides opportunities for skill specialisation in drugs, acquisitive crime or sex work.

Such features are commonly narrated as *'Stick wiv it bruv, it'll all come good in the end.'* In the street casino this is interpreted as 'Keep playing, you're bound to win at some point.'

New rules: altered social norms and new extremes

New internal pressures in the social field have altered the social norms of what is acceptable. Those seeking revenge will do whatever it takes to achieve their aims, be it attacking family members including mothers or employing extreme elements of the gang repertoire such as abduction or sexual violence.

The most noticeably altered social norm is intergenerational friction. The 'mentoring' role of olders for youngers is now somewhat diluted and youngers are more likely to challenge olders at a younger age, especially if they believe that the older in question has failed to achieve sufficient success or distinction, or is thwarting their ambition. Many aspirant youngers believe they are better at 'ganging' than their predecessors. Depreciated street capital for olders ensures an increased number of challenges by aspirant leaders. Increasingly youngers seek their own direct links to elders and opportunities for involvement in drugs businesses and other criminal activities.

Respect for 'old heads' is now more limited. Previously a younger accompanied by his mother was technically 'out of bounds' until he was alone; disrespecting the mother was considered unacceptable as a social norm. Now if the situation demands it, both are fair game.

Sudden rule changes

Successful challenges, altered social norms and realigned relationships can all lead to rule changes within the social field. Sudden rule changes in the game mean that young people are often caught unawares, especially if they live 'off the hood'. This places young people at increasing risk and brings an imperative to stay informed about current developments at all times.

Internal pressures: use of information and social networking sites

Rapid information transmission enabled by new technology has had a significant impact on the social field in recent years. New technology enables users to feel more connected to events. This feeling of immediacy encourages greater emotional investment, resulting in heightened responses to situations, more rapid retaliation and increased violence. Moreover, the use of social networking sites creates opportunities for generating street capital by providing a platform for individual/gang branding, as well as opportunities to provoke rivals and diminish their street capital. Mockery or online humiliation is now public, not private. In the social field, virtual information has the ability to:

- take on greater significance and have a higher emotional content;
- have wider repercussions in the social field;
- play out in unforeseen and uncontrollable ways;
- affect a wider range of agents, leading to a greater number of potential outcomes;
- be misread by a greater number of 'interested parties';
- lead to potential fatal results.

The centrality of information to the gang social field is of paramount importance. Information is used to build and strengthen social networks, street capital and reputations. It is used to challenge, enhance or secure one's field position, to diminish the street capital of others and to help young people risk manage their personal lives. Information is used in all tiers of the gang and within the wider network, creating an exclusive world that is very difficult for those outside the social field to break into or understand.

Normalisation of violence

In the neighbourhoods of SW9, gangs are no longer the aberrant 'other'. For many young people gang affiliation is a natural and logical progression. Their experiences at school, in the local neighbourhood and at home mean that violence is wholly normalised, expected and required in the social field. Indeed, violent aspects of the gang repertoire now include group rape, sexual assault, abduction, kidnap and torture.

Firearms now used across all three gang repertoires

In the social field of SW9, physical violence is the prime strategy for gaining reputation and building street capital and it is a feature of all three repertoires expressive, instrumental, and sanction. More importantly, recent changes in the social field mean that firearms are now used to support these strategies across all three repertoires.

Not winners, but losers

The factors listed above help explain the increase in violence in London SW9. This adhesive and constantly shifting gang landscape with its physical, metaphorical and relational boundaries confirms the social field (the street casino) as a threatening and dangerous environment for young people, representing, for many, a life controlled by fear in a landscape of risk.

It is a social field undergoing evolutionary change, not least through the profound impact of new technology, with its ability incessantly to transmit news and information, and to encourage users to analyse new developments, stay abreast of fast-changing situations, monitor personal reputations and street capital, assess risk, monitor tensions and develop strategies individually or as part of the gang. Survival involves continually sounding people out, using your networks to monitor all activity, gang-related or otherwise, separating fact from fiction and transmitting information to others immediately to accrue trust. All this requires constant monitoring of all information channels.

In this social field the 'information poor' suffer victimisation. Schoolteachers in SW9 report that one reason for low educational attainment is that information is constantly flowing into the classroom via mobile and smart phones. This, coupled with the heightened emotional responses invoked by this exchange of information leaves classrooms in constant turmoil. As information is shared, concentration wanes.

The fear of sanctions imposed by gangs, peers, police and others in authority puts enormous pressure on players in the street casino. The universal street code of not 'grassing' dictates that fear and anxiety cannot be shared. Accusations and rumours fly about what has been done and said, and what will be done. Interaction with police may be misconstrued as informing. Many young people worry about the police finding out and using their street names, because it implies some level of interaction. As a result, young people often just run when they are approached by police officers.

The range of sanctions – from rumour to murder – and all manner of variables in between are well understood by all players in the social field. For many young people, this necessitates and feeds their state of constant alertness and hyper-vigilance, a state of affairs that could be seen as analogous to a theatre of conflict or war (Sampson and Lauritson, 1994). Indeed, young people in the social field often refer to their environment as 'a war zone', and to themselves as 'soljas'. James Short (1997) refers to this as a 'soldier mentality', acquired to survive in an 'alternative cognitive landscape'. Those experiencing immediate risk remain in a state of constant readiness for physical violence, developing war-zone preparedness, which is highly stressful and mentally exhausting. This echoes dispatches from the front line in active war zones, where soldiers talk of developing a thousand-yard-stare, or the hyper-vigilance needed to block out all unimportant sensations and focus solely on the actions of the enemy. Such a view on the world must surely have a negative effect on the daily lives of young people, their education, relationships and health. Such is the stress of being compelled to play in the street casino. The daily agony of living with this stress was summed up by one gang younger, aged 15, in his comment "My life hurts."

References

Adler, P.S. and Kwon, S. (2002) 'Social capital: prospects for a new concept', *Academy of Management Review*, vol 27, no 1, pp 17-40.

Aldridge, J. and Medina, J. (2008) *Youth gangs in an English city: Social exclusion, drugs and violence*, ESRC End of Award Report, RES-00023-0615, Swindon: ESRC.

Aldridge, J. and Medina, J. (2010) *Youth gangs in an English city: social exclusion, drugs and violence*, ESRC End of Award Report, RES-000-23-0615, Swindon: ESRC.

Aldridge, J., Medina, J. and Ralphs, R. (2008) 'Dangers and problems of doing gang research in the UK', in F. van Gemert, D. Peterson, and I. Lien (eds) *Street gangs, migration and ethnicity*, Cullompton: Willan.

Aldridge, J., Ralphs, R. and Medino, J. (2011) 'Collateral damage: territory and policing in an English gang city', in B. Goldson (ed) *Youth in crisis? 'Gangs', territoriality and violence*, Abingdon: Routledge.

Aldridge, J., Shute, J., Ralphs, R. and Medino, J. (2009) 'Blame the parents? Challenges for parent-focused programmes for families of gang-involved young people', *Children & Society*, DOI: 10.1111/j.1099-0860.

Alexander, C. (2008) *(Re)thinking gangs*, London: Runnymede Trust.

Anderson, E. (1990) *The code of the street*, New York, NY: W.W. Norton.

Anderson, E. (1999) *Code of the street*, New York, NY: W.W. Norton.

Ansell, C. (2001) *Schism and solidarity in social movements: The politics of labor in the French Third Republic*, Cambridge: Cambridge University Press.

Atkinson, R.G. and Flint, J. (2002) *Neighbourhood boundaries, social disorganisation and social exclusion*, Glasgow: University of Glasgow.

Ball, S., Maguire, M. and Macrae, S. (2000) *Choice, pathways and transitions post-16: New youth, new economics in the global city*, London/New York, NY: RoutledgeFalmer.

Bannister, J. and Fraser, A. (2008) 'Youth gang identification: Learning and social development in restricted geographies', *Scottish Journal of Criminal Justice Studies*, vol 14, pp 96-114.

Baudrillard, J. (1988) *Selected writings*, Cambridge: Polity Press.

Barker, G.T. (2005) *Dying to be men: Youth, masculinity and social exclusion*, Abingdon: Routledge.

Batchelor, S. (2005) 'Prove me the Bam! Victimisation and agency in the lives of young women who commit violent offences', *Probation Journal*, vol 52, no 4, pp 358-75.

Batchelor, S. (2009) 'Girls, gangs and violence: assessing the evidence', *Probation Journal*, vol 56, pp 399-414.

Batchelor, S. (2011) 'Beyond dichotomy: towards an explanation of young women's involvement in violent street gangs', in B. Goldson (ed) *Youth in crisis? 'Gangs', territoriality and violence*, Abingdon: Routledge.

Baum, D. (1996) 'Can integration succeed? Research into urban childhood and youth in a deprived area of Koblenz', *Social Work in Europe*, vol 3, no 2, pp 30-35.

Becker, G. (1968) 'Crime and punishment: an economic approach', Journal *of Political Economy*, vol 76, no 2, pp 169-217.

Becker, H. (1963) *Outsiders: studies of the sociology of deviance*, New York: Free Press.

Becker, H.S. (1964) 'Personal change in adult life', *Sociometry*, 27, pp 40-53.

Beckett, H. with Brodie, I., Factor, F., Melrose, M., Pearce, J., Shuker, L. and Warrington, C. (2012) 'Research into gang-associated sexual exploitation and sexual violence – interim report', Luton: University of Bedfordshire.

Beckett, H. with Brodie, I. Factor, F. Melrose, M., Pearce, J., Pitts, J. Shuker, L. and Warrington, C. (2013) *'It's wrong ... but you get used to it'*, Report commissioned by the Office of the Children's Commissioner's Inquiry into Child Sexual Exploitation in Gangs and Groups, Luton: University of Bedfordshire.

Bennett, T. and Holloway, K. (2004) 'Gang membership, drugs and crime in the UK', *British Journal of Criminology*, 44, pp 304-23.

Berger, P.L. and Luckmann, T. (1966) *The social construction of reality: A treatise in the sociology of knowledge*, Garden City, NY: Anchor Books.

Berelowitz, S. Clifton, J., Firmin, C., Gulyurtlu, S. and Edwards, S. (2013) *'If only someone had listened'*, Office of the Children's Commissioner's Inquiry into Child Sexual Exploitation in Gangs and Groups, Final Report, London: Office of the Children's Commissioner.

Bourdieu, P. (1969) 'Intellectual field and creative project', *Social Science Information*, 8, pp 189-219.

Bourdieu, P. (1977) *Outline of a theory of practice*, Cambridge: Cambridge University Press.

Bourdieu, P. (1980) 'Le capital social: notes provisoires', *Actes de la recherché en sciences sociales*, vol 31 (January), pp 2-3, cited in J. Field (2008) *Social capital* (2nd edn), Abingdon: Routledge.

Bourdieu, P. (1984) *Distinction: A social critique of the judgement of taste*, translated by Richard Nice, Cambridge, MA: Harvard University Press.

Bourdieu, P. (1985) 'The genesis of the concepts of habitus and field', *Sociocriticism*, vol 2, no 2, pp 11-24.

Bourdieu, P. (1986) 'The forms of capital', in J.G. Richardson (ed) *Handbook of theory and research for the sociology of education*, New York, NY: Greenwood Press, pp 241-58.

Bourdieu, P. (1990) *The logic of practice*, Cambridge: Polity Press.

Bourdieu, P. (1991a) *Language and symbolic power*, Cambridge: Polity Press.

Bourdieu, P. (1991b) 'Le champ litteraire', *Actes de la recherché en sciences sociales*, vol 89 (September), pp 4-46, cited in D. Swartz (1997) *Culture and power: The sociology of Pierre Bourdieu*, Chicago, IL: University of Chicago Press.

Bourdieu, P. (1993) *The field of cultural production*, Cambridge: Polity Press.

Bourdieu, P. (1998a) *Acts of resistance: Against the new myths of our time*, Cambridge: Polity Press.

Bourdieu, P. (1998b) *Practical reason*, Cambridge: Polity Press.

Bourdieu, P. (1998c) *The state nobility: elite schools in the field of power*, Stanford, CA: Stanford University Press.

Bourdieu, P. and Wacquant, L.J.D. (1992) *An invitation to reflexive sociology*, Chicago, IL: University of Chicago Press.

Bourgois, P. (1995) *In search of respect: Selling crack in El Barrio*, Cambridge: Cambridge University Press.

Bradshaw, P. (2005) 'Terrors and young teams: youth gangs and delinquency in Edinburgh', in S.H. Decker and F. M. Weerman (eds) *European street gangs and troublesome youth groups: Findings from the Eurogang Research Program*, Walnut Creek, CA: AltaMira Press, pp 241-57.

Brass, D.J., Butterfield, K.D. and Skaggs, B.C. (1988) 'Relationships and unethical behavior: A social network perspective', *Academy of Management Review*, vol 23, no 1, pp 14-31.

Briggs, I. (2009) Presentation by Inspector Ian Briggs, RSPCA Status Dogs Summit, April.

Bullock, K. and Tilley, N. (2002) *Shootings, gangs and violent incidents in Manchester – developing a crime reduction strategy*, Crime Reduction Research Series Paper 13, London: The Home Office.

Bullock, K. and Tilley, N. (2008) 'Understanding and tackling gang violence', *Crime Prevention and Community Safety*, vol 10, pp 36-47.

Campbell, A. (1984) *The girls in the gang: A report from New York City*, Oxford: Basil Blackwell.

Campbell, A. (1990) 'Female participation in gangs', in C.R. Huff (ed) *Gangs in America*, Newbury Park, CA: Sage Publications, pp 163-82.

Castells, M. (1998) *End of millennium*, Malden, MA: Blackwell.

Centre for Social Justice (2009) *Dying to belong: An in-depth review of street gangs in Britain*, London: Centre for Social Justice.

Centre for Social Justice (2014) *Girls and gangs*, London: Centre for Social Justice.

Chambliss, W.J. (1973) 'The saints and the roughnecks', in W. J. Chambliss and M. Mankoff (eds) *Whose law, what order?*, New York, NY: John Wiley & Sons, pp 148-61.

Chesney-Lind, M. (1997) *The female offender: Girls, women and crime*, Thousand Oaks: Sage Publications.

Chin, K. (1996) *Chinatown gangs: Extortion, enterprise, and ethnicity*, New York: Oxford University Press.

Cloward, R.A. and Ohlin, L.E. (1960) *Delinquency and opportunity: A theory of delinquent gangs*, New York, NY: Free Press.

Cobbina, J.E., Like-Haislip, T.Z. and Miller, J. (2010) 'Gang fights versus cat fights: urban young men's gendered narratives of violence', *Deviant Behavior*, vol 31, no 7, pp 596-624.

Cohen, A.K. (1955) *Delinquent boys: The culture of the gang*, New York, NY: Macmillan.

Cohen, A.K. (1966) *Deviance and control*, Englewood Cliffs, NJ: Prentice Hall.

Coleman, J. (1986) 'Social theory, social research, and a theory of action', *American Journal of Sociology*, vol 91, no 6, pp 1309-35.

Coleman, J.S. (1994) *Foundations of social theory*, Cambridge, MA: Belknap Press.

Coleman, J.S. (1999) 'Social capital in the creation of human capital', in P. Dasgupta and I. Serageldin (eds) *Social capital: A multifaceted perspective*, Washington DC: World Bank.

Communities that Care (2005) *Findings from the Safer London Youth Survey 2004*. London: Communities that Care.

Conchas, G.Q. and Vigil, J.D. (2010) 'Multiple marginality and urban education: community and school socialization among low-income Mexican-descent youth', *Journal of Education for Students Placed at Risk*, vol 15, no 1, pp 51-65.

Conquergood, D. (1994) 'Homeboys and hoods: gang communication and cultural space', in L. Frey (ed) *Group Communication in Context: Studies of Natural Groups*, Hillside, NJ: Lawrence Erlbaum, pp 23-55.

Curry, G.D. and Spergel, I.A. (1992) 'Gang involvement and delinquency among Hispanic and African American adolescent males', *Journal of Research on Crime and Delinquency*, vol 29, pp 273-91.

Curry, G.D., Decker, S. and Pyrooz, D.C. (2014) *Confronting Gangs : Crime and Community* (3rd edn), Oxford University Press: New York

Daly, M. and Wilson, M. (1988) Homicide, New York, NY: De Gruyter.

Dasgupta, P. (2000) 'Economic progress and the idea of social capital', in P. Dasgupta and I. Serageldin (eds) *Social capital: A multifaceted perspective*, Washington DC: World Bank.

Davenport, J. (2014) '700 police launch dawn raids targeted at notorious Brixton-based gang', *London Evening Standard*, 8 April (www.standard.co.uk/news/crime/700-police-launch-dawn-raids-targeted-at-notorious-brixtonbased-gang-9095533.html).

Davies, A. (1998) 'Youth gangs, masculinity and violence in late Victorian Manchester and Salford', *Journal of Social History*, vol 32, pp 349-69.

DCFS (Department for Children, Schools and Families) (2010) 'Safeguarding children and young people who may be affected by gang activity', www.dscf.gov.uk/everychildmatters/earlyyears

Dean, M. (1997) *Tipping the balance, Search, No 27*, Spring, York: Joseph Rowntree Foundation.

Decker, S.H. and Curry, G.D. (2000) 'Addressing key features of gang membership: measuring the involvement of young members', *Journal of Criminal Justice*, vol 28, pp 473-82.

Decker, S.H. and Curry, G.D. (2002) 'Gangs, gang homicides, and gang loyalty: organised crimes of disorganised criminals?', *Journal of Criminal Justice*, vol 30, pp 1-10.

Decker, S.H. and Lauritsen, J.L. (2002) 'Leaving the gang', in R.C. Huff (ed) *Gangs in America* (3rd edn), Thousand Oaks, CA: Sage Publications, pp 51-7.

Decker, S.H. and Pyrooz, D.C. (2010) 'Gang violence worldwide: context, Culture, and country', in G. McDonald and E. LeBrun (eds), *Small Arms Survey 2010: gangs, groups and guns*, Cambridge: Cambridge University Press, pp 128-55.

Decker, S.H. and Pyrooz, D.C. (2011) 'Leaving the gang: logging off and moving on, 07/2011', in proceeding of: Strategies Against Violence Environments (SAVE), At Dublin Ireland.

Decker, S.H. and Pyrooz, D.C. (2011) 'Leaving the gang: logging off and moving on', proceedings of the Summit Against Violent Extremism (SAVE) held by Google Ideas and Council on Foreign Relations in June (www.cfr.org/counterradicalization/save-supporting-document-leaving-gang/p26590).

Decker, S.H. and Van Winkle, B. (1996) *Life in the gang: Family, friends and violence*, Cambridge: Cambridge University Press.

Decker, S.H. and Weerman, F. (2005) *European street gangs and troublesome youth groups*, Lanham MD: AltaMira Press.

Decker, S.H., Bynum, T. and Weisel, D. (1998) 'A tale of two cities: gangs as organised crime groups', *Justice Quarterly*, vol 15, no 3, pp 395-425.

Decker, S.H., Katz, C. and Webb, V. (2008) 'Understanding the black box of gang organisation: implications for involvement in violent crime, drug sales, and violent victimisation', *Crime & Delinquency*, vol 54, no 1, pp 153-72.

Demuth, C. (1978) *Sus, a report on the Vagrancy Act 1824*, London: Runnymede Trust.

Densley, J. (2011) 'Ganging up on gang: why the gang intervention industry needs an intervention', *British Journal of Forensic Practice*, vol 13, pp 12-24.

Densley, J. (2012a) 'It's gang life, but not as we know it: the evolution of gang business', *Crime & Delinquency*, doi: 10.1177/0011128712437912

Densley, J. (2012b) 'The organisation of London's street gangs', *Global Crime*, vol 1, no 1, pp 42-64.

Densley, J. (2012c) 'Street gang recruitment: signaling, screening and selection', *Social Problems*, vol 59, no 3, pp 301-21.

Densley, J. (2013) *How gangs work*, Oxford: Palgrave Macmillan.

Densley, J. and Stevens, A. (2014) '"We'll show you gang": the subterranean structuration of gang life in London', *Criminology and Criminal Justice*. Published online before print 14 February 2014, doi: 10.1177/1748895814522079

Deuchar, R. (2009) *Gangs: Marginalised youth and social capital*, Stoke on Trent: Trenham.

DiMaggio, P. (1988) 'Interest and agency in institutional theory', in L. Zucker (ed) *Institutional patterns and organizations: Culture and environment*, Cambridge, MA: Ballinger Publishing, pp 3-21.

DiMaggio, P. and Powell, W. (1983) The iron cage revisited: institutional isomorphism and collective rationality in organizational fields', *American Sociological Review*, vol 48, no 2, pp 147-60.

Downes, D.M. (1966) *The delinquent solution: A study in subcultural theory*, New York, NY: Free Press.

Durkheim, E. (1964) *The division of labor in society*, New York, NY: Free Press.

Ebaugh, H. (1988) *Becoming an ex*, Chicago, IL: Chicago University Press.

Esbensen, F.A., Deschenes, E.P. and Winfree, T.L. (1999) 'Differences between gang girls and gang boys: results from a multisite survey', *Youth and Society*, vol 3, no 1, pp 27-53.

Esbensen, F. A., Winfree, T. A., He, N. and Taylor, T.J. (2001) 'Youth gangs and definitional issues: when is a gang a gang, and why does it matter?', *Crime and Delinquency*, vol 47, no 1, pp 105-30.

Evans, K., Fraser, P. and Walklate, S. (1996) 'Whom can you trust? The politics of "grassing" on an inner city housing estate', *Sociological Review*, vol 44, no 3, pp 584-6.

Evans, K., Rudd, P., Behrens, M., Kaluza, J. and Woolley, C. (2001) 'Reconstructing fate as choice', *Young*, vol 9, no 3, pp 2-28.

Farrell, S. and Calverley, A. (2006) *Understanding desistance from crime: Theoretical directions in resettlement and rehabilitation*, Berkshire: Open University Press.

Farrington, D. (1995) 'The development of offending and anti-social behaviour from childhood: key findings from the Cambridge Study in Delinquent Development', *Journal of Child Psychology and Psychiatry*, vol 36, no 6, pp 929-64.

Felson, M. (2006) 'The street gang strategy', in M. Felson (ed.) *Crime and nature*, Thousand Oaks, CA: Sage, pp 305-24.

Field, J. (2008) *Social capital* (2nd edn), Abingdon: Routledge.

Firmin, C. (2009) 'Girls around gangs', *Safer Communities*, vol 8, no 2, pp 14-16.

Firmin, C. (2010) *Female Voice in Violence Project: A study into the impact of serious youth and gang violence on women and girls*, London: ROTA.

Firmin, C. (2011) *This is it, this is my life: the Female Voice in Violence Project*, London: ROTA.

Fleisher, M.S. (2006) 'Youth gang and social dynamics and social network analysis: applying degree centrality measures to assess the nature of gang boundaries', in J.F. Short and L.A. Hughes (eds) *Studying youth gangs*, Lanham, MD: AltaMira Press, pp. 86-99.

Fligstein, N. (1996) 'Markets as politics: a political-cultural approach to market institutions', *American Sociological Review*, vol 61, no 4, pp 656-73.

Fligstein, N. and McAdam, D. (2012) *A theory of fields*, Oxford: Oxford University Press.

Fukuyama, F. (1995) *Trust: the social virtues and the creation of prosperity*, London: Hamish Hamilton.

Fukuyama, F. (2001) 'Social capital, civil society and development', *Third World Quarterly*, vol 22, no 1, pp 7-20.

Furstenberg, F. (1969) *Der Aufteigsproblem in der modernen Gesellschaft*, Stuttgart: Ferdinand Enke Verlag.

Gangs in London (2011) http://gangsinlodnon.piczo.com

Garland, D. (2001) *The culture of control*, Oxford: Oxford University Press.

Gee, J.P. (2002) 'New times and new literacies: themes for a changing world', in M. Kalantziz, G. Varnara-Skoura and B. Cope (eds) *Learning for the future: New worlds, new literacies*, Melbourne: Common Ground.

Giddens, A. (1984) *The constitution of society*. Berkeley: University of California Press.

Goffman, E. (1959) *The presentation of self in everyday life*, Garden City, NY: Doubleday.

Goffman, E. (1961) *Asylums: Essays on the social situation of mental patients and other inmates*, Garden City, NY: Anchor Books.

Goffman, E. (1963) *Behaviour in public places: Notes on the social organization of gatherings*, Glencoe, IL: Free Press.

Goffman, E. (1974) *Frame analysis: An essay on the organisation of experience*, Cambridge, MA: Harvard University Press.

Goldson, B. (2011) *Youth in crisis? 'Gangs', territoriality and violence*, Abingdon: Routledge.

Gordon, R. (2000) 'Criminal business organisations, street gangs and "wannabe" groups, a Vancouver Perspective', *Canadian Journal of Criminology and Criminal Justice*, vol 42, no 1, pp 39-60.

Government Office for London (2004) *The London crime and disorder audit*, London: Government Office for London.

Graham, J.G. and Bowling, B. (1995) *Young people and crime*, Home Office Research Study No 145, London: HMSO.

Grund, T. and Densley, J. (2012) 'Ethnic heterogeneity in the activity and structure of a black street gang', *European Journal of Criminology*, vol 9, no 4, pp 388-406.

Hagan, J. (1993) 'The social embeddedness of crime and unemployment', *Criminology*, vol 31, pp 455-91.

Hagan, J. (1994) *Crime and disrepute*, Thousand Oaks, CA: Pine Forge Press.

Hagan, J. and McCarthy, B. (1997) *Mean streets: Youth crime and homelessness*, New York: Cambridge University Press.

Hagedorn, J. (1988) *People and folks: Gangs, crime and the underclass in a rustbelt city*, Chicago: Lakeview Press.

Hagedorn, J. (1998) 'Gang violence in the post-industrial era', in M. Tonry and M.H. Moore (eds) *Crime and justice, volume 24. Youth violence*, Chicago, IL: University of Chicago Press.

Hagedorn, J. (2007) *Gangs in the global city*, Urbana-Champaign and Chicago, IL: University of Illinois Press.

Hagedorn, J. (2008) *A world of gangs*, Minneapolis, MN: University of Minnesota Press.

Hallsworth, S. (2005) *Street crime*, Cullompton: Willan Publishing.

Hallsworth, S. (2008) 'Reasons not to be cheerful: New Labour's action plan for targeting violence', *Criminal Justice Matters*, vol 72, no 1, pp 2-3.

Hallsworth, S. (2011) 'Gangland Britain?: Realities, fantasies and industry', in B. Goldson (ed) *Youth in crisis?: 'Gangs', territoriality and violence*, Abingdon: Routledge.

Hallsworth, S. (2013) *The gang and beyond: Interpreting violent street worlds*, New York, NY: Palgrave Macmillan.

Hallsworth, S. and Brotherton, D. (2011) *Urban disorder and gangs: A critique and a warning*, London: Runnymede Trust.

Hallsworth, S. and Duffy, K. (2010) *Confronting London's violent street world: The gang and beyond. A report for London councils*, London: CESR, London Metropolitan University.

Hallsworth, S. and Silverstone, D. (2009) '"That's life innit": a British perspective on guns, crime and social order', *Criminology and Criminal Justice*, vol 9, no 3, pp 359-77.

Hallsworth, S. and Young, T. (2004) 'Getting real about gangs', *Criminal Justice Matters*, vol 55, no 1, pp 12-13.

Hallsworth, S. and Young, T. (2006) *Urban collectives: Gangs and other groups*, Report for the Metropolitan Police Service and Government Office for London, London: London Metropolitan University.

Hallsworth, S. and Young, T. (2008) 'Gang talk and gang talkers: a critique', *Crime, Media, Culture*, vol 4, no 2, pp 175-95.

Hallsworth, S. and Young, T. (2010) 'Street collectives and group delinquency: social disorganisation, subcultures and beyond', in E. Mclaughlin and T. Newburn (eds) *The Sage handbook of criminological theory*, London: Sage Publications.

Halpern, D. (2005) *Social capital*, Cambridge: Polity Press.

Hancock, L. (2003) 'Urban regeneration and crime reduction: contradictions and dilemmas', in R. Matthews and J. Young (eds) *The new politics of crime and punishment*, Cullompton: Willan Publishing.

Hanley, L. (2007) *Estates: An intimate history*, London: Granta Books.

Harding, S. (2010) 'Status dogs and gangs', *Safer Communities*, vol 9, no 1, pp 30-35.

Harding, S. (2012) 'Street government: the role of the urban street gang in the London riots', in D. Biggs (ed.) *The English riots of 2011: A summer of discontent*, Hook: Waterside Press, pp 193-215.

Harding, S. (2014) *Unleashed: The phenomena of status dogs and weapon dogs*, Bristol: Policy Press.

Hayward, K. (2004) *City limits: Crime, consumer culture and the urban experience*, London: The GlassHouse Press.

HBO (2002-07) The wire, Executive producer/writer David Simon.

Hirschi, T. (1969) *Causes of delinquency*, Berkeley: University of California Press.

HM Chief Inspector of Prisons, HM Chief Inspector of Probation and HM Chief Inspector of Constabulary (2010) *The management of gang issues among children and young people in prison custody and the community: A joint thematic review*, HMIP: London.

Hobbs, D., Hadfield, P., Lister, S. and Winlow, S. (2003) *Bouncers: violence and governance in the night-time economy*, Oxford: Oxford University Press.

Home Office (2006) *Group offending*. London: Home Office.

Home Office (2008) *Tackling Gangs Action Programme: A practical guide for local authorities, CDRPs and other local authority partners*, London: Home Office.

Home Office (2011) *An assessment of the Tackling Knives and Serious Youth Violence Action Programme (TKAP) – Phase ll* , Home Office Research Report 53, London: HMSO.

Hope, T. (1994) 'Communities, crime and inequality in England and Wales'. Paper presented to the 1994 Cropwood Round Table Conference Preventing Crime and Disorder, 14-15 September, Cambridge.

Hope, T. (1998) 'Community safety, crime and disorder', in A. Marlow and J. Pitts (eds) *Planning safer communities,* Lyme Regis: Russell House Publishing Ltd.

Hope, T. (2003) 'The crime drop in Britain', *Community Safety Journal*, vol 2, no 4, p 32.

Horowitz, R. (1983) *Honor and the American dream*, New Brunswick, NJ: Rutgers University Press.

Howell, J.C. (2012) *Gangs in America's communities*, Thousand Oaks, CA: Sage Publications.

Huff, C.R. (1990) *Gangs in America*, Newbury Park, CA: Sage.

IEP (Institute for Economics and Peace) (2013) UK peace index: Exploring the fabric of peace in the UK from 2003 to 2012 (www.visionofhumanity.org/pdf/ukpi/UK_Peace_Index_report_2013.pdf)

Imadfidon, K. (2012) *The Kenny Report*, London: Safer London Foundation.

Jacobs, B. and Wright, R. (1999) 'Stick up, street culture, and offender motivation', *Criminology*, vol 37, no 1, pp 149-73.

Jeffs, T. and Smith, M. (2008) 'Valuing youth work', *Youth & Policy*, no 100, Summer.

Jenkins, R. (2002) *Pierre Bourdieu* (revised edn), London and New York, NY: Routledge.

Joe, K. and Chesney-Lind, M. (1995) '"Just every mother's angel": an analysis of gender and ethnic variations in youth gang membership', *Gender and Society*, vol 9, no 94, pp 408-30.

Joe-Laidler, K. and Hunt, G. (2001) 'Accomplishing femininity among the girls in the gang', *British Journal of Criminology*, vol 41, pp 656-78.

Jones, G. (2002) *The youth divide*, York: Joseph Rowntree Foundation/York Publishing Services.

Katz, J. (1988) *Seductions of crime: The moral and sensual attractions of doing evil*, New York, NY: Basic Books.

Kennison, P. (2000) 'Being realistic about stop and search', in A. Marlow, and B. Loveday, (eds) *After MacPherson*, Dorset: Russell House Publishing.

Kintrea, K., Bannister, J., Pickering, J., Reid, M. and Suzuki, N. (2008) *Young people and territoriality in British cities*, York: Joseph Rowntree Foundation.

Kintrea, K., Bannister, J. and Pickering, J. (2011) 'It's just an area – everybody represents it', in B. Goldson (ed) *Youth in crisis?: 'Gangs', territoriality and violence*, Abingdon: Routledge.

Klein, M.W. (1971) *Street gangs and street workers*, Englewood Cliffs, NJ: Prentice Hall.

Klein, M.W. (1995) *The American street gang: Its nature, prevalence, and control*, New York, NY: Oxford University Press.

Klein, M.W. and Maxson, C.L. (2006) *Street gang patterns and policies*, Oxford: Oxford University Press.

LCPCG (Lambeth Community Police Consultative Group) (2010) *Whose shout? Engagement on community safety in Lambeth*, London: Lambeth CPAG, *www.lambethcpcg.org.uk*

LCPCG (2007-11) CPCG meeting minutes, *www.lambethcpcg.org.uk*

Lambeth First (2008) *Young and Safe Action Plan*, London: London Borough of Lambeth.

Lambeth First (2009) *Community Safety Ward Reviews 2009*, London: London Borough of Lambeth.

Lambeth First (2011a) *Lambeth Strategic Assessment 2011*, London: Lambeth First, Safer Lambeth Partnership, London Borough of Lambeth.

Lambeth First (2011b) *State of the Borough Report 2011*, London: London Borough of Lambeth.

Lambeth First (2012) *State of the Borough Report 2012*, London: London Borough of Lambeth.

LCPCG (Lambeth Community Police Consultative Group) (2010) *Whose shout? Engagement on community safety in Lambeth*, London: Lambeth CPAG, *www.lambethcpcg.org.uk*

LCPCG (2007-11) CPCG meeting minutes, *www.lambethcpcg.org.uk*

Lewin, K. (1936) *Principles of topological psychology*, translated by Fritz Heider and Grace M. Heider, New York: McGraw Hill.

Lewin, K. (1951) *Field theory in social science*, edited by Dorwin Cartwright, New York, NY: Harper & Brothers.

Lin, N. (2001) *Social capital: A theory of social structure and action*, New York, NY: Cambridge University Press.

London Councils (2011) *The gang and beyond: Addressing the impact of gang activity in the capital*, London: London Councils, www.londoncouncils.gov.uk

MacDonald, R. and Marsh, J. (2005) *Disconnected youth?*, Basingstoke: Palgrave Macmillan.

Mares, D. (2001) 'Gangstas or lager louts? Working class street gangs in Manchester', in M. Klein, H.-J. Kerner, C.L. Maxson and E.G. Weitekamp (eds) *Gangs in Europe: Assessments at the millennium*, London: Sage Publications.

Marshall, B., Webb, B. and Tilley, N. (2005) *Rationalisation of current research on guns, gangs and other weapons: Phase one*, London : UCL.

Martin, J.L. (2003) 'What is field theory?', *American Journal of Sociology*, vol 109, no 1, pp 1-49.

Matthews, R. and Pitts, J. (2007) *An examination of the disproportionate number of young black men involved in street robbery in Lewisham*, London: Children and Young People's Directorate and Lewisham's Youth Crime Group.

Matza, D. (1964) *Delinquency and drift*, New York, NY: John Wiley & Sons.

Matza, D. (1969) *Becoming deviant*, Englewood Cliffs, N.J: Prentice Hall.

Matza, D. and Sykes, G. (1961) 'Juvenile delinquency and subterranean values', *American Sociological Review*, vol 26, pp 712-19.

May, T., Cossalter, S., Boyce, I. and Hearnden, I. (2007) *Drug dealing in Brixton town centre*, London: Institute for Public Policy Research, Kings College, London.

McAdam, D. (2007) 'Legacies of anti-Americanism: a sociological perspective', in P. Katzenstein and R. Keohane (eds) *Anti-Americanisms in world politics*, Ithaca, NY: Cornell University Press, pp 251-69.

Mead, G.H. (1934) *Mind, self, and society*, Chicago, IL: University of Chicago Press.

Medina, J., Aldridge, J. and Ralphs, R. (2009) 'Youth gangs in the UK: context, evolution and violence', Paper presented to the Global Gangs Workshop, 14-15 May 2009, Graduate Institute, Geneva.

Medina, J., Cebulla, A., Ross, A., Shute, J. and Aldridge, J. (2013) *Children and young people in gangs: a longitudinal analysis*, London: The Nuffield Foundation.

Medina, J., Ralphs, R. and Aldridge, J. (2012) 'Hidden behind the gunfire: young women's experience of gang-related violence', *Violence Against Women*, vol 18, no 6, pp 653-61.

Merton, R. (1957) *Social theory and social structure*, Glencoe, IL: The Free Press.

Messerschmidt, J.W. (1993) *Masculinities and crime: Critique and reconceptualisation of theory*, Oxford: Rowan and Littlefield.

Messerschmidt, J.W. (2000) *Nine lives: Adolescent masculinities, the body, and violence*, Oxford: Westview Press.

Merton, R. (1938) 'Social structure and anomie', *American Sociological Review*, vol 3, no 5, pp 672-82.

Merton, R. K. (1968) *Social theory and social structure*, New York, NY: Free Press.

Miller, J. (2001) *One of the guys: Girls, gangs and gender*, New York, NY: Oxford University Press.

Miller, W.B. (1958) 'Inter-institutional conflict as a major impediment to delinquency prevention', *Human Organiszation*, vol 17, no 3, pp 20-3.

Miller, W.B. (1980) 'Gangs, groups, and serious youth crime', in D. Shichor and D.H. Kelly (eds) *Critical issues in juvenile delinquency*, Lexington, MA: Heath, pp 115-38.

Miller, W.B. ([1982] 1992) *Crime by youth gangs and groups in the United States*, Washington, DC: US Department of Justice, Office of Justice Programs, Office of Juvenile Justice and Delinquency Prevention.

Miller, W.B. (2001) *The growth of youth gang problems in the United States: 1970-98*, Washington DC: Office of Juvenile Justice and Delinquency Prevention.

Ministry of Justice Research Series 2/11, *Understanding the psychology of gang violence: implications for designing effective violence interventions*, Ministry of Justice, www.justice.gov.uk/publications/research.htm

Monks, S. (2009) *Weapon dogs: The situation in London*, London: Greater London Authority.

Moore, J. (1978) *Homeboys: Gangs, drugs, and prison in the barrios of Los Angeles*, Philadelphia, PA: Temple University Press.

Moore, J. (1991) *Going down to the barrio: Homeboys and homegirls in change*, Philadelphia, PA: Temple University Press.

Moore, J. and Vigil, J.D. (1989) 'Chicano gangs: group norms and individual factors related to adult criminality', *Aztlan*, vol 18, pp 31-42.

Morales, A.T. (1992) 'Latino youth gangs: Causes and clinical intervention', in L.A. Vargas and J. Koss-Chioino (eds) *Working with culture: Psychotherapeutic intervention with ethnic minority children and adolescents*, San Francisco: Jossey–Bass, pp. 129-54.

Morell, G., Scott, S., McNeish, D. and Webster, S. (2011) 'The August riots in England', www.natcen.ac.uk

Mullins, C.W. (2006) *Holding your square: Masculinities, streetlife and violence*, Cullompton: Willan Publishing.

NASUWT (National Association of Schoolmasters Union of Women Teachers) (2009) *Gangs and school*, Birmingham: NASUWT.

Newburn, T. and Stanko, B. (eds) (1994) *Just boys doing business: Men, masculinities and crime,* Abingdon: Routledge.

Ortiz, F. (2010) 'Making the dogman heel: recommendations for improving the effectiveness of dogfighting laws', *Standford Journal of Animal Law and Policy*, vol 3, pp 1-75.

Palmer, S. (2009) 'The origins and emergence of youth "gangs" in a British inner-city neighbourhood', *Safer Communities*, vol 8, no 2, pp 17-26.

Palmer, S. and Pitts, J. (2006) 'Othering the brothers', *Youth and Policy*, vol 9, pp 5-22.

Papachristos, A.V. (2005) 'Interpreting inkblots: deciphering and doing something about modern street gangs', *Criminology & Public Policy*, vol 4, no 3, pp 643-51.

Papachristos, A.V. (2009) 'Murder by structure: dominance relations and the social structure of gang homicide', *American Journal of Sociology*, vol 115, no 1, pp 74-128.

Park, R.E., Burgess, E.W. and McKenzie, R.D. (1925) *The city: Suggestions for investigation of human behavior in the urban environment*, Chicago: University of Chicago Press.

Parker, H. (1974) *View from the boys*, London: David & Charles.

Parsons, T. (1937) *The structure of social action*, New York, NY: McGraw Hill Book Company.

Patrick, J. (1973) *A Glasgow gang observed*, London: Methuen.

Pearce, J.J. and Pitts, J.M. (2011) *Youth gangs, sexual violence and sexual exploitation: a scoping exercise*, The Office of the Children's Commissioner for England, Luton: University of Bedfordshire

Pearson, G. (1983) *Hooligan: A history of respectable fears*, London: Macmillan.

Perri 6 (1997) 'Social exclusion: time to be optimistic', *Demos Collection*, 12, pp 3-9.

Phillips, S. (1999) *Wallbanging*, Chicago, IL: University of Chicago Press.

Pitts, J. (1998) 'Young people, crime and citizenship', in A. Marlow, A. and J. Pitts (eds) *Planning safer communities*, Lyme Regis: Russell House Publishing Ltd.

Pitts, J. (2003) *The new politics of youth crime: Discipline for solidarity*, Lyme Regis: Russell House Publishing.

Pitts, J. (2007a) 'Americanization, the third way, and the racialization of youth crime and disorder', in J. Hagedorn *Gangs in the global city*, Urbana-Champaign, IL: University of Illinois.

Pitts, J. (2007b) *Young and safe in Lambeth: The deliberations of Lambeth Executive Commission on Children, Young people and Violent Crime*, London: London Borough of Lambeth.

Pitts, J. (2008a) 'The changing shape of youth crime', *Youth and Policy*, no 100, pp 165-76.

Pitts, J. (2008b) *Reluctant gangsters*, Cullompton: Willan Publishing.

Pitts, J. (2011) 'Mercenary territory: are youth gangs really a problem?', in B. Goldson (ed) (2011) *Youth in Crisis? 'Gangs', territoriality and violence*, London: Routledge.

Pitts, J. (2012) 'Reluctant criminologists: criminology, ideology and the violent youth gang', *Youth and Policy*, no 109, pp 27-45.

Presdee, M. (2000) *Cultural criminology and the carnival of crime*, London: Routledge.

Prince's Trust (2004) 'New report reveals gaps in local support for the hardest to reach', Press Release, London: Prince's Trust.

Pritchard, T. (2008) *Street boys*, London: Harper Element.

Puttnam, R. (1993) *Making democracy work: civic traditions in modern Italy*, Princeton, NJ: Princeton University Press.

Putnam, R. (2000) *Bowling alone*, New York, NJ: Simon & Shuster.

Pyrooz, D.C. and Decker, S.H. (2011) 'Motives and methods for leaving the gang: understanding the process of gang desistence', *Journal of Criminal Justice*, vol 39, pp 417-25.

Pyrooz, D., Decker, S. and Webb, V., (2010) 'The ties that bind: desistence from gangs', *Crime & Delinquency*, http://cad.sagepub.com

Ralphs, R., Medina, J. and Aldridge, J. (2009) 'Who needs enemies with friends like these? The importance of place for young people living in known gang areas', *Journal of Youth Studies*, vol 12, no 5, pp 483-500.

Ruble, N.M. and Turner, W.L. (2000) 'A systemic analysis of the dynamics and organization of urban street gangs', *The American Journal of Family Therapy*, vol 28, pp 117–32.

Ruggiero, V. and South, N. (1995) *Eurodrugs: Drug use, markets and trafficking in Europe*, London: University College Press.

RSPCA (2009) 'New RSPCA figures show shocking rise in dog fghting on our streets', Press Release 21 May, RSPCA.

Salagaev, A., Shashkin, A., Sherbakova, I. and Touriyanskiy, E. (2005) 'Contemporary Russian gangs: history, membership and crime involvement', in S.H. Decker and F. M. Weerman (eds) *European street gangs and troublesome youth groups*, Lanham, MD: Altamira Press.

Sampson, R.J. and Groves, W.B. (1989) 'Community structure and crime: testing social disorganisation theory', *American Journal of Sociology*, vol 94, no 4, pp 774-802.

Sampson, R. and Laub, J. (1993) *Crime in the making: Pathways and turning points*, Cambridge, MA: Harvard University Press.

Sampson, R. and Lauriston, L. (1994) 'Violent Victimisation and offending: individual, situational and community-level risk factors', in A. Reiss and J. Roth (eds) *Social Influences volume 3: Understanding and preventing violence*, Washington DC: National Academy Press.

Sanchez-Jankowski, M. (1991) *Islands in the street: Gangs and American urban society*, Berkeley, CA: University of California Press.

Sandberg, S. and Pederson, W. (2011) *Street capital: Black cannabis dealers in a white welfare state*, Bristol: Policy Press.

Sanders, B. (2005) *Youth crime and youth culture in the inner city*, Abingdon: Routledge.

Sartre, J.P. (1963) *Search for a method*, translated by Hazel E. Barnes, New York, NY : Knopf.

Scarman, L. (1981) *The Scarman Report: The Brixton Disorders 10-12 April 1981*, Harmondsworth: Penguin.

Schalet, A. Hunt, G. and Joe-Laidler, K. (2003) Respectability and autonomy: the articulation and meaning of sexuality among girls in gang', *Journal of Contemporary Ethnography*, vol 32, pp 108-43.

Schneider, J., Rowe, N., Forrest, S. and Tilley, N. (2004) *Biting the bullet: Gun crime in Greater Nottingham*, Report to Nottingham CDRP, Nottingham: Nottingham City Council.

Schwendinger, H. and Schwendinger, J. (1985) *Adolescent subcultures and delinquency*, New York, NY: Praeger.

Scott, J. and Meyer, J. (1983) 'The organization of societal sectors', in J. Meyer and W.R. Scott (eds) *Organizational environments: Ritual and rationality*, Beverly Hills, CA: Sage Publications, pp 129-53.

Sharp, P., Aldridge, J. and Medina, J. (2006) 'Delinquent youth groups and offending behaviour: findings from the 2004 Offending, Crime and Justice Survey', Home Office Online Report 14/06, www.homeoffice.gov.uk/rds/pdfs06/rdsolr1406.pdf

Shaw, C.R., Zorbaugh, H., McKay, H.D. and Cottrell, L.S. (1929) *Delinquency areas*, Chicago, IL: University of Chicago Press.

Shaw, C.R. and McKay, H.D. (1931) *Social factors in juvenile delinquency*, Chicago, IL: University of Chicago Press.

Shaw, C.R. and McKay, H.D. (1942) *Juvenile delinquency and urban areas*, Chicago, IL: University of Chicago Press.

Short, J. (1997) *Poverty, ethnicity and violent crime*, Boulder, CO: Westview Press.

Short, J.F. and Hughes, L. (2010) 'Promoting research integrity in community-based intervention research', in R.J. Chaskin (ed) *Youth gangs and community intervention*, New York, NY: Columbia University Press.

Shover, N. (1996) *Great pretenders: Pursuits and careers of persistent thieves*, Boulder CO: Westview Press.

Shropshire, S. and McFarquhar, M. (2002) 'Developing multi agency strategies to address the street gang culture and reduce gun violence amongst young people', www.iansa.org/documents/2002/gang_culture_and_young_poeple1.pdf

Sibley, D. (1995) *Geographies of exclusion: Society and difference in the West*, London: Routledge.

Simon, J. (2007) *Governing through crime*, Oxford: Oxford University Press.

Smith, D.J. and Bradshaw, P. (2005) *Gang membership and teenage offending*, Edinburgh: University of Edinburgh.

Southgate, J. (2011) *Seeing differently: Working with girls affected by gangs*, London: The Griffin Society.

Spergel, I.A. (1964) *Racketville, Slumtown, Haulberg*, Chicago: University of Chicago Press.

Spergel, I. (1995) *The youth gang problem: A community approach*, New York, NY: Oxford University Press.

Squires, P. (2011) 'Young people and "weaponisation"', in B.Goldson (ed) *Youth in Crisis?: 'Gangs', territoriality and violence*, Abingdon: Routledge.

Sullivan, M. (1989) *Getting paid: Youth crime and work in the inner city*, Ithaca, NY: Cornell University Press.

Sullivan, M. (2005) 'Maybe we shouldn't study "gangs": does reification obscure youth violence?', *Journal of Contemporary Criminal Justice*, vol 21, no 2, pp 170-90.

Sutherland, E.H. (1947) *Principles of criminology* (4th edn), Philadelphia, PA: J.B. Lippincott.

Suttles, G.D. (1968) *The social order of the slum*, Chicago, IL: University of Chicago Press.

Stack, C. (1974) *All our kin: Strategies for survival in a black community*, New York, NY: Harper & Row.

St Cyr, J.L. and Decker, S. (2003) 'Girls, guys and gangs: convergence or divergence in the gendered construction of gangs and groups', *Journal of Criminal Justice*, vol 31, no 5, pp 423-33.

Stephens, P., Leach, A., Taggart, L. and Jones, H. (1998) *Think sociology*, Cheltenham: Stanley Thornes.

Streatham Guardian (2009) 'Three dangerous dog attacks a day in Lambeth', 2 April.

Stuart, J., Barnes, J. and Brodie, I. (2002) *Conducting ethical research* London: NESS.

Swartz, D. (1997) *Culture and power: The sociology of Pierre Bourdieu*, Chicago, IL: University of Chicago Press.

Sykes, G.M. and Matza, D. (1957) 'Techniques of neutralisation: a theory of delinquency', *American Sociological Review*, vol 22, pp 664-70.

Tannenbaum, F. (1938) *Crime and the community*, New York, NY: Columbia University Press.

Taylor, C.S. (1990) *Dangerous society*, East Lansing, MI: Michigan State University Press.

Taylor, T.J. (2008) 'The boulevard ain't safe for your kids ... youth gang involvement and violent victimisation', *Journal of Contemporary Criminal Justice*, vol 24, pp 125-36.

Thomson, R. (2000) 'Dream on: the logic of sexual practice', *Journal of Youth Studies*, vol 3, no 4, pp 407-27.

Thornberry, T.P. (1998) 'Membership in youth gangs and involvement in serious and violent offending', in R. Loeber and P. Farrington (eds) *Serious and violent juvenile offenders*, Thousand Oaks, CA: Sage Publications, pp 147-66.

Thornberry, T.P., Krohn, M.D., Lizotte, A.J., Smith, C A. and Tobin, K. (2003) *Gangs and delinquency in developmental perspective*, Cambridge: Cambridge University Press.

Thrasher, F. (1927) *The gang: A study of 1,313 gangs in Chicago*, Chicago IL: University of Chicago Press.

Tita, G., Cohen, J. and Endberg, J. (2005) 'An ecological study of the location of gang "set space"', *Social Exclusion*, vol 52, no 2, pp 272-99.

Toy, J. (2008) *Die another day: A practitioner's review with recommendations for preventing gang and weapon violence in London in 2008*, London: London Borough of Southwark.

Turner, V. (1974) *Dramas, fields, and metaphors*, Ithaca, NY: Cornell University Press.

UNISON (2011) 'New figures reveal £200m of youth service cuts', Press Release, 26 October (www.hscreformseries.co.uk/politics/28-unions/8446-new-figures-reveal-p200m-of-youth-service-cuts).

Van Gemert, F., Peterson, D. and Lien, I. (2008) *Street gangs, migration and ethnicity*, Portland, OR: Willan Publishing.

Venkatesh, S.A. (2011) www.streetgangs.com/academic/venkatesh_ paper.pdf 'Community justice and the gang: a life-course perspective', forthcoming in S.D. Levitt (ed) *Aging in an American street gang: Toward a life-course perspective on gang involvement*, Forthcoming in collection of articles to be published by American Bar Foundation.

Vigil, J.D. (1988a) *Barrio gangs: Street life and identity in southern California*, Austin, TX: University of Texas Press.

Vigil, J.D. (1988b) 'Group processes and street identity: adolescent chicano gang members', *Ethos*, vol 16, no 4, pp 421-45.

Vigil, J.D. (1993) 'The established gang', in S. Cummings and D.J. Monti (eds) *Gangs: The origins and impact of contemporary youth gangs in the United States*, Albany: State University of New York Press, pp 95-112.

Vigil, J.D. (2002) *A rainbow of gangs: Street-cultures in the mega-city*, Austin, TX: University of Texas Press.

Vigil, J.D. (2003) 'Urban violence and street gangs', *Annual Review of Anthropology*, vol 32, pp 225-42.

Vigil, J.D. (2010) *Gang redux: A balanced anti-gang strategy*, Long Grove, IL: Waveland Press.

Wacquant, L. (1992) 'Decivilisation and demonization: la mutation du ghetto noir americain' ('Decivilizing and demonizing: the remaking of the black American ghetto'), in S. Loyal and S. Quilley (eds) *The sociology of Norbert Elias*, Cambridge: Cambridge University Press, pp 95-121.

Wacquant, L. (2008) *Urban outcasts: The sociology of advanced marginality*, Cambridge: Polity Press.

Webb, E. Campbell, D. Schwartz, R. And Seehrent, L. (1996) *Unobtrusive Measures: Non-reactive research in the Social Sciences* Chicago Il: Rand Mcnally & Co.

Weber, M. (1915) 'Religious rejections of the world and their directions', in *From Max Weber: Essays in sociology*, translated and edited by H.H. Gerth and C. Wright Mills (1946), New York, NY: Oxford University Press.

Weerman, F.M. and Decker, S. (2005) 'European street gangs and troublesome youth groups: findings from the Eurogang research programme', in S.H. Decker and F.M. Weerman (eds) *European street gangs and troublesome youth groups*, Lanham, MD: Altamira Press.

White, R. (2013) *Youth gangs, violence and social respect*, New York , NY: Palgrave Macmillan.

Whyte, W.F. (1943) *Street corner society: The social structure of an Italian slum*, Chicago, IL: University of Chicago Press.

Winlow, S. (2001) *Badfellas: Crime, tradition and new masculinities*, Oxford: Berg.

Yablonksy, L. (1962) *The violent gang*, New York, NY: Macmillan.

Yates, J. (2006) '"You just don't grass": youth, crime and "grassing" in a working class community', *Youth Justice*, vol 6, no 3, pp 195-210.

Young, M. and Willmott, P. (1962) *Family and kinship in East London*, Harmondsworth: Pelican.

Young, T. (2009) 'Girls and gangs: shemale gangsters in the UK', *Youth Justice*, 9, pp 224-38.

Young, T. (2011) 'In search of the "shemale" gangster', in B. Goldson (ed) *Youth in crisis? 'Gangs', territoriality and violence*, Abingdon: Routledge.

Young, T., Fitzgerald, M., Hallsworth, S. and Joseph, I. (2007) *Guns, gangs and weapons*, London: Youth Justice Board.

Zorbaugh, H.W. (1929) *The Gold Coast and the slum: A sociological study of Chicago's Near North Side*, Chicago, IL: University of Chicago Press.

APPENDIX A

SW9 postcode

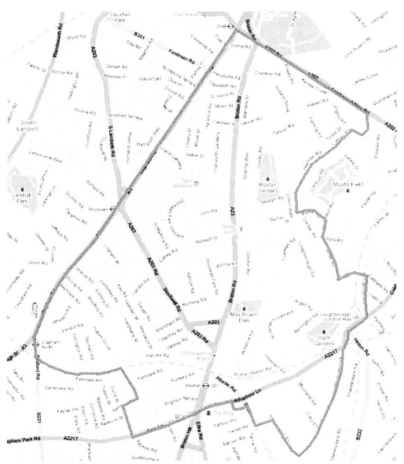

Map data © 2011 Google

APPENDIX B

Lambeth key crime types

Most serious violent (MSV) GBH (attempted murder and murder, wounding) increased by 26% from 21/11/09-21/11/10 (source: MPS*) – the largest rise, the highest volume and highest rate of MSV in London.
Where at least one suspect charged, 59% were GBH with intent; 38% for GBH/serious wounding; 83% of accused were male.

Knife crime offences increased by 16.4% (68 offences) for Apr-Nov 2010 compared to same period in 2009. Of the total 482 knife crime offences, 274 offences (56.8%) were personal robbery and 102 (21.2%) GBH with intent. Level of weapon use increased alongside firearms and knife seizures.
79% of all victims were male and 68.8% aged under 30. Suspects were 82.7% male; 71.1% aged under 30.

Gun crime has reduced by 24%, but Lambeth still has the second highest level of its most similar borough group after Southwark.

Serious youth violence (SYV) (any offence of most serious violence or weapon enabled crime, where the victim is aged 1-19, i.e. murder, manslaughter, rape, wounding with intent and causing grievous bodily harm) increased by 18% (01/04/10-21/11/10) (source: MPS). This is the highest rise in the MPS grouping of most similar boroughs and second highest in overall volume of SYV in London after Southwark. Youth victims increased from 96 to 158 (65%) on previous year: including 2 youth murders and 4 attempted murders, all featuring black victims and black suspects.
• 50% of all SYV offences are weapon-enabled personal robberies;
• 38% are GBH-related offences;
• 68% of offences involved a knife or bladed article and 6% involved a firearm fired;
• 28% of victims received an injury that was moderate to fatal.

Nearly 85% of SYV victims were male with young black victims significantly overrepresented as victims of stabbings and shootings; 67% of offenders were male, the oldest category for suspects was 18 years (12%) followed by those aged 16 years (10%); 54% of suspects were black, 9% were white. Intelligence indicates a large proportion of suspects were known gang members and associates.

Gangs and group violent offending
A high proportion of youth violence is attributable to gang tensions or is committed by individuals with gang links; 17% of Lambeth's stabbings and over 50% of shootings are gang-related. Sampling suggests that members of gangs are responsible for around 22% of Lambeth's violence against the person.
Victims of gang-related offences had median age of 20.
Main age range of victims was 15-20 years (65% or 20 victims), followed by 21-29 years (35% or 11 victims); 19 victims under 19 years, (youngest 15 years); 87% of victims were of black ethnicity. Majority of suspects were black and under age 30.

The report concludes that 'there is widespread but sporadic gang and group violent activity in Lambeth, centred in areas of social housing, and producing the high risks of serious youth violence and associated offending (e.g. related to drugs markets)'.

Note: *Metropolitan Police Service
Source: Lambeth First (2001a) (primary source MPS)

The Duluth Power and Control Wheel

DOMESTIC ABUSE INTERVENTION PROJECT

202 East Superior Street
Duluth, Minnesota 55802
218-722-2781
www.duluth-model.org

Example of gang evolution and fracturing: organised crime

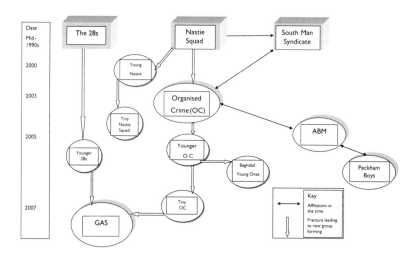

APPENDIX E

Approximate gang locations
in SW9 (July 2011)

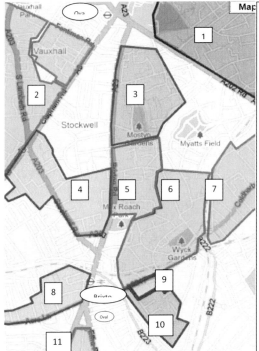

1. Wooly Hood
2. 031 Bloods known as O-tray One (ABS/G-street/Union Block)
3. Organised Crime
4. All Bout Money (Hotspot/SPE/DDC)
5. PDC (PIF/CFR/GAS)
6. CFR/GAS
7. Roadside Gs (YRS/TRC/C-Block
8. Acre Lane Campaign
9. Murderzone
10. GAS
11. Brixton Hill Bangers (NPG/P10)

The attached map is reproduced with kind permission by www.londonstreetgangs.com.

The dominant neighbourhood gang is listed (followed in brackets by subordinate groups or alternative names). The map shows all areas claimed by gangs and also all housing estates that are either part of larger gang territories. NB These areas are approximations only and are intended to give the reader an indication of approximate localities and proximities of gangs.

Source: Map Data (c) 2011 Tele Atlas. Downloaded 15 July 2011.

Timeline of known gangs in SW9

Date	Known gangs
1985-90	Various Yardie* gangs including Killerman Gold Posse; Young Raiders; the Untouchables; the Wackers; the Punishers; the 28s.
1991-95	The 28s; Kennington Posse.
1996-2000	PDC; New Park Gunnahs; Brixton Hill Bangers; Nastie Squad; South Man Syndicate.
2001-05	Organised Crime; PDC; Firehouse Posse; Cartel Crew; Kennington Black Mob; Nastie Squad; South Man Syndicate; Young Nastie Squad.
2007	ABM; Acre Lane Campaign; Alligator Crew; Bloodset Criminals; Brixton Yard Manz; Cartel Crew; Clapham Park Dred; the Crypts; Dipset Muslim; Fully Equipped; Gipset Taliban; G-Street; Hanna Town; Herne Hill Man Dem; Hot spot; Junction Boys; K Town Crew; Loughborough Soldiers; Man Dem Crew; Marcus Garvey Boys; Mash Force; Murderzone; Myatts Fields Posse; Organised Crime; 031 Bloods, (O-tray One); Pain in Full; PDC; Real Somalian Soldiers; RSS; Rema Crew; SMN Heathset; Southmandem; Stick em up Kidz; Stockwell Park Crew; S. Unit; Superstar Gang; Surrey Lane Soldiers; SW2 Boys; Thugz 4 Life; Tulse Hill Man Dem; Tulse Hill Thugz; Valley Crew; VMD; Young Thugz 4 Life.
2010	ABM; Acre Lane Campaign; Blenheim Gardens Squad; Brixton Hill Bullies; Corleone Family Riders; D Block; Front Line Bangers; GAS; Ghost Town; Gipset Crew; Murderzone; New Park Gunnerz; Organised Crime; PDC/PIF (Peel Dem Crew/Poverty Driven Children); 031 Bloods (O-Tray); Roadside Gs; South Man Syndicate; St Matthew's Boys; Tulse Hill Thugs; TN1 (Trust No-one).

Notes:

*Yardie: a term applied to Jamaican gangsters. The term itself derives from the (back) yards of the Garrison communities of Kingston, Jamaica.

This is not an exhaustive list. It represents the key groups that have come to the attention of statutory authorities. The groups listed in 1985-90 are thought to be exclusive Yardie posses and not necessarily urban street gangs.

Source: Pitts (2007b); London Borough of Lambeth (Community Safety Division); Lambeth Community Police Consultative Group (www.lambethcpcg.org.uk).

Index

Page numbers followed by *n* or *tab* refer to information in a note or a table respectively.

criminal damage and reputation
122–3
problems of departure from gangs
106
rented and social housing in
Lambeth 9–10
residence away from gang
neighbourhood 193–4
as shared space 152
see also neighbourhood
Huff, C.R. 34
humiliation of rivals 138, 144, 246,
283
hype and exaggeration 147, 250*tab*
hyper-vigilance and survival 191, 210,
285

I

identity
code switching 197–8
dual personas 198–9
leadership and collective identity 98
manufacture of gang reputation
125–7
and opposition to other groups 46
and reasons for departure from gang
105
and territoriality 33
see also reputation; self-promotion
illusio 52, 54, 55, 61*tab*, 62, 82, 269
immigrant communities in Lambeth
10
see also new arrivals in community
incumbents 48, 49
'independents' 185–6, 194–5, 216*tab*,
229
inducements to gang affiliation 178,
179
information acquisition and flow 164,
207–17, 249, 250*tab*, 272, 283
and advanced gang members 93
community engagement 208–9
and networks 208, 212–15, 230,
232–3, 237, 250*tab*
in school environment 284–5
and social capital 208
and social networking sites 87, 210,
215–16, 283
trading information 208, 211–12,
215, 216, 217*tab*
role of girls and young women
216*tab*, 230, 233–4, 237, 254
see also new technology; oral
transmission of information

informing *see* 'grassing'
initiation ceremonies 174, 184
Institute for Economics and Peace 17*n*
'institutionalisation' of gangs 30
instrumental repertoire 71, 73, 90, 97,
124, 137–42
see also economic capital;
entrepreneurial nature of gangs
inter-gang relations 88, 90–1, 95, 105,
195–6
see also group violence and gang
incursions
intergenerational transmission 26, 30,
173, 209
interpersonal and intra-gang disputes
and violence 26, 35, 119
and family of gang members 257–9,
282
and illusion of 'street family' 177–8
and personal advancement 101–2,
135–6, 190, 282
and 'postcode beefs' 159–60
relations between different tiers in
gang 88–9, 89–90, 90–1, 93, 98,
114–15, 116–17, 120, 282
set-ups and honey traps 232, 256–7
stabbing and departure 94–5
Islam and conversion of gang members
116, 247–8

J

Jill Dando Institute 32
Joe, K. 221
Johnston, Avril 78
joining a gang 27, 28–30, 38, 56, 87,
174–80, 184–5
appraisal of new members 209–10
girls and young women 221, 240
influencing factors 175–83
'forced' affiliation 30, 179–80, 246,
258–9
grooming 179, 275
protection as motivation 30, 36,
167, 170–1, 181–2, 193
school environment 169–70
recruitment as contested term 170,
174
transference to new gang 104–5,
183, 194
see also auditioning and testing
Joseph, Samantha 232, 257